T0114052

SEVEN DEADLY ECONOMIC SINS

You have heard of the Seven Deadly Sins: pride, greed, lust, envy, gluttony, wrath, and sloth. Each is a natural human weakness that impedes happiness. In addition to these vices, however, there are economic sins as well. And they, too, wreak havoc on our lives and in society. They can seem intuitively compelling, yet they lead to waste, loss, and forgone prosperity. In this thoughtful and compelling book, James Otteson tells the story of seven central economic fallacies, explaining why they are fallacies, why believing in them leads to mistakes and loss, and how exorcizing them from our thinking can help us avoid costly errors and enable us to live in peace and prosperity.

JAMES R. OTTESON is the John T. Ryan Jr. Professor of Business Ethics at the University of Notre Dame. He is the author of *Adam Smith's Marketplace of Life* (2002), *Actual Ethics* (2006), *The End of Socialism* (2014), and *Honorable Business* (2019).

Seven Deadly Economic Sins

Obstacles to Prosperity and Happiness Every Citizen Should Know

James R. Otteson

CAMBRIDGE
UNIVERSITY PRESS

CAMBRIDGE
UNIVERSITY PRESS

Shaftesbury Road, Cambridge CB2 8EA, United Kingdom

One Liberty Plaza, 20th Floor, New York, NY 10006, USA

477 Williamstown Road, Port Melbourne, VIC 3207, Australia

314–321, 3rd Floor, Plot 3, Splendor Forum, Jasola District Centre, New Delhi – 110025, India

103 Penang Road, #05–06/07, Visioncrest Commercial, Singapore 238467

Cambridge University Press is part of Cambridge University Press & Assessment, a department of the University of Cambridge.

We share the University's mission to contribute to society through the pursuit of education, learning and research at the highest international levels of excellence.

www.cambridge.org
Information on this title: www.cambridge.org/9781108824385

DOI: 10.1017/9781108915304

First published 2021
3rd printing 2021
First paperback edition 2023

A catalogue record for this publication is available from the British Library

Library of Congress Cataloging-in-Publication data
NAMES: Otteson, James R., author.
TITLE: Seven deadly economic sins : obstacles to prosperity and happiness every citizen should know / James R. Otteson.
DESCRIPTION: Cambridge ; New York, NY : Cambridge University Press, 2021. | Includes bibliographical references and index.
IDENTIFIERS: LCCN 2020024139 (print) | LCCN 2020024140 (ebook) | ISBN 9781108843379 (hardback) | ISBN 9781108915304 (ebook)
SUBJECTS: LCSH: Economics – Moral and ethical aspects. | Economics – Sociological aspects.
CLASSIFICATION: LCC HB72 .O79 2021 (print) | LCC HB72 (ebook) | DDC 330–dc23
LC record available at https://lccn.loc.gov/2020024139
LC ebook record available at https://lccn.loc.gov/2020024140

ISBN   978-1-108-84337-9   Hardback
ISBN   978-1-108-82438-5   Paperback

To Victoria Ellen, as she starts the next chapter of her life

CONTENTS

CONTENTS

CONTENTS

An old saying has it that if you lined up all the economists in the world end to end, they still wouldn't reach a conclusion.[1] There are lots of other jokes about economics in the same vein. President Harry Truman allegedly once said that he was in search of a one-handed economist, so that he would not have to hear from yet another economist: "on the other hand . . ." The truth is that economists disagree about a lot. Even Nobel laureate economists find themselves on different sides of all sorts of issues – on everything from inflation and deflation, the money supply, interest rates, and labor and health and environmental policy, to economic development, human motivation, and even rationality. They disagree on the importance and proper role of economic models, on whether their discipline is "value free," even on whether their discipline is a true or proper science.

On the other hand (pardon the joke), there are also some things that many economists agree on. What is curious about this latter fact is that the points of agreement seem to play so small a role both in political policy and in the wider public consciousness. People seem to be aware that economists disagree, that economists vote for different political parties, and that economists are not able to predict what the

---

[1] This is attributed, perhaps apocryphally, to George Bernard Shaw. See Rodrik 2015, 151.

market will do, which businesses will succeed, what the interest rates will be, or when the next recession will be – or what to do about it when it occurs. This gives people plenty of reason to be wary of what economists say and of economic expertise in general.

It is also true that if one reads the main works of some of the most prominent figures in the history of economics – Adam Smith, for example, or David Ricardo, John Stuart Mill, Karl Marx, or John Maynard Keynes – it quickly becomes clear that some of the most important aspects of their work bear little resemblance to the work of most contemporary economists. For one thing, where's the math? If you look at Smith's *Wealth of Nations*, or at Mill's *Principles of Political Economy*, Marx's *Capital*, or Keynes's *General Theory*, you will not find even one regression! The highly technical mathematical instruments economists employ today did not begin to appear until the late nineteenth century; they gained ground throughout the twentieth and today have all but crowded out anything that does not use them. Pick up a professional economics journal today and dip into it anywhere: chances are you will find mathematical formulas that only someone with extensive training can even read, let alone make sense of – and let alone apply to the real world in some beneficial or enlightening way. Unless one is oneself a trained economist, then, one could be forgiven not only for not reading most of what economists write, but for wondering whether, if they are so divided even among themselves, why anyone should bother listening to them.

And yet there are some basic principles that many economists agree upon. What's more, some of these fundamentals can not only be readily expressed and understood but would benefit humanity if more widely appreciated. That is what this book aims to explore. Each chapter focuses on an important principle of economics that, if more widely understood and implemented, would improve human life. In each case, however, the economic principles tend to be at odds with general and widespread impressions that non-economists have. Thus, I have framed each chapter in terms of what I will argue is an economic fallacy whose continued wide currency in the public's consciousness has negative effects.

Naturally, not all economists will agree with all the conclusions of this book. But its argument begins with widely accepted economic principles and builds on them in what I believe are plausible – I hope even compelling – directions. For full disclosure, I myself am a philosopher by training, not an economist. Most of my work falls into the field of "political economy," the eighteenth-century term for an integration of moral (or political) philosophy with the principles of economic reasoning and economic policymaking. I have studied and written extensively about Adam Smith (1723-1790), for example, as well as the history of economic thought. So, I am a student of economics who has come to appreciate the discipline by studying its history and the thought of its prominent figures. But that means that I am among what Nobel laureate economist Friedrich Hayek (1899-1992) called "secondhand dealers in ideas": I rely on the ideas of experts who have technical training to formulate my own nontechnical ideas. We are all, however, secondhand dealers in others' ideas to some (perhaps uncomfortably large) extent, since little of what we believe did we ourselves discover or demonstrate. My hope is that because my study of economics and the appreciation I have developed for its insights have come from the perspective of a humanities-trained moral philosopher, I can convey its central principles in a way that an educated non-economist can understand and appreciate.

Like politics, economics is one of those fields which everyone not only has an opinion about but often a very strong opinion – whether they have any training in economics or not. Consider the current debates about whether socialism or capitalism should be our system of economics.[2] Or about whether the legal minimum wage should be raised, whether billionaires are bad for the economy, whether we should place tariffs on Chinese goods, whether immigration should be open or trade should be free, whether healthcare should be nationalized, whether we should raise taxes or reduce our national debt, and so on: people often have very strong opinions about such matters – and yet most people do not know what economics has to say about the likely effects such policies would have. But one of the primary intellectual virtues is to know the limits of one's knowledge, and to proportion one's beliefs (and the strengths of one's beliefs) accordingly. These issues make an enormous difference in the lives of actual human beings, so we need to get them right. If economics can help – and on many issues, it can – then we should learn from it what we can.

The situation is perhaps analogous to medicine. About many issues – how to treat specific diseases, for

---

[2] For my own contribution to this discussion, see Otteson 2014.

example, whether one drug or another (or none) should be used, how to treat psychiatric illnesses (or even what counts as a psychiatric illness), what the causes are of various ailments and diseases, and so on – doctors will have differing opinions. And medical journals also frequently contain analyses that are difficult for laypersons to understand, let alone see the practical implications of. But the proper response to this variety of medical opinion and relative uncertainty about the import of medical experiments is emphatically not to forgo paying attention to doctors or to deny that there is such a thing as medical expertise. Instead, it is to seek a second opinion (or a third), and to look for areas of overlapping consensus. And, of course, the fact that medical professionals disagree about some things does not mean that they disagree about everything. On many issues – especially concerning the more routine and everyday ailments people face – there is indeed consensus and the paths of treatment are clear.

The same, I contend, holds for economics. Despite economists' disagreements about many issues, there are nevertheless some areas of overlapping consensus. There are some basic principles of economic reasoning that most economists agree on. This book will lay out several of them, including what I believe are the most important for improving human life. The discussion is thus addressed to the educated reader who is conscientious about wanting to understand how the world works and wants to make a good-faith effort to assess policy proposals and to vote responsibly and well, but who has not (yet) had the opportunity to explore the principles of economic reasoning to see what they hold and how they might help. Though the arguments in the following chapters are based on widely accepted principles of economics, in some cases they lead in perhaps surprising, even controversial, directions. I hope to convince you of the truth of what I will claim, but even if you end up disagreeing I hope you will develop an appreciation for the reasoning behind these economic claims, for how the claims are supported, and for what would be required to refute or deny them in good faith.

  The discussion of what I will argue are economic fallacies in what follows is also mixed with a fair bit of moral philosophy. Economics makes claims about human behavior and about human motivation, and human action is informed not merely by mechanical operations but by normative concerns regarding value. We are not robotic self-interested utility maximizers; we are also moral beings who make choices in part based on ethical conceptions of the right and the good. As Plato (428–348 BC) argued, our capacity to choose – we can say yes to an opportunity, but we can also say no – entails that we are accountable beings who are capable of providing reasons for our actions, thus morally responsible for our actions, and thus rightly held to account for them. A discussion of economic principles therefore must itself take account of our moral natures as free and responsible creatures who are capable of considering not only our own interests but those of others as well. The discipline of economics provides a powerful set of analytical tools to understand how human beings behave, but also how they should behave given their goals. The discussions that follow are aimed at helping us achieve our ends not merely as biological, physiological, or psychological, but as moral creatures who have not only ends but moral ends.

As you will soon see, my discussion is inspired by Adam Smith, who is widely considered the father of the discipline of economics but who was also, and primarily, a moral philosopher: he was the author of not only the now more famous 1776 *Wealth of Nations*, but also of an earlier book, the 1759 *Theory of Moral Sentiments*. As Smith's pioneering example demonstrates, an economics worth considering must integrate with our natures and values as moral beings. Though I do not agree with all Smith's conclusions, I aspire to model my work after his example of joining moral philosophy with economic reasoning, and of expressing economic principles in ways that any educated reader can understand and even appreciate.

If we want to figure out how to make good decisions in our own lives or how to improve society, we need to understand how economics can help. In many ways, it can. If you find, however, that you are, or were, an adherent to any of the (alleged) fallacies discussed in the following chapters, or if any of the claims made herein seem to you to fall outside the "Overton window" of commonly held acceptable opinion, I ask only that you hear me out. We may still end up disagreeing, but perhaps we might be in a position to have a more productive conversation. Whatever economic policies we end up supporting, my hope is that they will be informed by a better understanding of what economics might be able to contribute, ultimately, to a just, humane, and prosperous society.

Introduction

Why Care About Economics?

Even if you could not name them all, you have probably heard of the Seven Deadly Sins. Here is the standard list: pride, greed, lust, envy, gluttony, wrath, and sloth. Those seven are not the only sins there are, but because we are so susceptible to them – seemingly almost psychologically primed to be seduced by them – and yet they lead to so much harm in both individual lives and in society, they are wisely considered among the most important things we all need to beware. One need not be a Christian, or a subscriber to any particular faith at all, to see how easily we can succumb to them, how much mischief they can and do create in our lives, how beneficial it would be to us if we could resist them, and yet how much effort it takes to resist them. Just when we might think we have mastered one, we discover we are indulging others, with exactly the negative consequences we would predict. There is, unfortunately, no such thing as conquering them once and for all. They continue to recur, often when we least expect it, and when they do, they can seem so alluring, so self-promoting and even emotionally satisfying, that it is only after the fact that we might look back on our behavior and feel regret, embarrassment, even shame. In the heat of the moment, however, it can be a different story.

There are, however, central deadly *economic* sins as well. That is what this book is about. Committing these economic sins might not prevent you from getting into heaven, but what they can do is, like their sinful counterparts, wreak havoc – in our private lives as individuals and in our communities when they find their way into public policies. They are "deadly" mistakes in economic reasoning to which we seem psychologically susceptible and that can seem intuitively compelling, but, when viewed in the cool, objective light of dispassionate analysis, reveal themselves to lead to negative outcomes like waste, loss, and forgone prosperity. Because these can have real, if unintended and perhaps surprising, effects in people's lives, however, understanding both *that* and *why* they are fallacies is crucial.

In the chapters that follow, I lay out what I contend are seven central economic fallacies. I explain why they are fallacies, why believing in them leads to mistakes and loss, and how exorcizing them from our economic thinking can help us avoid costly errors and enable positive benefit. The book is designed not so much for economists or others who are already trained in or expert at economics – though they may be interested to see what a philosopher makes of their discipline – but, rather, for the educated reader who is concerned about economic matters and who wants to understand how economics can help us make better decisions in our private lives and in our public policies. It is aimed, in other words, at the educated citizen. Of course, there are many considerations that should go into deciding how, for example, to vote – everything from our moral values to prudential concerns to strategic reasoning. Economics cannot decide all of that. Even a firm understanding of the basics of economics will not tell you which party or candidate to support. But economics can help us understand how to evaluate the likely consequences of proposed policies; it can help us understand how prosperity is generated, and what endangers it; and it can help us see when a policy proposal that sounds good might not in fact be all that it is cracked up to be – as happens, alas, all too often. It can help us become not just better-informed voters but better reasoners about voting, and hence better citizens.

The book is based on the assumption that we all want a just and humane society – that, wherever we are on the political or economic spectrum, we all want a society whose public institutions protect justice and in which people are able to construct for themselves lives of meaning, purpose, and happiness. My argument will be that increasing prosperity – not just wealth, but widespread and increasing opportunity for flourishing lives – is a necessary prerequisite of a life worth leading and of public institutions worth supporting. Economics can help us achieve prosperity, even if it cannot tell us exactly what we should do with our prosperity. And economics can highlight several mistakes in reasoning that we are prone to make. Exposing those mistakes can enable greater prosperity and thus increase the chances of ever more of us leading genuinely flourishing lives. Or so I will argue.

Why Trust Economics?

I don't know you, of course, but I would be willing to bet that you have lots of opinions about economics. Some of your opinions you may hold strongly, and some of them you may believe are all but self-evident. That is true for most of us, including me. When you hear the word "socialism," for example, you may think of Scandinavian countries like Sweden or Norway, and thus attach positive associations to the term; or you may think of the former Soviet Union or contemporary Venezuela, and thus conjure negative thoughts. And whichever way your thoughts incline, you probably think the other side is making some clear mistake.

Curiously, however, many of us who have strong beliefs about economics have not had any training in economics. And consider our leading national politicians, or the people who pass laws or enact regulations on economic, banking, financial, or business institutions. The disheartening news is that most of them have not studied economics either. If most of us do not know much about the discipline of economics, and do not pay much (or any) attention to economists, why do we nevertheless have such strong economic opinions?

Part of the explanation is probably the general propensity we have to overestimate our knowledge. People who know little about Israel and Palestine may nevertheless have strong opinions about what to do regarding their conflicts; people who know little about medicine have strong opinions about vaccines or about who has and how to treat ADHD or depression; and so on. And many of us assume that because we know *something* well – our particular vocation or area of expertise, for example – then our opinions in other areas can be trusted as well. It is probably safe to say, however, that many (most?) of the people who have strong opinions about, say, whether we should raise the legal minimum wage have not reviewed the economic studies about it. Similarly with our opinions about sweatshops, "fair" vs. free trade, nationalization of healthcare, whether immigration is a net positive or not, and so on. Many of us have opinions about these and other economic matters, and we may vote in part on the basis of these opinions, but without knowing what economics has to say about them we are not in the best position to know whether our opinions are reliable or trustworthy.

We should not necessarily judge ourselves negatively, however, for not knowing about these matters. After all, we are all busy with other things that are much more consequential in our actual, everyday lives. Most of us simply do not have the time, for example, to read the Affordable Care Act (ACA) (has *anyone* actually read all 11,000-plus pages of it?). This implicates one of the ideas we will discuss in the chapters that follow, namely, *opportunity cost*: before deciding to spend any of our resources (including our time) on anything, we should think about what we are giving up to do so. Consider: the average person can read approximately half a page per minute; at that rate, it would take some 367 hours to read the ACA. If you were to read for eight straight hours a day, it would take you 46 days, or about nine work weeks, to read it. Is it worth it? Ask yourself what else you might do with those 46 days. And then ask yourself what it would gain you to have read it. You would know what's in it, but, to be honest, so what? As a single individual person, you could have had approximately zero effect on whether it passed – so why bother? And that is just one law; what about the thousands of others in effect and under consideration by just the federal government, not to mention those in effect or under consideration by state and local governments, and not to mention the tens of thousands of pages of federal, state, and local regulations and proposed regulations. Given the value to you of whatever else you could do, devoting your scarce time to reading those actual and proposed statutes, bills, and regulations would almost certainly not be worth it. Similarly with the literature on, say, the minimum wage. There are numerous empirical studies of various aspects and cases related to mandatory minimum wages: who, other than a trained economist who works in the field, should spend the time required to master them?

There is also, however, as paradoxical as it might sound, such a thing as *rational ignorance* – the idea that it is actually rational to remain ignorant of indefinitely many things. I do not know how satellite TV works, for example, or how to do a Tommy John surgery or how to file an amicus brief. Thankfully, however, I don't need to: there are others who do know those things, which relieves me of the burden of learning and frees me to learn about other things that relate more closely to what I actually do. If I were a satellite engineer or an orthopedic surgeon or an attorney, then I would know about the things concerned with what I did – but then I still would not know about the other things, or about the seventeenth-century Leveller movement or eighteenth-century British political economy (which I do know something about). Not having to know those other things enables me to focus my attention on a narrower range of things that connects more closely with my own interests and my own comparative advantage.

Comparative advantage is another concept we will discuss. The idea is that, although I might be able to be a satellite engineer if I spent a lot of time and energy training myself in the field, even if by some miracle I could be a better satellite engineer than at least some of the current satellite engineers, I probably could not be better by a sufficiently large margin to justify giving up what I already do and am already good at. So, the satellite engineer and I are probably both doing what we should be doing, that is, what enables each of us to contribute the value to society that we respectively can.

Just as business benefits from division of labor, then, so does knowledge. It is rational for each of us to specialize because it enables us to increase the output of whatever we work on. I could not write this book if I also had to make the word processing software I am using or if I also had to generate the electricity I am using; and if software engineers or electricity plant workers had to develop the disciplines of philosophy and economics on their own, they would not be able to make our computers work. This is true for knowledge as well. The geneticist relies on the chemist, the chemist relies on the physicist, the medical researcher relies on the biologist, the engineer relies on the mathematician, and so on. If any of them had to be experts in all those fields, they would not have any time or opportunity to make the contributions to their own fields that they are actually capable of. But they *can* make those contributions if others are taking care of the other things for them. Thus, everyone benefits from division of labor – yet another claim of economics we will explore.

There is a lot that economists do not know, but there are some things that economists have been able to figure out. Because so much of our lives depends on economic policy and because so many of the decisions we make, both individually and in the public realm, have economic implications, we should pay attention to what economics can teach us. It is a discipline, a field of inquiry, with its own specialties and subspecialties, and no one could – or should: remember rational ignorance! – become a master of all of it. But some of the principles of economics would, if more widely understood and appreciated, help us make not only better decisions in our own individual lives but also make better social and public decisions about laws, regulations, and policies. If only those of us who are not trained economists could find a ready way to learn some core economic fundamentals without having to go back to school and major in economics.

Plan of the Work

That is where this book aims to help. It presents several principles of economics, focusing on areas where their insights can be expressed without technical jargon and where exposure of the fallacies can enable significant improvement in both individual and public life. So, it largely avoids esoteric topics, specialized discussions, and – you may be relieved to learn – where math is required. I will argue that there is a series of economic fallacies that hinder our thought and, unfortunately, inform our policy. Getting rid of them will enable far better decision-making in our individual lives, as well as far better public policy. It may also help us to focus our energies on areas where we can contribute the most value to ourselves and to society – and to have public institutions that reward us for doing so.

The book has seven main chapters, each addressing a commonly held economic belief or set of beliefs that I will argue are in fact fallacies. Here is the list.

Chapter 1 addresses the "Wealth Is Zero-Sum Fallacy," or the idea that the only way a person or group can get wealthy is by impoverishing some other person or group. In fact, in a market-based commercial society, wealth is positive-sum, meaning that both (or all) parties to mutually voluntary transactions benefit. By contrast, gaining wealth through what we will call *extraction* is indeed zero-sum, or even negative-sum; gaining wealth through what we will call *cooperation*, however, is positive-sum and win–win. This chapter also addresses the worry that the rich in a commercial society might hoard, thereby preventing others from benefiting as much as they otherwise might. At the end of the book, I provide a list of references and suggestions for further reading for Chapter 1 and all the other chapters.

Chapter 2 addresses the "Good Is Good Enough Fallacy," or the idea that if some proposed course of action (or allocation of resources) would, or at least could, lead to a good outcome, then we should therefore do it. In fact, examining the potential good that would ensue from a proposal is only part of the question; the other part is what we would have to give up to do it. Because all actions and allocations involve tradeoffs, we need to estimate the opportunity cost and compare it to the prospective benefit, and then consider moving forward only if the likely proposed benefit outweighs all likely costs, including opportunity cost. That is easier said than done, however, and the implications of considering opportunity cost are surprisingly far-reaching.

Chapter 3 addresses what we will call the "Great Mind Fallacy," or the idea that there is some person or group that possesses the relevant knowledge to know how others should allocate their scarce time or treasure – and is incentivized and motivated to get it right. In fact, third parties, even expert third parties, are typically not in possession of the detailed personal knowledge required to know how other individuals should allocate their resources. They may know averages or trends based on aggregated data, but because they do not know you or your situation, they typically cannot know what is right for you to do. They are also often incentivized in ways that do not motivate them to get things right.

Chapter 4 addresses the "Progress Is Inevitable Fallacy," or the idea that innovation, increasing wealth, and economic progress are natural or inevitable. In fact, economic progress has occurred only very recently in human history, and it is dependent on fairly specific – and historically rare – cultural norms and institutional arrangements. It is thus fragile and delicate, and could easily be slowed, stopped, or even reversed.

Chapter 5 addresses the "Economics Is Amoral Fallacy," or the idea that economic calculation is cold and inhumane, proceeding without regard for human beings or the real welfare and interests of those whose lives it affects. In fact, the principles of economic reasoning not only incorporate real human interests and values, including moral values, but they might even be capable of illuminating the best ways to address and realize them.

Chapter 6 addresses the "We Should Be Equal Fallacy," or the idea that inequalities in income or wealth are necessarily bad or worrisome and thus should necessarily be reduced. In fact, people's differing abilities, skills, interests, and values should be expected to lead to differential levels of material wealth. Moreover, because they can enable people to complement one another, they can play an important role in enabling and encouraging cooperative mutual benefit. There is one conception of equality, however – what I will call *equal moral agency* – that we should support and that our public institutions should recognize and protect.

Chapter 7 addresses the "Markets Are Perfect Fallacy," or the idea that commerce and markets can solve all problems. In fact, markets face several challenges, including collective action problems and negative externalities, and there are some areas of human life – in families, for example – where market features like private property rights, competition, and negotiation are inappropriate. So, markets cannot solve all problems, and they introduce their own peculiar kinds of problems. Markets are good at addressing some kinds of problems, however, so the proper way to evaluate them is by examining them objectively, warts and all, and seeing how they stack up against actually available alternatives.

The last chapter is the Conclusion, which offers an argument for the importance of privacy – and respect for privacy – for treating others as persons of dignity and for recognizing them as moral agents equal in this respect to us. It addresses what I call the "I Am the World Fallacy" (a bonus eighth fallacy!), or the idea that my values, preferences, and tolerances are correct not only for me but also for others as well. In fact, each person is not only precious and valuable but unique, and the proper signature of choices one person should make might well apply to no others. Each of us therefore needs a private realm in which to develop his or her unique identity, and we should respect others' expression of their identities in the same way that we want others to respect ours. Such respect reflects a moral imperative arising from individuals' dignity as equal moral agents but can also lead to economic growth, vitality, and prosperity.

Finally, in a brief postscript, I indicate one important limitation of my discussion of economic fallacies, connected with my reliance on the perhaps controversial moral principle of equal moral agency. I close with a few summarizing words about why I think getting the fundamentals of economics right is so important.

As I shall try to show, the economic fallacies discussed in the following chapters have proven not only harmful but persistent. I have framed them around fallacies that "every citizen should know," but the purpose in exposing them is not only to enable better voting. As I shall also try to show, belief in the fallacies can also lead to bad decisions in our private lives – according to our own considered values. Economics offers a powerful set of analytical and decision-making tools. We must use our values, including especially our moral values, to point them in the right direction, as it were, but if we ignore or fail to use them, we open ourselves up to all manner of needless, even if well-intentioned, mistakes. We will never be able to make all decisions perfectly, of course, and no set of public institutions will ever be perfect. What we can do, however, is avoid at least some central mistakes, and thus what we can hope for is improvement, if not perfection. In this, economics can help. But we have to get it right.

1

Wealth Is Positive-Sum

Give me that which I want, and you shall have this which you want, is the meaning of every such offer; and it is in this manner that we obtain from one another the far greater part of those offices which we stand in need of.

Adam Smith, *The Wealth of Nations*

Introduction

Many believe that prosperity is a zero-sum game. A *zero-sum game* is one in which for every winner there is a loser. Think of sports or other competitive games. When the Chicago Cubs finally won the World Series in 2016, it meant that the Cleveland Indians lost. If you and I play chess, whichever of us wins, the other loses. Because markets are competitive, and because firms (and individuals) compete against each other, some of them will succeed and others will fail. This can make it seem as if markets, like baseball or chess, are zero-sum. One firm or one individual succeeds, but at the expense of other firms or individuals. And if one person were to succeed tremendously – perhaps she becomes a billionaire – it might seem that the only way she could have done so is by defeating a lot of other people: how else could she have gotten all that money?

That might be how it seems, but that is not how it is – or at least not necessarily how it is. Voluntary exchanges in a properly functioning market economy are actually positive-sum, not zero-sum, and the wealth they create is positive-sum as well.

Be Positive

If you have something I want – anything from your labor to your love to your laptop – there are two main ways I can get it from you. The first is by taking it forcibly from you. I could assault you and take it; I could steal it from you when you are not looking; or I could defraud you out of it – promising to pay you in the future, but after you give it to me, I do not pay. If I steal your laptop from you, it is +1 laptop for me, but –1 laptop for you: +1 plus –1 is zero, hence the name "zero-sum." This has been the tried-and-true method of procurement for most of human history. As soon as one person or group gets sufficient power over another person or group, they kill, conquer, and steal whatever the losing side has (or had).

Think of the "great" civilizations of the past. How did the Egyptian pharaohs build their awe-inspiring pyramids? It took a lot of labor and capital to build them; where, and how, did they get it? Answer: they conquered others, enslaved them, and forced them to labor. Or think of the Roman Empire, with its impressive Colosseum, aqueducts, roads, and vast territory: how did it achieve all of that? Answer: conquest, slavery, and theft. The examples could be multiplied almost without limit. In fact, as the great Scottish philosopher and political economist David Hume (1711–1776) put it, virtually all human civilizations, empires, and governments everywhere in the world "have been founded originally, either

15

on usurpation or conquest, or both, without any pretence of a fair consent, or voluntary subjection of the people" (Hume 1985 [1748], 471). We today may look upon their pyramids and colosseums and great walls with admiration and even awe, but we do not have to speculate long to imagine what the conquered and the enslaved who built them thought of them. In any case, all of these are examples of zero-sum exchange.

The Romans, for example, were not so much creating new wealth as taking wealth from other places and concentrating it in Rome. Imagine I built a sandcastle on the beach, and then proclaimed: "Look at my creation! Look at all the new sand I created!" Well, no. I did not create any new sand; I merely moved it from elsewhere and concentrated it here. I contributed my labor, and I organized the sand into a new, and perhaps impressive or even beautiful, configuration, but I did not make any new sand. Similarly with pharaohs, caesars, emperors, and kings and all their "creations." In fact, these kinds of exchanges might actually be *negative*-sum, not even zero-sum, because inevitably valuable assets are lost in the process – life, liberty, and property are often destroyed, leading to net loss.

Let us call such zero- (or negative-) sum exchanges *extraction*.[1] Their key defining features are: (1) they are involuntary, meaning that the conquered, the enslaved, and the victims of fraud or theft did not consent; and (2) they are not mutually beneficial, meaning that only one side of the transaction benefited – but at the expense of the other side.

[1] Following the terminology of Acemoglu and Robinson 2012.

For almost all human history, until approximately A D 1800, average per-capita wealth in the world was consistently extremely low: worldwide, the average was between $1 and $3 (in contemporary dollars) per person per day. Humanity's historically preferred method of extractive transaction is the main reason why: when we are just stealing from one another, there is no net increase in wealth. Wealth moves from one place to another, but without overall increase. And given the almost constant historical threat of predation, there has been an abiding pressure against creating anything much at all. If one person or group started to generate wealth, chances increased that someone else would come along and take it – and perhaps kill or enslave them in the process. So, despite occasional isolated locations or pockets of wealth creation in human history, there was no overall, general, sustained increase in wealth.

But there is another way to get what one wants from another: make an offer of exchange that the other party is free to accept or decline. Consider again the example of your having a laptop that I would like. Instead of stealing it from you, I could offer to buy it from you. If we agree on a price, and we exchange the laptop for the money we agreed to, then we have not a zero-sum (or negative-sum) exchange, but a *positive-sum exchange*. Both sides – that is, each of us – benefited from it. For consider: if you did not value the money I offered you for your laptop more than you valued the laptop, you would not have agreed to the exchange; and if I did not value the laptop more than I valued the money I offered you for it, I would not have agreed to the exchange. If the exchange was mutually voluntary, however, then it must also have been mutually beneficial: we both benefited, according to our respective schedules of value. Positive value (for me) plus positive value (for you) equals positive value (for us both): hence the name "positive-sum."

Suppose you go into Starbucks and order a double pumpkin spice mocha latte. The barista says "that'll be $5"; you hand over the $5, and you get the latte. Which of you benefited from that exchange – you, or Starbucks? Answer: you both did! If either you or Starbucks did not benefit from it, or did not believe you would benefit, you would not have agreed to the exchange. If Starbucks asked you for $50 for the latte, you would have said "no, thank you" and gone elsewhere; if you offered $1 for the latte, Starbucks would have said "no, thank you" and moved on to the next customer. So the fact that you both agreed on a price of the exchange, $5, means that you both, according to your own respective schedules of value, believed you benefited from it.[2] Such mutually voluntary and mutually beneficial exchanges are positive-sum and increase the total amount of benefit, or prosperity, in the world – even if only by a small, incremental amount. Let us call these mutually voluntary and mutually beneficial exchanges *cooperation*.[3] The more such cooperative exchanges take place, the more value there is in the world; as such small, incrementally beneficial exchanges are repeated millions and even billions

---

[2] We could be mistaken, however. Though voluntary transactions tend to track mutual benefit, there are cases in which we might voluntarily engage in transactions that do not in fact benefit us. I return to this issue shortly.

[3] Following David Rose's terminology; see Rose 2011 and 2019.

of times in a country or around the world, they begin to generate significant increases in prosperity.

Be Moral

Let us step back and ask a bigger-picture question. Which is more moral – extraction or cooperation? If the answer seems obvious, as I hope and trust it is, it has not been so obvious to people throughout most of our history. In fact, it constituted a great leap forward in human morality to consider that the morally superior way to deal with others is to engage in cooperative exchanges, transactions, and partnerships instead of extractive. The sad and ugly fact is that for most of our history, people simply did not regard asking permission from others as a requirement of morality. But it *is* a moral require-ment – at least if we accept the moral premise that all human beings are *equal moral agents*. If we do not accept that premise, then extraction, as well as morally repugnant behaviors like racism, sexism, xenophobia, and so on, may be licensed. But once we do accept it, then it becomes clear that the proper, indeed the only properly moral, way to deal with others is to treat them as our moral peers, equal in dignity and agency to us, which entails never engaging in involuntary extraction but only in voluntary cooperation.

I submit that a fundamental moral premise that should inform all our dealings with others is recognition of their equal moral agency. We may not force, mandate, coerce, or defraud them, either into giving us their land or posses-sions or into laboring for us. Our moral equality thus entails that a decision to coerce others requires special moral

justification, and must meet a very high justificatory burden –
typically only in cases where the person in question has
already engaged in unjustified coercion toward another, in
other words, as punishment for prior wrongdoing. No matter
how much we might want what another has, no matter how
much what they have might benefit us, we must respect their
equal moral agency as reflected in their right to say "no, thank
you" to us and go elsewhere.[4] I call this the *opt-out option*.
Possession of equal moral agency means that every person,
however rich or poor and of whatever high or low social
status, has the right to decline any offer or proposal to, or
demand we might make of, them. Morality requires respecting others' opt-out option. That means that the only
exchanges we may make with them are cooperative.

Cooperative exchanges are therefore more moral
than extractive exchanges. But which lead to greater prosperity? Because extractive exchanges are at best zero-sum,
whereas cooperative exchanges are positive-sum, only cooperative exchanges lead to increasing overall prosperity. The
more positive-sum exchanges we have, the more of our preferences, desires, and needs are met. And there is a multiplier
effect: as more of our preferences, desires, and needs are met,
we are enabled to turn our attention to yet other preferences,

---

[4] As Adam Smith writes, "To disturb [our neighbor's] happiness merely
because it stands in the way of our own, or to take from him what is of real
use to him merely because it may be of equal or of more use to us, or to
indulge, in this manner, at the expense of other people, the natural
preference which every man has for his own happiness above that of other
people, is what no impartial spectator can go along with" (Smith 1982
[1759], 82).

desires, and needs; and the more positive-sum exchanges are executed, the more overall value – whether in time or treasure – we have to meet these further preferences, desires, and needs. We have, hence, a virtuous cycle upwards in which ever more value is created and ever more prosperity is generated. As millions and billions of such positive-sum transactions are executed around the world, there is ever more prosperity available to direct toward yet further ends. This leads to what Nobel laureate Edmund Phelps (2013) calls "mass flourishing."

Cui Bono?

Wealth and prosperity that are generated cooperatively are thus not zero-sum; they are positive-sum. Their increase does not entail extracting from one party to give to another party; it does not entail a loser for every winner. On the contrary, it is *extraction* that involves one party benefiting at the expense of another party. *Cooperation* involves both parties benefiting.

Cooperative exchanges do not, however, entail that everyone benefits – only those who are parties to the transaction. If I cooperatively buy from or work for you, each of us benefits. But suppose I could have bought from one of your competitors or suppose someone else wanted to work for you, but you hired me instead. Your competitor and the disappointed prospective employee did not benefit from our exchange; only we did. But did our exchange make the other party *worse* off? No: it left them exactly as they were. They did not benefit from our exchange, at least not directly, as they expected or perhaps hoped that they would, but they were not thereby made worse off. No costs or injuries were visited upon them; they were left in exactly the same position in which they were prior to our exchange – namely, hoping to exchange or partner. Thus, cooperative exchanges do not benefit everyone, at least not directly. They benefit only those parties to the exchange, though they do not worsen the situations of others.

This is an example of what economists call a Pareto improvement:[5] at least one person was made better off, while no other person was made worse off. It is important to keep in mind that hoping for a beneficial exchange or partnership and then not getting it does not constitute a cost or injury. Because others are not entitled to, and have no right to, our time or treasure – the principle of equal moral agency means they have no right to us (without our consent) – they cannot claim an injury or demand compensation if we choose to patronize or partner with someone else. They may be disappointed, and they may have had their hopes dashed, but people protected by the principle of equal moral agency are entitled to choose with whom to exchange, transact, or partner. But disappointment at not receiving a benefit is not a cost or injury, since the disappointed party did not actually possess anything that has now been lost; they only hoped to acquire some additional new thing, and now they will have to look elsewhere to acquire it.

Let me illustrate this claim with an example. Consider dating and marriage.

---

[5] So-called for Vilfredo Pareto (1848–1923), who is credited with formulating the idea.

Suppose Jack and Jill are in love and decide to marry.[6] But Joe was also in love with Jill and hoped to marry her. When Jill marries Jack instead of Joe, was Joe injured? Is he entitled to some compensation from either Jack or Jill? No. Jill's decision might have disappointed Joe, but Joe has no right to Jill – no right to her love or affection or companionship – and hence he has no basis on which to demand compensation. Unless we claim that Joe's interests are more important than those of Jack or Jill, or that Joe is himself somehow more important than either Jack or Jill, Joe will have to seek his companionship elsewhere. The principle of equal moral agency prevents us from granting Joe any special status or privilege; his moral agency, along with his preferences, desires, and needs, are important, but no more important than those of anyone else. He is a unique and precious individual, a valuable and irreplaceable seat of consciousness and agency and hence dignity, and therefore he deserves respect; but the same applies also to Jack and Jill, and to everyone else. The partnership between Jack and Jill (i.e., their marriage) is positive-sum, meaning each of them benefits from it (presumably: otherwise they would not have agreed to marry). It does not mean that everyone benefits from it – Joe does not – but neither Joe nor anyone else is positively injured. Joe is left in exactly the same position in which he was before, namely, looking for, hoping for, desiring someone to marry.

Change the example slightly. Suppose Jack and Jill have been dating for some time; Jill believes she loves Jack and Jack believes he loves Jill. Jack decides he wants to ask Jill to

---

[6] I elaborate on this analogy in Otteson 2014 and 2017.

marry him, and so he asks her to dinner next Saturday night, at which he intends to ask her; Jill agrees to go to dinner with him, wondering whether Jack will ask her to marry him – and she decides that if he does ask, she will say yes. In anticipation, Jack buys an engagement ring and looks forward to their dinner. On the Friday before their portentous Saturday date, however, Jill happens to run into Joe at a coffee shop – and there is a spark. They spend the rest of the day with each other, talking, walking, breaking bread; indeed, they talk all night. As the sun is coming up the next morning, Joe looks at the beautiful sunrise, he looks at the beautiful Jill, and he says: "Jill, I have never met anyone like you before. No one's ever had an effect on me like this before. I can't believe what I'm about to say, but, let's get married! Let's go to a justice of the peace right now and get married!" Jill is stunned, and her head begins to whir, but as thoughts fly around in her mind, she replies, "Yes!" And they get married that very day.

Now think for a moment about poor Jack. Has he suffered some bad luck? Obviously yes – the very week he decides to ask his longtime girlfriend to marry him, she just happens to meet some stranger with whom she decides to elope? That seems pretty bad luck. Is the disappointment he now feels justified? Again, obviously yes: he loves her; he had devoted time and energy into his relationship with her, and he had hopes and expectations that their love and partnership would be formalized and would continue indefinitely into the future. All that has now come to an unexpected end. But: Is Jack owed any compensation? Should he be able to sue Jill to compensate him for the future love and affection he antici- pated getting from her that he will now not get? Should he be able to sue Joe for – well, for what? Trespass? Or should the state pass a law that says that people like Joe should not speak to or ask to wed people like Jill, or that if people like Joe do so he (or Jill, or taxpayers, or anyone else) must compensate Jack?

The answer to all these questions is no. And the reason, crucially, is because Jack had no right to Jill. Jill is a free person. She gets to decide to whom to give or from whom to withhold her love, affection, time, and partnership. Even if her decision leads some others to experience disappointment or disaffection, and even if her decision was prompted by luck – a chance encounter with another person – nevertheless as a moral agent equal to everyone else, she gets to decide whom to marry and whom not to marry (and whether to marry at all). So, is Jack owed anything? If you are a friend of Jack's, perhaps in virtue of your friendship you have some obligation to him: perhaps you should take him for a beer and console him. Perhaps you should introduce him to another potential mate. But you may not visit any cost on or injury to Jill or Joe, without violating their equal moral agency. Bad luck and reasonable disappointment, therefore, do not by themselves constitute injury requiring or licensing forced compensation.

What does this have to do with economics? Precisely the same reasoning applies to market exchanges. Suppose you own a coffee shop, and I have been patronizing your shop every morning for some time. Both you and I expect our mutually voluntary and mutually beneficial transactions to continue indefinitely into the future. But suppose one day a new coffee shop opens across the street from yours. I decide to try it, and I discover, to my surprise, that I like it better – I like the coffee better, the prices better, the ambience better, the service better, or some combination. In any case, I stop going to your shop. Suppose others stop patronizing you as well, and thus the former success of your business does not continue. Perhaps you have to lay off some workers; perhaps you even go out of business altogether. Are you owed compensation? Were you injured by your subsequent loss of business? The answer to both questions is no, and for the same reason: you had no more right to me and my resources, or to your other (former) patrons and their resources, than Jack has a right to Jill and her affection. We are all equal moral agents entitled equally to make choices, and to take our love and other resources with us.

But our choices no longer to patronize you do not constitute the imposition of a cost or injury on you. Each day that you opened your shop, you hoped for customers. Unless you had some voluntary contract or other promise with your customers, each day you had only the hope, and perhaps expectation, of getting customers. If today you get fewer customers, those who did not patronize you did not take any resources from you. They did not steal from or defraud you; they did not violate a promise to or contract with you; they did not trespass on or otherwise use your property without your consent. They simply chose to go elsewhere. So, you may well be disappointed, but they caused you no loss; they only did not give you a gain, the gain you were hoping for but were not entitled to demand. If your business subsequently does not enjoy the success it once did, that will no doubt constitute a real and genuine disappointment to you, but the absence of a hoped-for gain is not a loss. You were instead left in exactly the same position where you started when you opened today: hoping for customers, hoping for positive-sum exchanges.

A worry one might raise is whether a disappointed party might not be negatively affected after all because of the reduction in the number of available options. It is not just that Jack is disappointed that Jill decided to marry Joe instead of him; he now has one fewer option available to him in the world. Similarly, if a company hires you instead of me, the total set of options available to me, even if numerous overall, has now been reduced by one. Does that not negatively affect me, or constitute a cost to me? It is true that the set of options for a disappointed party has been reduced, but that worry is mitigated by two factors. First, for most people most of the time, there are so many other potential options that the reduction by one, even one that a person really wanted, is minimal relative to the entire set. There will be lots of other possibilities – and new possibilities arising all the time. In a modern market economy, it is like someone claiming a bit of sand on the beach to build a sandcastle: if you want to build a sandcastle too, you cannot use *that* sand, but you can just use other sand. Similarly if someone buys the car, house, condo, and so on that you wanted: you may have lost an option, but there will still be other options, even if they are not equally valuable to you; and in any case new options are being created continuously. Of course, human beings are each unique, irreplaceable, and more valuable than any good, service, or anything else. But along with their uniqueness and irreplaceability comes their equal moral agency, which entails their right to make choices – even those that disappoint you.

Positive-sum exchanges, then, will not satisfy everyone. But they will satisfy the parties to them. And those who are not satisfied are not positively harmed; they remain in precisely the same position in which they were. So, while not everyone benefits from positive-sum exchanges, at least some do; and the more of such exchanges there are, the more benefit is created.

The Story of Humanity's Wealth

Earlier I said that disappointed third parties would not benefit from first- and second-party cooperative exchanges "at least not directly." Here is what I meant by that. You are not *directly* benefited if I choose to patronize a shop other than yours – or if I choose to work, partner, marry, transact, or exchange with someone other than you – but you are benefited *indirectly* by living in a society in which not only are such positive-sum cooperative exchanges encouraged but zero-sum extractive exchanges are prohibited. For not only does that mean that no one may extract resources unwillingly from you, which would constitute a genuine – and direct – cost or injury to you, but you also benefit indirectly from living in a society in which positive-sum exchanges, and the prosperity to which they lead, are executed. You may not have been able to execute this one particular exchange, but the prosperity generated by the millions and billions of other positive-sum exchanges in your society means that your overall standard of living will go up regardless. A society of increasing prosperity means more value creation, and hence more opportunity for you to achieve your ends, than you could enjoy from living in a society in which prosperity is not increasing (or is declining).

It turns out that this is the story of the wealth that has been created in the world since approximately A D 1800. It was around that time, in some specific parts of the world, that the idea began to spread that cooperative exchanges are not only allowable but morally commendable, and that extractive exchanges are not morally neutral but morally objectionable. As that idea spread, more and more positive-sum exchanges took place, leading to the explosion in wealth that the world has seen over the last two centuries. And that increase in wealth has been not only spectacular but historically unprecedented.

The average person alive in 1800 was no wealthier than the average human alive 100,000 years ago: both lived on less than $3 per person per day in contemporary dollars. [7] By contrast, the average person alive in the world today enjoys $48 per day, a 16-fold real increase. In the United States today, people on average enjoy $164 per day, an incredible 55-fold real increase. In 1900, approximately 90 percent of all people on earth lived at the low historical average of under $3 per person per day, which the United Nations defines as "absolute poverty." [8] Today, that proportion stands at approximately

---

[7] This section draws on resources including: Clark 2007; Maddison 2007; Chandy and Smith 2014; McCloskey 2016 and 2019; Mokyr 2016; Roser and Ortiz-Ospina 2017; Yunus 2017; Pinker 2018; Rosling, Rosling, and Rönnlund 2018; World Bank 2018; Davies 2019; Meyer et al. 2019; and Otteson 2019.

[8] The United Nations describes "absolute poverty" as "a condition characterized by severe deprivation of basic human needs, including safe

9 percent, and it is falling rapidly. Indeed, we are on the brink of reducing the proportion of people living at absolute poverty to zero – an incredible achievement, though one that almost no one seems to know about. Although the gains worldwide have been uneven, with some places enjoying a much greater increase in prosperity than other places, almost all of us are gaining, with more gaining each year. And the difference this makes in the lives of the poorest among us is the most striking. The pharaoh, the emperor, and the king have long been able to get what they wanted and to arrogate to themselves a life that was unreachable by the vast majority of others – but by extraction. The prosperity to which positive-sum exchanges in markets have led has benefited not so much them as it has everyone else. This is why Phelps (2013) calls it "mass flourishing": for the first time in human history, even the low, the disrespected, and the disenfranchised have been able to improve their conditions, and to an extent never before seen.

Things are not perfect, of course. There will always be problems in a world of imperfect creatures and limited, if increasing, resources. Our vastly increased resources are still outstripped by our seemingly infinite and often conflicting desires, and of course there is still that 9 percent of people living at the tragically low historical level of absolute poverty. But the good, indeed great, news is that nearly seven billion people have been able to rise above those historical levels of poverty and achieve levels of prosperity, longevity, life

drinking water, sanitation facilities, health, shelter, education and information"; see Mack 2016.

satisfaction, literacy, peace, food security, freedom, and the expectation of a better future that previous generations could only have dreamed of.

The Rich and the Poor

The first fallacy that needs to be exposed, then, is that wealth creation is zero-sum. The generation of wealth in markets is actually positive-sum: it is not win–lose; it is win–win. But exposing that fallacy also implicates other, related fallacies. One relates to the familiar refrain that "the rich get richer and the poor get poorer." That is what happens in an extractive regime. When people's persons, property, and voluntary promises are not protected, when people can be assaulted, encaged, or enslaved, stolen from or trespassed upon, or defrauded or had their contracts or promises breached, then whoever is more powerful or vicious can victimize the less powerful or the virtuous. Throughout much of human history, this is exactly how the rich got rich: they violated what we might call the three pillars, or the "three Ps," of justice – the persons, property, and promises – of others in order to enrich themselves at the latters' expense. No voluntary consent was given or sought, and no mutual benefit accrued – only benefit for one extracted from another. In such cases, unfortunately repeated throughout human history and still occurring in the world today, the rich do indeed get richer not just *while* the poor get poorer but by *making* the poor poorer.

As we have seen, however, that is not what happens with cooperative exchanges like those in markets. There, both sides benefit. But consider a few questions.

31

Suppose A and B voluntarily decide to exchange. Perhaps they both benefit, but do they benefit to the same degree? Could it not be true that A benefits more, even much more, than B benefits? Yes, it could be true. In reality, it is hard to know exactly to what degree the parties to a voluntary exchange benefit – partly because it is very difficult to measure, or even to know what exactly to measure. *Value* and *benefit* are not discrete entities that can be counted, and it is not clear that they are the kind of entity, like water, that can be gauged. Because they cannot be weighed or counted, it is not clear how terms like *how much* even apply to them. (We could ask people to make personal estimates, but it is not clear what exactly whatever they might respond would indicate.) But there is one thing we can know: they must have benefited to at least some extent. We know that because if they did not benefit – if they did not receive what they believe to be some net positive increase in value – they would not have done it. All human action is costly. It takes energy to do anything, and because energy, like other resources, is limited, and people tend not to expend energy for no reason, we must assume that if a person does something she has some reason for it, some benefit or value she believes she is accruing or will accrue for her action. Hence, if she did not think she would benefit from buying a product or service, if she did not think she would benefit from working for this company or that one, if she did not think she would benefit from this partnership or transaction, and so on, she would not have done it.

That does not mean she cannot be mistaken. We are all fallible, and we all do things that do not pan out the way we hoped, expected, or anticipated. We also often do things that, after the fact, we wish we had not done. So, not all voluntary transactions end up being mutually beneficial, or at least as beneficial as we had hoped. At the moment of decision to act, however, we hope to achieve something. More specifically, we hope to achieve some value or benefit. If A and B exchange or partner voluntarily, each of them expects to benefit from doing so. Perhaps one of them will end up benefiting more than the other. But that would not change the fact that they both believed they would benefit to at least some degree.

If either or both decided after the fact that they did not actually benefit from the exchange – or perhaps not enough to justify the transaction – then they will not do that again. Next time they will look elsewhere, or seek different terms, and so on. Because, however, third parties typically do not have the local, personal information about A and B that would be required to know whether an exchange will in fact end up being mutually beneficial to them, third parties are usually not in a position to second-guess A's and B's decisions. But A and B do possess the local, personal knowledge about their own situations. A and B might still be mistaken, but they stand a much better chance of getting it right – that is, of making a good decision that is likely to lead to their benefit – than is anyone who does not know them or their circumstances. Of course, it is very difficult for anyone to know with certainty what will in fact end up benefiting them. A good way of discovering benefit-producing transactions is to let the individuals who are best positioned to know make decisions in their own cases, and then learn from their experiences, good or bad. Thus, allowing individual persons and parties to make economic decisions in their own cases is usually a better way to discover mutual benefit, and ensuring protection of each party's opt-out option disciplines everyone to seek not only their own benefit but others' benefit as well.

But perhaps A is a large corporation with billions of dollars in assets, whereas B is a single individual who is, relative to A, far poorer. Perhaps A is Starbucks, and you are B; perhaps it is true that you both benefit when you buy a latte from Starbucks, but Starbucks is much richer than you, and so perhaps it benefits much more from the sale than you do. Or perhaps Starbucks has far less to lose than you do if the two of you do not successfully exchange, giving them more leverage. All that might be true. Yet your opt-out option remains your right, and it is decisive for you. At the point of exchange, both you and Starbucks are moral equals, even if unequal in wealth.

What about the barista who serves you? Perhaps Starbucks is benefiting from the sale, but is the barista? Yes, the barista is benefiting as well. We know that because if the barista did not believe he was benefiting, or at least benefiting sufficiently to keep working there, he would quit. Now, maybe he does not have many other options, or perhaps he simply does not like his other options; perhaps he thinks this is the best option for him right now but nevertheless believes he should be doing better – that he should be getting paid more, or get a promotion, or receive better benefits, and so on. There is a good chance the barista does believe that he should be paid more than whatever he is getting paid, because that is what everyone believes, no matter where they work or how much they are getting paid. We all want more, and we may all believe we deserve more, but neither of those entails that we are not gaining from whatever we are doing now. Again, otherwise we would not do it. The only way to doubt this is by assuming that the person in question is either not rational – that is, is not capable of understanding her own circumstances and taking action to improve her situation, whatever it is – or is choosing based on inauthentic preferences. But being poor, or poorer than another, does not therefore mean that one is not rational. One person not making as much as another person does not mean that the former is less intelligent or less virtuous than the latter. Some discussion of poverty relief, and of economic policy in general, seems indeed premised on an assumption that the poor are somehow lesser, that the fact that they are poor means they are not capable of taking proper care of themselves or making good decisions in their own lives.[9] Such a view might flatter the sensibilities of the rich, but it seems a prejudicial insult to the poor.

Although we all sometimes make poor choices, it is, in fact, exceedingly difficult to know, especially from the outside or from afar, whether a person's choices are based on inauthentic preferences. What would the standard be for telling when a person is choosing based on authentic preferences? The temptation would be to decide based on the substance of the choices a person makes. If he made choices different from what we would make in his situation, does that necessarily mean his choices are inauthentic? But he is not us – and therein lies the danger: it is all too easy to decide that my preferences should be your preferences, and to judge you according to the degree to which your actual choices coincide

[9] For critical assessments of poverty-relief policy, see Easterly 2007 and Coyne 2013.

with my imagined choices were I in your shoes. The worry here is prejudice: others make, or are making, choices based on inauthentic preferences because their choices are not those I would make – in other words, my preferences are superior to theirs. But just as being poor does not necessarily mean one is irrational, making different choices from those that person A would make does not by itself mean that B's preferences are bad, irrational, or inauthentic.

It turns out that a great deal of poverty – not all, but a great deal – is the result of roadblocks that are placed in the path to prosperity. We will discuss this in more detail later, but making it difficult or impossible for people to own property or to start businesses, targeting the poor for violations and fines, preventing them from entering markets, enacting or endorsing regulation that already existing firms can pay but new entrants cannot, and so on – all of which goes on at local, federal, and global levels today – are examples of extraction. They are ways of enabling some to profit, or profit more, from preventing competition and protecting market share for some at others' expense. The poor particularly suffer from such restrictions, but consumers also lose because they keep prices artificially high and because they stifle the entrepreneurship, innovation, diversity of ideas, and creativity that open markets and open competition allow. The story of increasing worldwide wealth over the last two centuries has resulted precisely from allowing ever more people to engage in mutually voluntary and mutually beneficial transactions *without* third-party interposition.

To a perhaps surprisingly large extent, the poor could rise out of poverty all on their own if only we would let them.

We know this because they have done and are doing it now. Consider the history of Hong Kong, for example, in comparison to mainland China, or that of South Korea and of North Korea, and consider how the former in each comparison grew so much wealthier, in such a short time, relative to the latter. Before undertaking to do something for the poor, then, perhaps we should first stop doing things to the poor. They are not science or engineering experiments, and they are not children requiring adult supervision. They are human beings, equal in dignity and moral agency to us: let them have and use their agency.

Hoarding

In a properly functioning market economy – one, that is, in which all transactions are mutually voluntary and mutually beneficial, and in which every party to any transaction retains an opt-out option or the right to say "no, thank you" and go elsewhere – any successfully executed transactions lead to gain for both (or all) parties to them. Thus, the idea that one person can get wealthy only at the expense of another, or only by making another poor – that is, that wealth is necessarily zero-sum – is a fallacy.

A related fallacy, however, is connected to the common "haves vs. the have-nots" phrase, namely, that if someone has wealth, then that person is the only one who benefits from it. When we speak of "the rich" who "own" or "possess" or "accumulate" wealth, or when we speak of how much the rich "have," we may be assuming that the rich not only acquired their wealth through extraction but are hoarding it.

37

They "have" it and are not sharing. If there are people who do not have wealth, however, then hoarding it seems clearly wrong – the rich should share. As many put it, the rich should "pay their fair share," usually in taxes, out of a duty not of charity but of fairness or justice. Perhaps the rich have benefited from living in a country whose institutions have allowed them to grow rich; or perhaps they have benefited from luck in the form of good parents or good schools or good infrastructure – none of which can they claim to have created or chosen on their own, and hence for none of which can they claim moral credit or entitlement. If some are richer than others, perhaps much richer than others, then it might seem only fair that they should "give back" to their communities, either in thanks for their lucky good fortune or in repayment for the opportunities they exploited when others did not have the chance.

Jeff Bezos is currently the wealthiest person in the world, with a net worth estimated, as of this writing, at $130 billion. As astonishing as that number is, it does not make him the wealthiest person ever. Over the last 500 years, there have been at least six people wealthier than Bezos, and perhaps (depending on estimates) a handful more. At their peaks, the inflation-adjusted wealth of several Americans probably topped that of Bezos: Cornelius Vanderbilt (1794–1877) is estimated to have had a net worth of between (in contemporary dollars) $105 billion and $205 billion; Vanderbilt's son William Henry (1821–1885) inherited and increased his father's fortune to as much as $239 billion; and the wealth of Henry Ford (1863–1947) is estimated to have been between $188 and $199 billion. As high as those numbers are, they pale in comparison to the two wealthiest Americans of all time: Andrew Carnegie (1835–1919), whose net worth at its peak would equal roughly, in contemporary dollars, $310 billion; and John D. Rockefeller (1839–1937), whose net worth at its peak would be roughly equivalent today to a staggering $336 billion. And yet none of them can hold a candle to the single wealthiest person in the world over the last 500 years, the German merchant, banker, financier, and mining rights owner Jakob Fugger (1459–1525), whose total wealth at its peak is estimated to be roughly equivalent to an incredible $400 billion today – roughly *triple* Bezos's wealth.

What on earth did they do with all that wealth? Did they really need all of that? In the cases of the earlier historical figures especially, when they were building their fortunes the world was full of desperately poor people, and the differentials between their wealth and the wealth of the average of the rest of the world was on the order of hundreds of thousands to one. When Carnegie sold his holdings in U.S. Steel in 1901, his resulting net worth is estimated to have constituted some 4 percent of the wealth of the entire United States, making him approximately 150,000 times as wealthy as the average American at the time and some 200,000 times as wealthy as the world average. It is difficult to contemplate such numbers and not feel resentment, even revulsion. There was no way for Carnegie to have used all that wealth, no reasonable way to imagine that he could possibly have needed it. It may be true that in the last third or so of his life he gave much of it away to various good charitable causes – universities, libraries, hospitals, churches, and so on – but what could possibly justify his having all that in the first place?

I suggest that the mere possession of wealth, however, even a great deal of wealth or a great deal more wealth than many (most, almost all) others, does not by itself rise to the level of injustice or justify moral condemnation. A moral judgment would instead turn on answering the question of how the person got his wealth. Was it through force, fraud, theft, imperialism, cronyism, conquest, or usurpation – in other words, was it through involuntary *extraction*? Or was it through mutually voluntary and mutually beneficial exchanges, or *cooperation*? The answer to that question makes all the moral difference: the former is immoral, but the latter is not. If one wants to condemn another's wealth, one would have to show not just that the wealth is large or is more (even a great deal more) than what others have, but, instead, one would have to show that it was acquired through immoral means. Actual historical examples – including Carnegie and virtually every other person in the pantheon of what the contemporary philosopher Peter Singer (2009) calls the "superrich" – admit of various judgments, with many arguing that extraction played at least some role in the generation of virtually all their fortunes, though there is disagreement about whether, and if so to what extent, they did benefit from extraction. But to whatever extent extraction did play a role, then we would be justified in condemning it morally.

I propose to put aside judgment of any particular historical figure, however, and instead make a more general claim: the wealth of the rich does not – at least in a market economy – benefit only themselves. It will certainly benefit them, but many others will benefit as well. The reason is that, despite the way we often speak and perhaps think of the matter, the wealth is not "distributed" to anyone, and their "holdings" are not literally held by them. Take these in turn.

We often speak of "wealth distribution," as, for example, when we speak of how much wealth is distributed to the top 1 percent in America or how worldwide wealth is distributed across the globe. When we speak this way, we can imagine that the wealth is sitting in some people's pockets or in their backyards, or perhaps hoarded in some countries as opposed to others, and that it was either handed out to them by someone or something, or that it was gathered by them, like sand from a beach and piled in a heap. In a market economy, however, there is no person or agency that has the wealth and dispenses it to some as opposed to others. As we have seen, it has often happened in human history that a pharaoh, emperor, king, or warlord confiscated, stole, or otherwise wrested wealth from others, and then oftentimes distributed the booty to his family, friends, or foot soldiers. All that is extraction. By contrast, in a properly functioning market economy, which operates under attitudes that condemn extraction and institutions that punish it, the only way to get wealth is by producing, generating, or creating it in voluntary cooperation with others. In other words, in a market economy, the only way one can benefit or enrich oneself is by benefiting or enriching others – simultaneously, if not always to the same degree.[10]

---

[10] One can also get wealthy by receiving others' wealth as a gift, as many who inherit their wealth do. In a market economy based on cooperation, however, the wealth anyone would receive as a gift would itself have had to be generated through mutual benefit.

I am speaking literally, not figuratively or metaphorically: by "producing" it I mean that before there was no wealth and now there is. Suppose you and I are blacksmiths who make pins. Alone I can make twenty pins per day and you can make twenty pins per day. If we partner and work together, by dividing the labor we can make not forty but sixty. Adding more voluntary partners to our venture, and further dividing the labor among us to enable further specialization, increases the productive gains not linearly but exponentially. If we voluntarily partner with eight other people, then, according to estimates Adam Smith made based on his own observations (Smith 1981 [1776], 15), the ten of us could make upwards of 48,000 pins per day, or the equivalent of some 4,800 pins per person – an increase in production of 23,900 percent! Now, do any of us by ourselves need 4,800 pins per person per day? Of course not. So, what do we do with the remainder? We sell it. If our ten-person pin-making shop is now producing 48,000 pins per day, the vast majority of which we are selling in markets, then the total supply of pins in society is increasing dramatically. What happens to the price, other things equal, as the supply increases? The price comes down. What happens as the price comes down? More and more people can afford the pins.

Now, pin-making may seem like a trivial matter (Smith himself calls it a "trifling" example), but the same logic applies to other goods produced in markets. If people are allowed to partner and cooperate, they will discover ways to divide the labor and specialize. Dividing the labor enables increasing production for, as Smith enumerates, three principal reasons: (1) each worker increases his dexterity and skill, because by focusing on a smaller range of tasks he gets much better at them; (2) time is saved that would otherwise be lost by switching from one task to another; and, perhaps most importantly, (3) specialization enables the development of new ideas, expedients, and innovations to improve and expand production. Thus, the pattern observed in pin-making would hold elsewhere as well: division of labor and specialization, thus increased production, thus decreased prices, thus increasing numbers of people who can afford them, and thus an increasing standard of living.

As more and more people can engage in these entre-preneurial ventures and partnerships, more and more goods and services will follow these patterns of increased production and decreased prices, which means there will be an increasing overall supply of goods and services in society. The Adam Smithian prediction would be that as attitudes and institutions supporting and encouraging cooperative transactions spread, more and more people would rise out of humanity's historical norm of poverty, perhaps reaching heights that in his day no one could have dreamed of. It was an audacious prediction to make in 1776, when Smith published his *Wealth of Nations*. And yet what has unfolded in the subsequent 245 years?

The Labor Theory of Value

A belief that economics long ago abandoned but that continues to recur is a labor theory of value. One of its proponents was Karl Marx (1818–1883), but another was none other than Adam Smith. They were both wrong, however, despite how intuitively plausible the labor theory of value, or LTV, might seem. It is important to see why.

Let us view our pin-making example from a different angle. Suppose I decide I want to open a pin-making shop, and I borrow money to buy a warehouse, equipment, and supplies, and to hire you and nine other people. Your jobs will be to execute the various operations required to make the pins: as Smith describes it, one person "draws out the wire, another straightens it, a third cuts it, a fourth points it, a fifth grinds it at the top for receiving the head" and so on (Smith 1981 [1776], 15). Suppose we then begin to manufacture our tens of thousands of pins per day, and, the market being favorable, we sell them at a profit. Who gets that profit? I, the owner, do. What do you and the other workers get? A wage. Is that fair? If one subscribes to an LTV, it might seem quite unfair – even unjust.

Both Marx and Smith thought that the ultimate origin and source of value is human labor. Consider the difference between open land left in the condition in which nature created it and that same field that has been cultivated by human labor. An acre of land with naturally occurring apple trees on it might produce a bushel or two of apples; but an acre of land with apple trees that are deliberately planted and cultivated for maximum productive output will produce many times that amount. In the seventeenth century, John Locke (1632–1704) estimated that the addition of human labor in the form of farming and active cultivation could add ten times, one hundred times, even one thousand times the value that would have been produced by the same land if left to nature's devices (Locke 1980 [1690], sects. 37, 40, and 43). That meant that human labor accounted for between nine-tenths and nine hundred and ninety-nine thousandths of the value created for others to use or consume. It is easy to conclude – indeed, it can seem all but self-evident – that labor is not only what creates value but perhaps even that labor *is* value. The former is what Smith thought, and the latter is what Marx seemed to think.

Now come back to the pin-making shop I started and in which you and others work for me for a wage. If it is labor that creates value, then it is the workers who are creating the value because they are the ones laboring. If, however, the profit goes to me (the owner) instead, then it seems as though I am exploiting the laborers and arrogating to myself, perhaps even stealing, what rightfully belongs to them. For consider: if it was the workers' labor that created, or perhaps constitutes, the value, then what right do I have to profit from it? Shouldn't the profit go to them instead?

It turns out that the LTV is false, however. But before coming to that, an unnoticed aspect of the example should be pointed out: the owner of the shop also contributed labor! It was the owner who had the idea, who hired the workers, who manages the workers and supplies, who pays the bills, and who sells in the market. It is also the owner who took out the initial loans of capital, at his own risk, and who therefore stands not only to profit if things go well but also to lose if things go poorly. And it is he who bears the responsibility of meeting payroll. All of these require skill and labor, under both risk and uncertainty, which goes some way toward explaining why, in those relatively rare occasions that a business succeeds, the entrepreneur also profits, just as the workers do who are receiving their wages.

But the LTV is actually false. To see why, consider as an example a painting from Van Gogh. How much is it worth, or what is its value? Perhaps he worked on the painting for a month; in his day, a month's worth of labor might have been valued at a couple hundred dollars or so. But the painting today might sell for millions. How do we explain the discrepancy? Or compare the value of a Van Gogh today to the value of something I might paint. Perhaps I spent twice as long making my painting as Van Gogh did making his, and yet his is worth orders of magnitude more than mine – indeed, than anything I could possibly produce, no matter how much time I spent on it. Again, how do we explain the discrepancy? The answer lies in the element of the scenario that we left out of the above discussion: other people. The worth of a painting, or a pin, is determined not by how much labor you, I, or anyone else put into it, but, rather, by how much others value it. In other words, it is *other people's* schedules of value that determines the worth, and the price, of things – not what you, I, or any other laborer wants.

If we were to subscribe to an LTV, we would be unable to understand everyday occurrences of people valuing things differently and of their being willing to pay different amounts for the same thing. We would be unable to account for the fact that some things on which people might labor enormously could end up having no value – something that happens, alas, all too often. The philosopher Robert Nozick (1938–2002) offered this example: if I take some driftwood I found on a beach and cover it with pink enamel paint, I will surely have labored on it, but it would appear that by doing so I have not added any value; indeed, I may well have *decreased* its value (Nozick 1974, 175). The LTV cannot explain or even make sense of such common examples. The LTV would also be unable to explain why firms go out of business, as nearly 80 percent of new businesses in the United States do within two years of their founding. Presumably the people who started and worked at those businesses labored, indeed probably labored very hard, at them; on the LTV, they will therefore have created a great deal of value. Why, then, would they go out of business? Are those of us who choose not to patronize them guilty of error, or even injustice, for not recognizing or respecting the labor value in their goods or services?

Yet these phenomena are intelligible at once if we reject the LTV and instead assume a subjective theory of value, or STV. The STV holds that what any production, any good or service, is worth depends on the judgment of others – specifically what others, or at least one other, is willing to give up or sacrifice for it. The answer to why a Van Gogh painting is worth more than an Otteson painting is not because of the labor each of us put into his respective creation; it is, rather, because of how other people value our respective creations. The reason the driftwood coated in pink enamel paint is worthless is not because the painter did not labor on it, but because no one else values the creation. The reason so many businesses go under is not because their owners or employees did not labor on, or in, them; it is instead because other people – customers, clients, and prospective customers and clients – did not value their offerings sufficiently to be willing to part with whatever resources they would have had to sacrifice to procure them. And so on. The upshot is that value is subjective, meaning tied to and dependent on individuals' respective personal valuations. Pick any creation, any production, any good or service whatever: some people will value it highly, others will value it less, and others will value it not at all; some indeed will assign it a negative value – they might be willing to pay *not* to have, see, hear, or experience it. (If you had ever heard me play the piano, you would understand immediately.) And all of them may be making the correct valuations, according to their own individual schedules of value.

Relate this discussion to our pin-making shop. Whether the shop manages to be profitable, and to whatever degree it manages to do so, depends on the extent to which it is offering a good at rates or under conditions that others value – that is, that others believe would provide them a net increase in value, after subtracting whatever they would have to sacrifice or trade off for it. Assuming that our partnership in the shop is voluntary and cooperative, all of us were willing to sacrifice some of our time and treasure in return for whatever each of us agreed to receive. As long as no extraction – no force, fraud, or theft, no misrepresentation or breach of contract – was involved, the default assumption is that each of us believed that he or she benefited, or would benefit, from the partnership, which is why we agreed to the partnership in the first place. If after a while any of us believes that the value we are contributing to the enterprise is not being fully recompensed by whatever return in profit, wages, benefits, and so on we are receiving, we are welcome to renegotiate – or at least attempt to renegotiate. As equal moral agents to everyone else, each of us has the right to propose, request, or argue for whatever she would like, or whatever she believes is fair or just or right.

Because others are equal moral agents as well, however, they may also similarly negotiate. But they also, like us, retain their opt-out option, which means they retain the right to say "no, thank you" to us if they choose. Moral equality is a two-way street. We may not like, or we may come not to like, the choices others make, whether they be customers who choose to patronize our competitors or employers who choose not to remunerate us as we believe they should. In the absence of extraction, breach of contract or promise, and so on, others' choices that disappoint or disaffect us would therefore not rise to the level of injustice warranting (enforceable) compensation. Jill's choice to marry Joe rather than Jack disappoints Jack, but Jack is entitled to no compensation from Jill (or Joe) because Jill (and Joe) are equal moral agents to Jack and thus get to decide to whom to give or from whom to refrain from giving their affection. You may wish you got paid more, and you may believe you deserve to be paid more; but if your employer will not pay you more, she has just as much right to that decision as Jill does about whom to marry.

But you may also exercise your opt-out option too. If you believe that your employer is mistreating you or undervaluing your contributions, quit – and take your skills, your labor, your time, and your treasure elsewhere. Of course, most of us do not like the prospect of taking such drastic action, and doing so would undoubtedly be accompanied by high costs, if nothing else in time, in anxiety, and in psychological discomfort. These are real costs, which should not be discounted or depreciated. When contemplating taking such a step, then, we will have to factor those costs into our reckoning as well, and they may well mean that we should remain in less-than-ideal situations longer than we would (ideally) like. Because, however, others, as equal moral agents to us, are entitled to make their own decisions about with whom to partner or transact and under what conditions, we must respect their choices – even when we disagree with them, and even when they are ultimately making the wrong choices.

If the owner of a business is profiting handsomely, and her employees believe they should be paid more, they therefore have the right to request or negotiate for more. They also have the right to quit, or threaten to quit (even as a group), if they do not get what they want. But they must respect her opt-out option as well. She, like her employees, will have to make decisions based on complicated calculations about what the best use of her limited time and treasure is, always under risk and uncertainty. There is no more guarantee she will get it right than her employees are guaranteed that their choice to stay or to leave will be turn out to be right for them. Beyond whatever they have mutually voluntarily agreed to, however, the employees are not entitled to her resources, and hence they are not entitled to any specific package of wages, benefits, or other compensation regardless of the labor they do or will contribute.

Trickling Down?

The good news is that in a market economy employees will typically have many options. There are some 30 million businesses in the United States today, with more coming into (and of course many also going out of) existence continually. Employees can also start their own businesses if they would like. Because in market economies overall prosperity continues to rise, that means there are not only continually more options from which to choose and more potential opportunities to pursue, but there are also more resources overall to enable ever more entrepreneurial activity, and ever more needs, preferences, and goals to be met and satisfied.

This raises the issue of capital accumulation and profit. The argument has been that individuals and firms that succeed in properly functioning market-based economies will have done so by cooperative mutual betterment. Their profit will be honest, and honorable, because it resulted from, and resulted only from, their having simultaneously made others better off – as judged by those others. The prosperity, and capital, that would grow from honest profit is, then, ultimately a consequence of improving others' lives.

As we have seen, however, the increasing capital does not merely sit in a bank vault somewhere; people typically do not keep their wealth in coffee cans buried in the backyard, stuffed into their mattresses, or in their pockets. Instead, they save, invest, or spend it. They put it in (interest-bearing) bank accounts; they buy stock or put it in pensions, mutual funds, 401(k)s, or IRAs; or they buy various goods and services with it. In each case they are putting their wealth in a position to help yet others, including others they do not know. What does the bank do with the money you put into your account? It lends it out to others, so that they can buy cars or homes, so they can send their children to college, so they can start their own businesses, and so on. When you put your money in mutual funds or 401(k)s, what happens to that wealth? It is invested in other people's businesses, enabling them to engage in research and development, improve their facilities, or buy equipment and supplies; to hire more employees, pay them more, or give them more generous health, education, insurance, or other benefits; to try new ventures or experiment with innovations; or some combination. In other words, it enables other people to search for ways to improve their own and others' situations more or better. Thus, the more capital people have, the more they can enable others to improve their lives – and the more of this, the better.

Is this story, however, just a warmed-over version of a discredited "trickle-down" theory of economics? Is the argument, reduced to its basics, that we should just let rich people get as rich as they want, but don't worry, some scraps will (eventually) make their way to the poor as well – and that the poor should be content and even happy with whatever the rich deign to bestow upon them? The term "trickle-down economics" was applied in particular to the economic policies of former U.S. president Ronald Reagan, who seemed to endorse (or at least was described as endorsing) similar sentiments, claiming that rising wealth concentrations among the rich were fair, just, and right (see, for example, Quiggin 2010, chap. 4). If the richest 10 percent in society saw their wealth double, while the poorest 10 percent saw their wealth increase by a meager 2 percent (say), the trickle-down position seems to be that the poor would have no grounds to complain. They were benefiting too, after all, weren't they?

Consider also that some people who succeed in life do so at least in part because of sheer good luck. Maybe they were born into wealthy families or inherited wealth; maybe they were loved, fed, and cared for, were sent to good schools and were well educated, and were introduced to good networking opportunities; maybe they were born in safe, healthy communities and environments; and so on. Others, however, are not so lucky. Thus, it might seem that at least some portion of the success of the former is due to no virtue of their own, while at least some portion of the relatively less success of the latter is due to no fault of theirs. But if some of what you have is due to good fortune for which you bear no responsibility, how can you claim to deserve or be entitled to it? And if some portion of my more straitened circumstances is due to bad fortune for which I bear no responsibility, how can you claim that I do not deserve or am not entitled to more? If we are all equal moral agents, equally possessed of dignity and equally deserving of respect, why should some prosper through good luck while others suffer from bad luck? Even if both our situations are improving (though at different rates), still it would seem that in neither case is the relative level of success in life fair, right, or just.

I believe the conclusion is correct: it is not fair. The harder question, however, is: What should be done about it? If someone should be made to compensate someone else, who should be made to pay and who should be benefited? And how can we do this without making things worse – without, for example, making some pay who should not, and benefiting some who deserve no benefit?

The fact that one person has less wealth than another does not by itself answer any of these questions. Suppose I tell you that A has one hundred times as much wealth as B. What follows from that? Or, what follows morally from that? Unfortunately, nothing. The reason is that we do not yet have an account of how A got her wealth, and we have no account of why B has so much less. Did A get her wealth through extraction (force, fraud, theft, and so on), or through cooperative, mutually voluntary and mutually beneficial exchanges only? The answer to that question should make all the difference in our moral evaluation of her situation – and without knowing those particularities, including the history that led to it, we cannot answer that question. We also do not yet know why B has so much less. Was he stolen from or defrauded, or was he prevented from owning property, starting a business, entering a market, or competing with others? A moral evaluation of B's position turns on the answers to these questions as well.

We also do not know what the absolute condition of B is. Perhaps B has only a tiny fraction of A's wealth, but in absolute terms he is many times wealthier than the United Nation's definition of "absolute poverty" of about $3 per person per day. Tiger Woods has a net worth estimated at approximately $800 million – about 1/138th, or 0.7 percent, of that of Jeff Bezos. That means that, relative to Bezos, Woods is extremely poor. But it would seem absurd to claim on that basis that some of Bezos's wealth should be redistributed to Woods. Despite Woods's extreme poverty relative to Bezos, by any reasonable or objective standard, he is, in absolute terms, doing quite well. Thus, a person's absolute condition should affect our evaluation as well.

Granting that luck, good or bad, affects people's prospects and relative success in life also does not, by itself, mean that we should, or even can, do anything about it. Not all rich people have acted badly, and not all poor people have been wronged. Although luck figures into everyone's life, it figures in different ways and to differing degrees, and people's choices about how to deal with or respond to luck have a profound effect on the courses of their lives. How would we go about learning the peculiarities in specific cases, and apportioning our redistribution from the lucky to the unlucky accordingly? Is there any way we could do so without inadvertently punishing some who do not deserve to be punished, or benefiting some who do not deserve to be benefited? Even if we could imagine some ideal political mechanism that could operate according to a morally correct set of governing principles, how could we be sure, or even reasonably confident, that whatever governmental agency we would charge with interpreting, applying, and executing the procedures we had envisioned would actually do so according to our intent? This last question we might call a "political-economic" question, and there is a large economics literature examining all the ways, to borrow Robert Burns's phrasing, the best-laid schemes o' mice an' men gang aft agley – that is, all the ways that the actual (not theoretical) functioning and the real (not imagined) results of centrally administered government agencies fail to live up to our expectations and why.[11]

---

[11] There is now an entire field of economics dedicated to studying this phenomenon, specifically applying economic principles to non-market (including governmental) decision-making, called "public choice,"

So it is, or might well be, unfair, but unfortunately it is unclear what we can do to remedy the situation. Centralized experts or administrators typically do not have the morally relevant knowledge to know whether or how to intervene, and the mechanisms at their disposal are unlikely to match our considered judgments about what should be done. Does that leave us, however, with no alternative? Must the poor just resign themselves to accepting their unfortunate lots in life?

Thankfully, no. It turns out that our lives are in almost all material respects far better for living in societies with market economies than our lives would be in societies without them. People in market economies are not just wealthier, but they live longer, have higher literacy and education rates, enjoy more peace and less conflict, protect the environment better, have more access to goods and services and healthcare and food and water, are freer, and report higher overall satisfaction with their lives. The differences are substantial: people living in the forty or so countries with the most market-based economies are on average an order of magnitude wealthier than those living in the forty or so countries with the least market-based economies; their life expectancy at birth is over twenty years longer; far higher proportions of them have indoor plumbing, electricity, air conditioning, access to the internet, access to healthcare, the ability (and leisure) to travel abroad; and so on. The poor in particular do much better: the poorest 10 percent in the

complete with Nobel Prize winners (e.g., James Buchanan in 1986) and a dedicated peer-reviewed journal – *Public Choice* – which has been published since 1966. See also Schuck 2014.

quartile of most market-based countries enjoy on average nearly ten times the income that the poorest 10 percent earn in the quartile of least market-based countries. The *poorest* 10 percent of the population in Hong Kong, for example, are wealthier than the *richest* 10 percent in Cuba (Gwartney et al. 2018; Monnery 2019). These are not small things. Indeed, they can make tremendous differences in the quality of life.

The more important point, however, is that the only hope we have been able to discover of enabling people to ascend out of poverty and of improving their opportunities to create lives of meaning and purpose for themselves, for their families, and for their communities, are market-based economies that encourage and reward cooperative partnerships and transactions and that discourage and punish extractive. The production of wealth enables all of us – especially the poorest among us – a chance at a better life. Given the growing empirical evidence gathered over the last forty years or so (see the sources at the end of this book), it appears that might be their only hope for genuine and lasting material improvement. This evidence seems to demonstrate that the institutions of a market economy, and the attitudes and culture that support and sustain them, are the keys to widespread and real improvement in people's lives.

Who Benefits Most?

Perhaps it is true that both the rich and the poor benefit from living in such an economy; but do the rich benefit more? The philosopher John Rawls (1921–2002) argued that the principles of justice, or "fairness" as he called it, require that inequalities may be allowed only if their primary beneficiaries are the least-advantaged in society. If a system of political economy allowed only the top 1 percent to benefit, while the situations of the other 99 percent remained unchanged, then, on Rawls's view, this inequality would be unfair and hence unjust. On the other hand, if a system of political economy allowed the top 1 percent to benefit, but thereby enabled the other 99 percent to benefit even more, then this would be fair and hence just. A market economy arguably satisfies this standard more than any other system of political economy we know of.

There were enormous gaps between the wealth of the pharaoh and the rest of his society, between Caesar and the rest of his society, and between most kings and the rest of their societies. In those kinds of societies, what little overall wealth they had was extremely concentrated in only a few hands, and was typically accumulated and enforced by extraction. During the only time in human history that overall wealth has increased substantially, however – just the last couple centuries or so – the primary beneficiaries have been the poor, not the rich. It has historically been the poorest in society who have been closest to the subsistence margin, whose lives were so poor that, as Adam Smith described in the eighteenth century, people would sometimes face the horrifying decision of which of their children or elderly to expose to the elements so that the rest of them could survive (Smith 1981 [1776], 10). What did even modest increases in wealth mean to the poor? Maybe their children could eat today; maybe they could buy their children a pair of shoes; maybe they could send their children to school, even only to learn to read and do arithmetic, instead of needing them to hunt or work in the fields as soon as they were able. Those of us lucky enough to be alive today, or lucky enough to live in the wealthier regions of the world today, might have a hard time appreciating just how agonizing and backbreaking poverty can be, even at what was the historical norm for humanity.

But consider this from another angle. How much additional benefit in your life would an extra $1,000 per year make? It would certainly make some difference, but if you are reading this book that extra $1,000 would likely not change your life very much. Indeed, the difference might be barely perceptible. But how much difference would that same $1,000 per year make to a person who is currently living on $1 per day? It would be transformative. As Hans Rosling (Rosling et al. 2018) documents, it could make the difference between traveling only on foot (barefoot), and getting a bicycle (and a pair of shoes); between cooking with an open flame by burning gathered wood, and cooking with propane; between your children making five trips per day gathering water from a waterhole an hour away, and doing so only once per day with a five-gallon bucket and spending some of their liberated time doing schoolwork with light from a bulb; between eating the same gray low-nutrition porridge for every meal, and at least occasionally eating meals with some meat and vegetables; between sleeping on dirt floors, and sleeping on a mattress; between scavenging in trash dumps, and working in a local garment firm and for the first time in your family's history bringing home a regular and predictable salary. The amount of wealth that enables these transformations might seem small to us who are already far wealthier, but it can literally mean the difference between life and death for those at humanity's historical norms of poverty.

Jeff Bezos no doubt travels, eats, and is accommodated far more luxuriously than you or me, but the marginal difference between the quality of his life and yours or mine likely pales in comparison to the difference in the quality of life an extra $1,000 means to the poorest on earth. So, while it may well be true that a market economy can enable billionaires and Bezoses, it also enables more and more people to ascend from the previous levels of $1 per person per day to $2 and $4 and $8 per person per day. That is real and significant improvement – and the only thing that has accomplished it in the entirety of human history are markets and the spreading belief in the morality of cooperation and the immorality of extraction. If we care about improving the situation of the poor – as I believe we should – then it is they who deserve our concern first. The rich will take care of themselves; cooperative market exchanges, however, and the public institutions that protect them, have been the only real, substantial, and sustained method of poverty relief we have ever discovered. We should not take them lightly or deprecate them; we should celebrate, protect, and extend them. That means advocating for cooperative exchanges that are positive-sum and value-creating. If the market economies that enable such exchanges also enable some of us to enjoy more wealth than others, then that enables just that more prosperity with which we can attend not only to our needs but help others as well. Our wealth does not relieve us of obligations toward others; rather, it enables us to more fully execute those obligations. Growing wealth helps every-one, especially the poor, and the poor deserve nothing less.

Conclusion

The production of wealth in a market-based commercial society is positive-sum, not zero-sum. It is based on exchanges whose defining characteristics are that they are mutually voluntary and mutually beneficial; they are examples of coop-eration, as opposed to extractive exchanges, which benefit one party at the expense of others. It is thanks to the spread of cooperative exchanges that we owe our relatively recent but historically unprecedented increases in prosperity worldwide, and it is thanks to the prior prevalence of extraction that humanity remained so long at levels of wealth that the United Nations describes as "absolute poverty."

Cooperative exchanges are not only productive of increasing prosperity, however; they are also more moral than extractive exchanges. They respect each person's opt-out option, or the right of any person to say "no, thank you" to any offer or proposal, and as such treat each person as a person of dignity and possessed of an equal moral agency. An economy in which all transactions are cooperative thus reflects the moral principle of equal agency, in addition to allowing all participants in it to increase their prosperity – if not necessarily to the same degree.

Increasing overall wealth especially benefits the poor-est among us most, for it is they who are most in need of resources with which to improve their situations. Throughout human history, the richest in society have been able to acquire the goods and services they wanted – though, at least before around 1800 or so, primarily through extraction. It is only since that time, as belief in the moral superiority of cooperative exchange over extractive exchange spread, that what Phelps (2013) calls "mass flourishing" appeared in the world and has continued, and accelerated, to this day.

2

Good Is Not Good Enough

*More houses would have been built, more lands would have
been improved, and those which had been improved before
would have been better cultivated, more manufactures
would have been established, and those which had been
established before would have been more extended; and to
what height the real wealth and revenue of the country
might, by this time, have been raised, it is not perhaps very
easy even to imagine.*

Adam Smith, *The Wealth of Nations*

Introduction

Throughout most of human history, the total amount of
usable resources people had at their disposal was consistently
low – the contemporary equivalent of between $1 and $3 per
person per day. One cannot do much with that. Could you live
today on, say, $3 per day? To furnish you with all your needs –
from food, clothing, and shelter, to music, coffee, graduate
school, that new pair of shoes, and the next iPhone? You
might be able to survive, but only barely; you would likely
have to give up an enormous number of the things you enjoy
in life today – and you had better hope you do not get sick or
break a bone. The proportion of human beings living at that
historical low level, however, is today lower than it has ever
been. It has been beaten back to only 9 percent of people

today, and is falling. We are thus on the precipice of, for the first time in human history, eliminating absolute poverty from the planet.

The increasing wealth human beings have generated in the last two centuries is thus historically unprecedented. It is now in excess of $128 trillion dollars, or some $17,500 per person per year – compared with the approximately $1,000 per person per year throughout more than 99 percent of human history. That means that people alive today can afford far more goods and services, can meet far more of their needs and desires, and put far more resources toward their goals and ends, than ever before. That is a great good in itself – it has alleviated a great deal of the misery, pain, suffering, drudgery, and premature death that characterized human life for virtually all of its history – even if, of course, it has not solved all problems and there remains much work to be done, many problems yet to be solved, and many frontiers of human possibility yet to be traversed. Today the levels of adult literacy worldwide, the levels of stable and predictable access to potable water and nutritious food, the levels of access to healthcare and electricity, the levels of environmental stewardship and sustainable use, the levels of opposition to sexism and racism and homophobia and xenophobia and violence and torture, the levels of self-reported happiness and overall satisfaction with life, the levels of longevity and reduction of infant death and death in childbirth, the levels of vaccination and education of children, and the levels of peace – in a word, the levels of prosperity and flourishing – are higher than they have ever been (McCloskey 2016 and 2019; Pinker 2018; Rosling et al. 2018; Davies 2019). Please take a moment to take those stupendous facts in: however bad things might seem, these measures of human flourishing are now at levels *higher than they have ever been.*

All this unprecedented prosperity allows us to do many more things than previous generations could have dared to hope or even imagine. Consider how much benefit to your life just one recent invention creates: the global tele-communicator in your pocket or purse, which not only allows you to communicate immediately with almost anyone any-where on the planet but gives you instantaneous access to virtually the entirety of human knowledge. What you can find out, what skills you can learn, and with whom you can start friendships or partnerships are now almost unlimited, and in any case orders of magnitude greater than what your grand-parents or anyone else in human history could have enjoyed. Amidst all this unprecedented prosperity, however, a problem remains: however increasingly plentiful our wealth has become, our desires still outstrip them. There remain goals and ends still unachieved, needs and desires still unmet. Indeed, it seems to be a fixed feature of the human condition that no matter how much we have, we still want more.

It is also the case that resources, however large, can-not be put to more than one use at the same time. You may have the money to buy either a latte or a bagel, but that same $5 cannot go to both at the same time. You might be able to afford to send your children to college or buy yourself a Ferrari, but you probably cannot do both (even if you can do both, you cannot do both with the same $250,000). And there are also the issues of our time, our labor, and our love. Any hour, day, week, month, and so on that you spend doing one thing is an hour, day, week, month, and so on you cannot spend doing anything else – it is gone forever. If you decide to work for one firm, you cannot also decide to work for another firm. If you decide to marry this person, you cannot also decide to marry anyone else (well, not in most places, at least – but you get the point: if you give your love to one person, there are indefinitely many other potential mates to whom you will have decided not to give your love).

That means we have to make choices, and choices involve tradeoffs. To get one thing, we will have to give up getting indefinitely many others. However much wealth one has, one still has to make choices, and sometimes those choices can be painful ones. Our rising wealth may have alleviated, for at least the vast majority of humanity today, the wrenching choice Adam Smith observed in the eighteenth-century Highlands of Scotland, where people were forced by their extremely straitened circumstances sometimes to decide which of their children or elderly to expose to the elements – in other words, to let die – so that their other children or family members could survive. But Americans today might have to make difficult choices between, for example, buying a house with enough bedrooms for the number of children they have or sending their children to private schools. Or between buying a car and getting tutoring or in-home care for their special-needs child. Or between going to the family reunion this year or paying down their student loan debt. Or between spending more hours at work and spending more hours with the family. And so on. It is not that some of these are bad choices and others good, which would make the decisions far easier; the choices might all be good ones, which makes the decisions much more difficult. As Nobel laureate Thomas Sargent (2007) put it, "Individuals and communities face trade-offs." We cannot have it all, alas.

How, then, do we make such choices? How *should* we make them? These kinds of decisions depend on numerous factors, including our schedules of value (what matters to us, what our hopes and dreams and ambitions are, and so on) and our available resources (how much time, money, and so on we have). Since we cannot do all the things we would like, we must make choices: how should we do so?

Be Rational

The fact that our desires outstrip our resources entails that we must make choices. That fact implicates an important concept in economics, one that can help us begin to think through how to make such choices, namely: *opportunity cost.*

Opportunity cost is the value of whatever you have to give up in order to do the thing you choose to do. More specifically, it is represented by the value to you of the most highly valued alternative. Consider, as an example, your time. Your time on earth is absolutely limited: there was a moment when it started, and there is, I am sorry to say, a moment when it will end. However long the duration is between those two points, you cannot create any more of it than there will be.[1] That means that time is among your most precious

---

[1] I pass over in silence recent claims that future technological breakthroughs might enable us to live much longer, perhaps indeed

SEVEN DEADLY ECONOMIC SINS

resources, maybe the most precious. Every hour, day, week, month, or year you spend doing one thing is not only gone forever but also cannot be spent doing something else. So we must choose wisely how to spend our time: if you spend it doing something that provides benefit but that is less valuable than other ways you might have spent your time, then you are making a mistake – according to your own schedule of value. The concept of opportunity cost is a way of estimating the value (to you) of your sacrifices, in the hopes that you can make better decisions about what to do.

In a canonical 1945 article called "The Use of Knowledge in Society," Nobel laureate economist Friedrich Hayek (1899–1992) began his discussion by asking, "What is the problem we wish to solve when we try to construct a rational economic order?" In some sense, this is the fundamental question of all economics or all political economy. If that is Question 1, however, we should first address a prior question, perhaps Question 0: What *is* a "rational economic order"? We would need to know what that is before we can even begin thinking about how to achieve (or "construct") it. Take those three terms in succession.

By *rational*, Hayek does not mean wise, virtuous, or reasonable. Hayek's use of the term, which is consistent with most use of it in social science generally, refers to means–end rationality. That is, we first specify a goal; then we investigate

forever; see, for example, Canavero 2014 and Benatar 2016, part 4. If we could live forever, for example through transplants or cloning, we would effectively eliminate opportunity cost – which would change everything. Perhaps exploring that possibility deserves its own book.

what steps or actions are required to achieve it or make progress toward it, and what steps or actions would take us away from it. Any proposed step or action would be "rational" if it helps achieve the goal, and "irrational" if it does not. So, this conception of rationality is neutral with respect to the goals themselves; it makes or implies no judgment about whether the goal is good, right, prudent, reasonable, and so on. It says simply: If x is your goal, and A, B, and C would help you attain x, but D, E, and F would take you away from x, then it is rational to pursue A, B, and C and irrational to pursue D, E, and F.

By *economic*, Hayek is referring to the resources, including human, available to us, as well as the goods and services available in society, and the choices we must make regarding them. Because these resources are scarce relative to our desires and ends, choices must be made. *Economic* can refer not just to obviously "economic" goods and services like the things you buy in a store, but to all the goals you have – love, beauty, knowledge, everything. All the things you desire, all of which are costly in time or treasure to you or someone else (or both) to produce or procure or use or enjoy, are susceptible to evaluation and deliberate choice about how valuable they are relative to other things you also want, given the limited resources available to achieve them.

Finally, by *order*, Hayek means the ranking of our ends (goals, values, desires, preferences, and so on) and the allocation of our scarce resources to them. The order is the ranked set of decisions we make regarding which of our ends are most important, which are second-most important, which are third-most important, and so on, and the patterns of allocations of all the resources we have at our disposal to achieve them.

Putting all three terms together, then, what Hayek means by a "rational economic order" is the allocation of our scarce resources to our most important ends first, then to our second-most important ends second, and so on down the list. Our economic order is rational if we allocate our scarce resources according to the actual hierarchy of value we have, irrational if we do not. If I spend time doing things that are less valuable to me than other things I could be doing, or if I spend money on goods or services that are less valuable to me than other things I could be spending my money on (or to saving or investing my money), then I am acting irrationally according to my own schedule or hierarchy of value. It means I am devoting resources to things that I myself believe are less valuable than other things to which I could devote them; I am sacrificing higher-valued ends for the sake of lower-valued ends, contradicting my own values. Thus, I can achieve the wisest or best or most productive use of my limited resources by, first, figuring out what my schedule of value is, and then, second, allocating the resources at my disposal according-ly. The same is true for society: a society has a "rational economic order" if it allocates its resources to its most impor-tant ends first, then second, and so on, and does not expend resources toward lower-valued ends at the expense of higher-valued ends.

That brings us to Hayek's Question 1: How do we achieve a "rational economic order," not only in our own individual lives but for all society? This is a weighty question:

since our resources are limited, making "irrational" choices about expending them means sacrificing more important ends. No one should do that, and no society should do that – and if either does so for long, it can mean not just forgone gains but, at the limit, ruin. If the Soviet Union devotes too much of its resources to building tanks and not enough to food, people will starve as thousands of tanks molder in fields (as actually happened); if a college student spends too much time socializing with friends instead of studying, then she will struggle or even fail out (as, unfortunately, often happens); if workers spend too much time checking social media instead of doing their work, their company will suffer lost productivity (which is an increasing problem in America and elsewhere today); and so on. Now, if the Soviet Union decides that manufacturing tanks is more important than its people eating, or if it means more to a college student to socialize than to get good grades, and so on, then their respective decisions are "rational" according to the Hayekian definition of the term; if not, then the decisions are "irrational."

How to achieve a rational economic order is a difficult question. Hayek's claim is that it can be achieved only by allowing decentralized economic decision-making by individuals who respond to freely emerging prices. I will explain this further in a moment, but for now the important point to realize is that we must always consider opportunity cost if we are to have even a hope of achieving a rational economic order. Because every choice involves opportunity cost – meaning every choice to do one thing involves giving up indefinitely many other things – to know whether we are choosing well we need to account for what we are giving up. It is not enough to show that what we decide to do is a good thing or would lead to benefit. There are many things we might do that might be good, lead to benefit, or create value. What we need to know instead is whether what we are considering is not merely *good* but *better than* the other good things we would have to sacrifice to do it.

The Broken Window

Many of the decisions about allocating our resources that we make as individuals, and many of the decisions that governments make about allocating resources, proceed on the basis of looking at only one side of the balance sheet. By that I mean that they consider whether this thing they are contemplating is good or would lead to benefit, and if they are or would, then the decision is made to move forward. But they did not look at opportunity cost. They did not consider what those resources that are to be dedicated to the end in question might otherwise have done. For that reason, they do not in fact know whether this use is better than – not just good, but better than – other uses of the resources. They therefore do not know whether this is what should be done, and thus they do not know whether the decision is consistent with a rational economic order.

Consider a famous example from the nineteenth-century French parliamentarian and political economist Frédéric Bastiat (1801–1850). In his 1850 essay *What Is Seen and What Is Unseen*, Bastiat offers the following scenario. Suppose one James Goodfellow has a shop with a storefront window. And suppose his son, Jimmy, throws a rock through the window, breaking it. Now Mr. Goodfellow must replace the window. Bastiat's question: Is Jimmy actually an economic creator? After all, to replace his window, Goodfellow must now pay a glazier, giving the glazier business he did not have before. Suppose the new window costs $100. Now the glazier has an additional $100 in business, and Goodfellow has a new window. That seems like economic productivity. So, what we might have considered *destructive* behavior seems actually to be *productive* behavior. Should we therefore encourage more breaking of windows?

No, we shouldn't. The benefit to the glazier of $100 and the benefit to Goodfellow of a new pane of glass are what Bastiat calls the "seen" benefits. But what is "unseen"? What is unseen is the opportunity cost – that is, what Goodfellow would have done with that $100 if he had not been forced by little Jimmy's action to put it toward a new window. Perhaps, as Bastiat suggests, Goodfellow might have been planning on buying a new pair of shoes, or some books for his personal library. The "unseen" cost, or opportunity cost, is the value of the shoes or books that Goodfellow now has to give up to buy the new pane of glass.[2] If we looked only at the "seen" benefits, we might be inclined to think that destruction is actually profitable. But when we also consider the "unseen" costs, we realize that that conclusion is based on an incomplete assessment of the full situation. Once we have taken a full

---

[2] Goodfellow also loses time: the time now required for him to investigate and procure the windowpane could have been spent doing something else that he preferred.

accounting, it becomes clear that, as Bastiat claims, "Destruction is not profitable" (2017 [1850], 406).

Suppose you wonder, however, what difference it makes if the $100 went to a glazier or if it went instead to a cobbler or bookseller. As long as money is circulating, what difference does it make, perhaps from the perspective of the overall economy, where it goes? Somebody, after all, whether a glazier, cobbler, or bookseller, is getting $100 in business.

It turns out it does make a difference, in two important but distinct ways. First, it makes a difference to Goodfellow: he did not want to buy a new windowpane! He could, after all, already have done so if he wanted to, but he wanted to buy shoes or books instead. If he now must redirect that $100 away from something he valued more highly (shoes or books) to something he values at a lower level (windowpane), then he has lost value (to himself). The difference in value to him between the benefit he would have gotten from the shoes or books and what he gets from the windowpane constitutes a loss to him. It is "unseen," since he did not actually buy the shoes or books and hence did not actually realize the benefit from them, but it is no less real for being unseen. It is his opportunity cost. Even if someone else – the glazier, for example – benefits, Goodfellow still loses that forgone benefit.

Second, when we speak of money circulating in an economy, that is what economists call "flow," not what they call "stock." Yes, $100 is flowing through the economy, and whether it goes to a glazier or to a cobbler, it is still flowing. But consider the stock, or the overall quantity of resources or goods in the economy. Focus for the moment just on the products that Goodfellow owns. After the windowpane was broken, he would have a (new) windowpane; if the pane had not been broken, however, he would have had an (already existing) windowpane *and* a new pair of shoes or new books. So, the overall stock of products at Goodfellow's disposal was diminished by Jimmy's destructive act by the amount of a pair of shoes or new books. To think otherwise is to commit what is now called the "Broken Window Fallacy," or to make the mistake of thinking that destruction is, or can be, a net positive in an economy.

The Broken Window Fallacy applies not just to Goodfellow, however, or to any particular individual, but to society generally. Whenever a natural disaster occurs – a hurricane or tornado or flood, for example – inevitably one hears pundits or commentators say something along the lines of: "Well, the $100 million in damage the hurricane caused was bad, but the good news is that now people can rebuild, generating new business!" That commits the Broken Window Fallacy. The question such commentators fail to ask is what could have been done, or would have been done, with that $100 million if the hurricane had not struck. If people had wanted to use that money to rebuild, they could have already decided to do so. The fact that they had not decided to do so, however, suggests that in their judgment that was not the best use of their resources. They had other things, more highly valued things, in mind to do with their resources. So, although it might be true that after rebuilding they received some benefit – maybe things were rebuilt more sturdily, for example – nevertheless, whatever benefit they received from rebuilding constitutes less value to them than whatever else they would have done with the money. And we know that because the only reason they decided to dedicate resources to rebuilding was because of the unfortunate and destructive hurricane that struck.

Public Works

Should your city subsidize the construction of a professional sports stadium? Should it operate public golf courses, have public libraries, subsidize arts festivals and presentations, construct or buy multi-use arenas, sponsor job retraining programs, or subsidize childcare? All of these seem like good ideas, at least in principle, and chances are that your local community supports or engages in some combination of them. States add higher levels of programs: healthcare and retirement subsidies, state parks, research grants, subsidies to various industries and firms and universities and schools, city and county infrastructure grants, pensions for state workers, food and nutrition provision and subsidies, and so on. The federal government has yet more programs. Usually it is fairly easy to see who benefits from them: recipients of aid, people without adequate (or desired) food or retirement or health-care or education, the businesses and their workers who get state-sponsored contracts, and so on. So, what's the problem?

Unfortunately, there is a problem, or at least a potential problem. It is not that these things are not, or might not be, good ideas in themselves. It is, rather, that all of them are funded by reallocation of resources from citizens – and we do not know to what uses those citizens might otherwise have put them. To know whether any of these uses of resources, and whether any of these government programs, are good uses of our limited resources, we must estimate the opportunity cost. That is, we must: (1) estimate, in good faith, the likely benefit of such expenditures; (2) estimate, again in good faith, the likely opportunity cost, or the benefit we are forsaking or sacrificing in order to engage in such expenditures; and then (3) compare the two. Which is likely to lead to greater benefit? If all we have done is (1) and ignored (2) and (3), then we cannot know for sure. Suppose my teenage son says he wants me to buy him a car, and he lays out all the benefits of his having a car at his disposal – and believes that he has thereby ended the discussion. In fact, however, he has left out a crucially required part of the calculation: what benefit would the money that would be spent on a new car have otherwise generated for the family? What tradeoffs, and what sacrifices, would we have to make, to buy the car? Until we know that, we cannot know whether we should buy the car. Similarly with sports stadiums, public libraries, and all the other potential public projects: we cannot know whether we should do them until we have made a good-faith estimate of what we would have to give up to pay for them, and we have compared the two.

Now, this is often very difficult to do, since the immediate payoff – the stadium, the library, the car, and so on – is visible, tangible, and hence easy to imagine; while the sacrifices, which do not yet exist or are not readily known, are hence more difficult to imagine and estimate. Because resources are scarce, however, allocation in one direction means deciding not to allocate them in other directions. That means there are costs, opportunity costs, even if they are unseen. And that means that until we have estimated the opportunity cost we cannot yet know whether this proposed use of these resources is something we should pursue.

Be Local

In his 1776 *Inquiry into the Nature and Causes of the Wealth of Nations*, Adam Smith set himself the task of figuring out why some places were becoming wealthy and others were stagnating or declining. He was able to canvass an improbable number of historical examples and marshal an impressive amount of empirical evidence – remember, this was the eighteenth century, before the internet, computers, telephones, or even electricity – in coming to his conclusions that protections of private property, open markets, and free trade were the keys to increasing prosperity. He argued that natural resources, climate, geography, infrastructure, education, and demography could help, but they were not by themselves sufficient either to initiate or sustain economic growth.

That last item, demography, is important to underscore. To his great credit, Smith, unlike many of his contemporaries and many people before and since, did not believe that there were natural differences among human populations across the world. There were no superior and no inferior races.[3] All people were roughly equally rational and thus were roughly equally capable of improving their situations –

---

[3] A century later, Charles Darwin, in his 1871 *Descent of Man*, could still believe in a natural ranking of human races. See Darwin 1981 (1871), 158–84.

if only they were allowed. Smith's argument instead is that economic growth had been inhibited by bad institutions and practices, chief among them myriad forms of extraction. Some people were not allowed to own property; some were not allowed to start their own businesses; some people were not allowed to work in certain occupations or to buy, sell, or trade; and some people were continually subject to confiscation, expropriation, and predation. Smith's solution was as simple in its description as it was difficult to implement: give everyone, of whatever class or station, the right to own property, and respect that right; let anyone, of whatever class or station, start any business he liked, and offer his goods or services to anyone he wanted; let anyone, of any class or station, compete in an open market with anyone else; and let anyone, again of any class or station, trade or partner with anyone he liked, whether a fellow citizen or a foreigner. In this way, Smith thought, all people would be able to improve their own situations, and a growing general prosperity would ensue.

It was, as I said, a simple formula,[4] but it has proved exceedingly difficult to implement, and people's skepticism about other people's abilities to make good choices on their own behalf has continued to limit the potential benefits that could accrue from it. An implication of Smith's argument was that there should be a government that would protect what

---

[4] Smith called it indeed "the obvious and simple system of natural liberty": "Every man, as long as he does not violate the laws of justice, is left perfectly free to pursue his own interest his own way, and to bring both his industry and capital into competition with those of any other man, or order of men" (1981 [1776], 687).

Smith called "justice": namely, protecting everyone's person, everyone's property, and everyone's voluntary promises or contracts (Smith 1982 [1759], 84). *Person*: no one may assault, kill, or enslave another. *Property*: no one may trespass upon, steal, confiscate, expropriate, destroy, or despoil another's property. And *promise*: no one may be held responsible to comply with any demand or fulfill any agreement if it was not voluntarily entered into; if two (or more) parties do enter into voluntary agreements, they should be held to them; and third parties should not interfere uninvited into first and second parties' voluntary agreements.

The protection of this tripartite conception of justice was, Smith thought, the primary duty of government. To do so, Smith argued that the government should have three parts: first, a military that could protect against foreign aggression (that is, that could ensure the protection of justice against foreign malefactors); second, a police and court system that could protect against domestic aggression and adjudicate disputes impartially (that is, that could ensure the protection of justice against domestic malefactors); and third, the provision of "certain publick works" that would benefit substantially everyone in society but that could not be provided by private enterprise (Smith 1981 [1776], 687–8).

This third duty of government requires a bit more exploration, particularly as it relates to an important insight Smith had about "local knowledge." Some commentators believe that Smith's third duty of government, to provide "certain" public works, is the leading edge of the proverbial wedge – licensing the government to engage in positive wealth or resource redistribution, or, depending on one's perspective, licensing the government to engage in tyranny and banditry. But Smith had two surprisingly stringent criteria for what could qualify as a public work to be provided by the government. First, it must be something that would benefit substantially all citizens, not merely one person or one group at the expense of the other. As Smith wrote, "To hurt in any degree the interest of any one order of citizens, for no other purpose but to promote that of some other, is evidently contrary to that justice and equality of treatment which the sovereign owes to all the different orders of his subjects" (1981 [1776], 654). In other words, it would have to be a positive-sum improvement, not merely an extractive transfer of wealth or a disregard of opportunity cost. Second, it would also have to be something that could not be provided by private enterprise – not merely that it is not currently being provided, or that is not being provided in the way some might prefer: it had to be unable to be provided at all by private enterprise.

Smith proposed these two criteria as conjuncts, not disjuncts: a proposed public work had to meet *both*, not merely one or the other. Upon reflection, it would appear that not many proposed public works would qualify. Would a sports stadium, public park, or library qualify? Apparently not: there are privately provided stadiums, parks, and libraries. Would a university qualify, or healthcare? But there are private universities, and there are private hospitals, medical care, and health insurance. Would unemployment insurance or retirement benefits or poverty relief or care for the homeless or indigent qualify? Again, there are numerous private, both for-profit and not-for-profit, entities dedicated to these ends. And similarly for many other of the public

81

works provided by local, state, and federal governments. It would seem, then, that the Smithian government would be quite small by contemporary standards, and would do exceedingly little beyond protecting people's persons, property, and promises after all.

Smith's principal justification for taking this position was based on his historical and empirical survey of governments and experiments in government around the world and over the centuries. His survey led him to conclude that those countries whose governments limited their activities to the protection of the "three Ps" of person, property, and promise were the countries in which prosperity increased. By contrast, those governments that did not respect and protect their citizens' three Ps, almost no matter what else they did, would create disincentives to prosperity – and thus would either slow their growth, stagnate, or even, if the violations of the three Ps were sufficiently widespread or severe, decline. Though the data at Smith's disposal were quite limited by contemporary standards, investigative work since Smith's time has corroborated his claim (Landes 1999; McCloskey 2006, 2010, 2016, and 2019; Deaton 2013; Phelps 2013; Scheidel 2017; Diamond 2019). So, it seems he may have been on to something.

But Smith had another argument for why third-party, and in particular government, interventions into private citizens' economic decisions should be limited. I call it his "Local Knowledge Argument": "What is the species of domestick industry which his capital can employ, and of which the produce is likely to be of the greatest value, every individual, it is evident, can, in his local situation, judge much better than any statesman or lawgiver can do for him" (1981 [1776], 456). Smith went so far as to make this bold claim:

> The statesman, who should attempt to direct private people in what manner they ought to employ their capitals, would not only load himself with a most unnecessary attention, but assume an authority which could safely be trusted, not only to no single person, but to no council or senate whatever, and which would nowhere be so dangerous as in the hands of a man who had folly and presumption enough to fancy himself fit to exercise it.
>
> **(ibid.)**

So, granting a government official or agency the authority to interpose in private persons' economic decisions could not "safely be trusted," and would moreover exhibit "folly" and "presumption." Why?

One of the things that Smith believes he observed about human beings is that they are self-interested. They are not exclusively self-interested, however, and for Smith one's "self-interest" includes the interests of others one cares about – one's family, friends, community, and so on. But whatever one's aims or values in life and whatever one's current situation or condition, Smith thought that it was a permanent feature of human nature that one would seek to improve one's condition. So, everyone seeks to improve his situation and condition, and to achieve his goals, aims, ambitions, values (including moral values), and preferences more completely, more extensively, and more richly. This means, for Smith, that no statesman or lawgiver is required to superintend people's motivations to improve their situations – they already do that themselves.

83

SEVEN DEADLY ECONOMIC SINS

And because individuals will themselves suffer the consequences if they make bad decisions, they are naturally disciplined to do the best they can in a way that statesmen and
lawgivers, who would not directly suffer negative consequences
from bad decisions, are not.

Smith's "Local Knowledge Argument" can be captured in a simple three-step syllogism:

1. Each person is in unique possession of knowledge regarding her own goals, desires, ambitions, and values, as well as
   the opportunities, responsibilities, constraints, tradeoffs,
   and opportunity costs she faces.
2. To be used wisely, scarce resources must be allocated
   according to a ranked hierarchy of value (that is, one's
   limited resources should be expended first to one's most
   important values, second to one's second-most-important
   values, and so on).
3. Therefore, the person best positioned to make wise use of
   her scarce resources is the individual herself.

The argument does not assume that individuals are infallible.
Rather, the claim is that they are *relatively better positioned* to
make decisions in their own cases because they have more
intimate and immediate knowledge of their own situations
than third parties have. Each of us makes mistaken decisions
in his or her own case, frustratingly often. But the further
away from us someone is – and thus the less about us someone knows – the less likely is he to know what decisions we
should make. Our close family and friends know a lot about
us, but even they do not know everything; more distant
friends and acquaintances know yet less about us; and most

of the world knows nothing at all. What can your congress-person or senator, for example, know about you? What can people in agencies in Washington, DC know about what decisions you should make, how you should allocate your time and treasure, what values are most important for your well-being and what are less important? Smith's answer: they can know virtually nothing. If they are making decisions for you – or are constraining your choices, incentivizing your choices, nudging your choices, and so on – there is thus little hope they can get it right, and certainly far less hope they could get it right than you could get it right for yourself.

Each of us possesses knowledge about his or her own situation – that is, each of us possesses "local knowledge" – that others do not possess. That makes it "folly" for a statesman or legislator to think that he will know better what you should do than you will. But Smith also claimed it was "dangerous" to empower such a statesman or lawgiver and it was "presumption" for them to think they could do it. Because the government agent does not know you or your situation, his only recourse would be to imagine it. But when he tries to imagine your situation, having no actual knowledge or facts on the basis of which to fill out his picture of you and your life, on what basis, then, will he fill out that picture? On the basis of his *own* life. He will imagine that you are more or less like him – with his sensibilities, his preferences, his values, and so on. If he then decides to intervene into your economic decisions, it will have been based on his assumption that you are, or perhaps that you should be, just like him. That is what Smith means by "presumption," and it is no compliment. It is for the government agent to imagine that his own sensibilities, preferences, values, and so on are right not only for him but right for everyone else too. It is to elevate his own character and aspirations above that of all others and to depreciate the character and aspirations of others.

Smith claims that such an authority "could safely be trusted, not only to no single person, but to no council or senate whatever" and "would nowhere be so dangerous as in the hands of a man who had folly and presumption enough to fancy himself fit to exercise it" (1981 [1776], 456). Why is it "so dangerous"? For two reasons. First, because there is no limit to this authority over others. The triggering events that would precipitate exercise of this authority could be every single decision any citizen makes that the government agent believes is wrong. How many such decisions would there be? Which of your past, current, and future decisions might run afoul of the agent's judgment? It is impossible to know. It would thus be impossible to plan your life or rest secure in your person, property, or promises, and impossible to be a free person of dignity, equal in your moral agency to others – all others, including the government agent.

Second, what kind of person do you imagine would be most attracted to wielding this kind of authority over others? In Smith's view, most decent people would recoil at the thought of superintending the private decisions of their fellow citizens. But not all people would recoil at the thought of it; some would embrace and even relish it. Which type are more likely to avoid such an authority, and which are more likely to seek it out? Smith's argument is that the people who get themselves into such positions of power over others are often those we would least want in those positions – because they will tend to wield their power as extensively as they possibly can.[5] They will seek to expand, not diminish, their power; they will seek more, not fewer, resources; they will seek to grow, not limit, the scope of their authority. One thing history seems to teach us is to be wary of one person or group being given power to intervene into the decisions and choices of peaceful citizens. The idea that such power would be used only judiciously, sparingly, and wisely seems naïve and inconsistent with human experience – just consider the injustices, expropriations, and exploitations, and the cruelty and inhumanity, that have marred human behavior throughout history when one group has power over another – and, as Smith suggests, it would be folly to hope that the next one will somehow be better and different from all the previous. In fact, it is more than mere folly: as Smith says, it would be "dangerous."

To complete the discussion of the Local Knowledge Argument, and to relate it to our discussion of economic fallacies, the fallacy in this case would be to believe that we are, or any of us is, in a position to know better what our fellow citizens should do with their time and treasure than they themselves are. They are free moral agents too, equal in their agency to us, and so they deserve our respect, not our correction. Beyond that, however, we are in no epistemic position to second-guess them and their choices. An objective look at the limitations of our own knowledge – how difficult is it to know whether we are making good decisions even in our *own* lives, let alone in those of anyone else? – reveals that in

---

[5] See Hayek 2007 (1944), chap. 10 for an articulation of a similar argument.

fact we are typically in no position to judge what is good for others. We do not possess the detailed, personal, contextualized, historical information that is required to know what constitute good choices for others; we do not know what their goals or aspirations or values or preferences are; and we do not know what constraints and responsibilities and tradeoffs they face. Except under extraordinary circumstances, then, we should adopt as our default assumption that people have reasons for what they do and are in a better position to decide what choices to make in their own circumstances than we are for them from ours.

Medicine on Mars

One of the key elements of knowledge about others that we typically do not possess is their opportunity cost. Perhaps it would be good for them to quit their job or get new skills training. Perhaps it would be good for them to go the gym today or not eat at McDonald's. Perhaps it would be good for them to recycle or buy an electric car, get tutoring for their child or move into (or out of) the city, get an apartment rather than buy a house, get married or get divorced, and so on. Think of people you either know personally or about whom you have read or seen news stories: you probably have opinions about such matters as those and many more. The Local Knowledge Argument would caution you against forming too strong an opinion, however, because your lack of familiarity with all the relevant particulars of their lives means you might well be wrong, and you should apportion your beliefs, and the strength of your beliefs, to the actual knowledge you have, not just your assumptions or speculations.

But let us stipulate, for the sake of argument, that your (or mine, or anyone else's) opinions about what others should do in cases like these would, if adopted, lead to benefit or improvement in their lives. Does that mean they should do it? Does it mean we should nudge, incentivize (or disincentivize, as the case may be), or even coerce them into doing it?[6]

Not necessarily. And one reason is because of opportunity cost. The fact that course of action A would lead to benefit for me does not yet mean that I should do A. A's benefit to me is, or should be, a necessary element of any reason I would consider doing A, but I cannot yet know whether I should do A until I consider B, C, D, and all the indefinitely many other things I might do instead and reckon their potential benefit to me as well. If I decide to do A, I forgo B, C, D, and so on. What if one of those other options would yield yet greater benefit to me than would A? In that case, if I decided to do A regardless, I would be forsaking greater benefit, and sacrificing some of my scarce resources, to pursue a lesser value. Thus, the fact that A, or any other courses of action you or others might nudge me into, would provide me benefit does not yet conclude the case and does not yet mean I should do it.

Because our resources are scarce, opportunity cost is real. We ignore it at our peril. But this applies not just to

---

[6] For arguments defending paternalistic nudging, see Thaler and Sunstein 2009; Ubel 2009; Thaler 2015; and Conly 2013 and 2016. For criticism, see White 2013; and Rizzo and Whitman 2020.

decisions individuals make in their own private lives, but to larger policy and social decisions we make. Let me give an example to illustrate.

Suppose you very unfortunately have a rare fatal disease, and there is no known cure. Left untreated, it is going to kill you. But suppose that a Mars probe discovers an element that does not exist on earth but that, we discover, could cure your otherwise fatal disease. What a happy discovery! We should therefore initiate a program to travel to Mars, mine that element, bring it back to earth, and process it so that it can become the life-saving treatment you need. The government – or perhaps an international coalition of governments – should immediately organize and finance it. Right?

Well, not so fast. The cost of doing so would likely be huge, perhaps trillions of dollars. No one wants to contemplate suggesting that your life should be sacrificed for money. (If it makes it easier to consider the horror of such a judgment, imagine that the afflicted person is not you but your child; would you not demand that everything be done to save your child, regardless of the cost?) Insurance, healthcare, and litigation routinely, in fact, estimate the costs of lives when they provide (or decline) benefits at certain specific prices, when they provide (or decline) care, or when they make payouts or agree to settlements in cases of wrongful death. The reality of opportunity cost forces us to ask what can be uncomfortable, even distressing, questions: What else might be done with those trillions of dollars if they were not spent on procuring the Mars medicine for you (or your child)? What benefit could those resources otherwise provide to others? Because what we are contemplating is not you spending your own money, but, rather, governments spending other people's money as well, we must ask: What benefit would that money have generated in those others' lives, or in the lives of their children and communities?

Wealth does not occur naturally; it is not spontaneously generated, and it does not exist in unlimited proportions. It is scarce and must be produced by human beings, with their limited time, resources, and skills, all of which could be expended in other directions. If what we are contemplating is trillions of dollars, as the Mars medicine would require, that is a lot of potentially forgone benefit that we would not only have to assess but whose opportunity cost we would have to reckon. The fact that moving forward with the Mars medicine program would benefit you hence unfortunately does not by itself justify the required sacrifice of other benefit from those resources. We would need to know what that sacrificed benefit would be.

This is an extreme case, obviously – a very great benefit to you, with a very large required cost to others – but the point it makes is generalizable. The possible existence of a medical treatment does not by itself justify procuring and administering that treatment, just as the possible provision of any benefit from any given course of action does not by itself justify pursuing that course of action. When governments undertake to provide benefits, or when they compel private actors (individuals, groups, firms, or industries) to provide benefits, the worry thus arises not just – as the Local Knowledge Argument would suggest – from skepticism that they will or can get it right from afar, but from the worry that they have not sufficiently considered the opportunity cost of their actions.

Healthcare requires resources. Everything from the money for the treatment to the money that went into developing the treatment (and the cost of all the blind alleys and dead ends of failed experiments in the development of medicines and therapies and treatments), and the time and energy and expertise and training of all the medical professionals involved. Doctors, nurses, technicians, maintenance and janitorial and secretarial staff, and so on do not, after all, and cannot work for free: they must provide for themselves and their families too. Not to mention all the chemists, engineers, and researchers (and their staffs) who work in laboratories and for pharmaceutical companies and medical device manufacturers – and all the millions of people who invest in those companies, or whose retirements, pensions, and 401(k)s are invested in them and who are depending on them to increase the value of their investments. And all the others who depend on them for medical services as well. And so on. The number of people implicated in such a wide, extensive network of interdependence involved in something as vast as the "healthcare system" is mind-boggling, and to justify the expenditure of Mars medicine would require that we estimate all the forgone opportunities and benefits that it would entail across this entire, vast network. That is exceedingly difficult, perhaps impossible, to compute – even to estimate – but thus exceedingly difficult to justify.

All of us want good things for ourselves and for others. Yet the amount of our own scarce resources that we would be willing to expend for others, including others unknown to us, is itself limited. Because our resources are scarce, it has to be. That means we will often have to make hard decisions, sometimes tragically hard decisions, about giving up one benefit, even a very great benefit, for the sake of some other yet greater benefit. These decisions are not easy. Sometimes they are indeed incredibly difficult, particularly because they are often made at risk of loss and under uncertainty about the outcomes. The reality of opportunity cost means, however, that we cannot avoid making them. Our limited knowledge, particularly about the future, means we often get them wrong, but we have an even greater chance of getting them wrong when we do not even attempt to estimate opportunity cost. Ignoring opportunity cost means that we risk forgoing even greater benefit, and suffering even greater loss.

Tradeoffs

A final aspect of the Good Is Not Good Enough Fallacy is tradeoffs. Because our resources are scarce and our desires outstrip our resources, every decision we make involves a tradeoff. Every dollar or minute we spend in one way means trading their benefit off against some other way we could have spent that dollar or minute. No one likes to think of tradeoffs, because no one likes the idea that we cannot have everything we want. Think of all the things you wanted to be when you grew up: oceanographer, medical doctor, president, professor, rancher, professional hockey player. Those are what I wanted to be when I grew up. You will have your own list, but neither of us could be all the things we wanted to be. We had to make tradeoffs. Or think of larger moral, social, or political goals one might have: liberty, security, equality, prosperity, happiness, virtue, and so on. Perhaps we can make improvements, at least incrementally, on many or even all those margins, but given our scarce resources of time, talent, and treasure we cannot pursue all these goals, or maximize for all these variables, at the same time. Some of them will, at the margins, have to be preferable to others, which means we will have to make tradeoffs.

Consider just one important moral, social, and political goal: equality. As Nobel laureate Amartya Sen has asked, "Equality of what?"[7] Do we mean equality of opportunity? Equality before the law? Equality of individual liberty? Equality of material resources? Equality of condition? Equality of welfare? Equality of capability? As Sen shows, championing any one of them will entail, in at least some ways, sacrificing others. We cannot have equality of material resources, for example, without sacrificing at least some equality before the law – some will have to have their resources taken from them so that it can be given to others, which means the law will have to treat different people differently, granting legal rights to some that it denies to others. Similarly, equality of resources will conflict with equality of welfare, because some people require more resources – perhaps they are disabled, for example – to enable them to enjoy the same welfare as others who require less resources. Equality of capability will run afoul of equality of resources because

[7] See Sen 1995. We discuss this further in Chapter 6.

94

some will require greater education, training, or other assistance in order to fulfill their capabilities than will other people. As Sen argues, there can therefore be no such thing as endorsing equality *simpliciter*.

And so it goes with all the other values we might champion, whether moral or economic, whether private or public. For each of them a tradeoff is involved. And because different people have different schedules of value, they will have different ideas about what tradeoffs they would be willing, or would regard as appropriate, to make. The fact of human diversity, and of the plurality of human values, means that these differing ideas about tradeoffs will conflict, and because it will never be the case that all people have the same schedule of value, these conflicts are and will be an enduring feature of the human condition. And sometimes these conflicts can be violent. If we are to have a hope of minimizing such conflict, however, each of us must engage in good-faith deliberation about his or her own schedule of value, and as a community we must engage in good-faith deliberation not only of benefit but of opportunity cost. This will not solve all our problems, but it can help prevent us from even greater loss than we might otherwise experience. And, because it relies on taking people's real needs and desires into account, it might also stand a chance of reducing some of the conflict in human life.

Conclusion

The fact that a proposed course of action would lead to a good result is necessary but not by itself sufficient to justify doing it.

We must show not only that the proposed course of action would lead to a good result but in addition that it would lead to a better result than the other available alternatives. To determine that, we need to know its probable benefits as well as its probable costs – including the opportunity costs. A "rational economic order" requires that our scarce resources be allocated first to their most important uses, then to their second-most-important uses second, and so on, which means we must estimate the potential payout of various options of resource allocation, as well as the costs, including opportunity costs, involved, and then decide accordingly.

Because opportunity cost is "unseen," however, meaning that forgone uses of our resources are not actually realized and hence must be merely imagined, it is easy to neglect or forget them. But opportunity cost cannot be evaded by being ignored, and it is no less real for being unseen. Any proposed expenditure of our resources, whether by private or public means, can be accurately assessed only once opportunity cost and all other costs, as well as likely benefits, are estimated.

Adam Smith's local knowledge argument holds that individuals tend to have more intimate and detailed knowledge of their own situations, and of those situations with which they are personally familiar, than they do of others' situations. Individuals know their own values, desires, goals, and preferences, the opportunity costs they face and the risks they are willing to take, and the obligations, responsibilities, and constraints they face, better than others do. Hence, it is individuals themselves who are typically better positioned to know how their resources should be expended to enable them to achieve their goals, including their moral goals. Third parties have a much lower chance of knowing what decisions individuals should make, and hence are typically ill-positioned to make decisions for them. The political-economic institutions required for individuals to exploit their local knowledge and to make good decisions in their own cases and for the benefit of willing others are primarily protections of individuals' persons, property, and voluntary promises.

Because resources are scarce, all decisions involve tradeoffs. That includes not only strictly economic decisions but moral ones as well: for any moral value we might champion, there will be others that will therefore take a backseat. Construction of a rational moral order, then, like the construction of a rational economic order, requires ranking our moral values and allocating our scarce resources accordingly, with a full reckoning of the tradeoffs and opportunity costs involved.

3

There Is No Great Mind

The man of system . . . seems to imagine that he can arrange the different members of a great society with as much ease as the hand arranges the different pieces upon a chess-board. He does not consider that the pieces upon the chess-board have no other principle of motion besides that which the hand impresses upon them; but that, in the great chess-board of human society, every single piece has a principle of motion all its own.

Adam Smith, *The Theory of Moral Sentiments*

Introduction

In Chapter 2 we discussed the "Local Knowledge Argument," or LKA, which claims that, because individuals are in possession of detailed knowledge about their own localized situations, they are typically better positioned to make decisions about how to allocate their own resources than are third parties. This chapter looks at a related claim, in the form of what I will call the "Great Mind Fallacy," or GMF. The GMF has two aspects. Its first aspect is to believe that there is some person or group of people who possesses enough information, and is endowed with sufficiently superior character, that we can safely entrust with the authority of crafting policy for citizens. Its second aspect is to endorse public policy that could succeed only if such people were in charge of administering the agencies and mechanisms required to effectuate the beneficial results we hope for from them.

One potential criticism of the LKA that we did not address in Chapter 2 is that people are, in fact, imperfect reasoners. As the field of behavioral economics has lately been demonstrating, people are routinely bewitched by a large number of cognitive errors and biases that negatively affect their reasoning and hence the choices they make. Might it not be the case, then, that sometimes experts do know what is good for us – even better than we ourselves do? If they can figure out how and when we are likely to make mistakes in our reasoning, perhaps they can nudge, or even shove, us to make better decisions.

The provision of information on which people can base their decisions is a good and noble aim, and our increasing knowledge of human biology, psychology, health, nutrition, and so on indeed does portend better decision-making. What we discuss in this chapter, however, is not mere provision of information aimed at improving decision-making.[1] It is rather the prospect, increasingly supported today, of overriding people's preferences and decisions and inducing them to make choices different from what they otherwise would have. That presumes a level of knowledge for the expert inducers, on the one hand, and a level of faith in them, on the other, that I will argue are unwarranted. It requires a belief in Great Minds that do not in fact exist.

---

[1] The procurement and provision of information are themselves costly, however, which means that they, too, would be subject to opportunity cost analysis. For a seminal treatment, see Stigler 1961.

Experts and Expert Knowledge

In their influential 2009 book *Nudge*, Nobel laureate Richard Thaler and Cass Sunstein claim that because we now know that people are not perfect reasoners, one aim of public policy should be to take account of our predictable mistakes by proactively structuring the choices available to us so that we are more likely to make the right choices. If left to our own devices, they argue, we would not save enough for our retirement; we would drive too fast; we would engage in impulse buying that would harm our budgets; we would drink too much alcohol; we would let momentary weakness lead us to forgo a workout at the gym and instead eat a doughnut, despite our desires to maintain good fitness; and we would make many other mistakes in addition. Thaler and Sunstein's goal is to thread the needle between respecting free choices while at the same time encouraging us – sometimes subtly and even unconsciously, sometimes not so subtly – to make the choices that even we ourselves, if we could reflect dispassionately, would endorse. They call their position "libertarian paternalism," which sounds paradoxical but reflects their desire to protect free choice (the "libertarian" part) while at the same time "nudging" us to make good decisions (the "paternalism" part).

Thaler and Sunstein claim that "well-established findings in social science" demonstrate that we routinely "make pretty bad decisions," and their wish is to help people instead make the decisions they would make "if they had paid full attention and possessed complete information, unlimited cognitive abilities, and complete self-control" (2009, 5). That seems like a high standard. The decisions we would make if we paid *full* attention, possessed *complete* information, and had *unlimited* cognitive abilities and *complete* self-control? Although one might worry that such a standard could authorize a dystopian world of a governmental Big Brother manipulating us according to its whims and preferences, Thaler and Sunstein insist that their goal is merely "to influence choices in a way that will make choosers better off, *as judged by themselves*" (2009, 5; italics in the original).

Now, a claim of "don't worry – you'll thank us later" might not assuage concerns associated with empowering third parties, including governments, with the power to coerce, to act as "choice architects" (2009, 11) for us, and to engineer the choices we imagined we were free to make. But at least Thaler and Sunstein add "libertarian" to their "paternalism." Others have argued for abandoning the freedom to choose altogether and opting instead for unvarnished paternalism. Medical doctor Peter Ubel (2009), for example, argues that endorsing free individual choice might have been appropriate in the eighteenth century because there did not then exist expert knowledge in health, medicine, and nutrition. Perhaps in the eighteenth century we could endorse Adam Smithian free markets as a discovery device, allowing individuals to experiment and innovate to make trial-and-error attempts to find and achieve paths of flourishing and success. As Ubel claims, however, today we do possess expert knowledge about these matters, or at least many of them. And where we do, allowing people the freedom to experiment is not morally laudable: it is cruel – like setting a five-year-old child loose in the woods and telling her "Good luck!" If we, or at least some of us, know what are better, and what are worse, choices to make, and if we know not only that people are likely to make mistakes but also what kinds of mistakes and in which kinds of situations they are likely to make them, then we should compel them to avoid mistakes and make good choices. Ubel argues that we should not let the negative connotations associated with "paternalism" deter us from doing the good for others that we know we could.

Philosopher Sarah Conly argues that we should abandon altogether the idea of "autonomy" or individual free choice, which she holds to be merely an antiquated relic of prescientific thinking. She invites and embraces the government to actively engage in paternalistic decision-making regarding everything from saving for retirement to the number of children she (or rather we) should have (Conley 2013 and 2016). As she says, she is not trained in financial investing or in nutrition or child psychology or medicine, so how could she be expected to make good decisions in such cases for herself? Because, she reasons, most other people too are in states of ignorance about these and many other topics relative to experts, she concludes that we should abandon our romantic attachment to free choice and instead welcome government paternalism by experts.

Is there in fact such a thing as expert knowledge? Of course there is. Are there many areas of knowledge in which any given individual is ignorant, and in which there exists a substantial asymmetry of knowledge between what the individual consumer, patient, or citizen knows and what the seller, provider, or expert knows? Again, yes. Does that mean we should support libertarian paternalism, or perhaps outright paternalism? No, it does not.

Let me emphasize that the case against (libertarian) paternalism does not rely on the claim that experts do not actually know what they are talking about. Of course, like everyone else, experts do get a lot of things wrong. Consider, as just one example, some of the claims that recognized experts made about the future of humanity and of the world at and shortly after the first Earth Day, which took place in 1970. Harvard biologist George Wald: "civilization will end within 15 or 30 years unless immediate action is taken against problems facing mankind"; Stanford biologist Paul Ehrlich: "The death rate will increase until at least 100–200 million people per year will be starving to death during the next ten years"; *Life* magazine: "Scientists have solid experimental and theoretical evidence to support . . . the following predictions: In a decade, urban dwellers will have to wear gas masks to survive air pollution . . . by 1985 air pollution will have reduced the amount of sunlight reaching earth by one half."[2] Many other examples could be adduced of experts making claims about what will happen if present trends continue – but of course "present trends," particularly of large-scale phenomena that comprise or are heavily affected by human behavior, rarely continue exactly as we might predict. People change their behavior, scientists update or change their understandings and their models, new evidence arises, prior consensuses are abandoned and new are formed, and so

---

[2] See Perry 2018 for these and other examples.

on. If you are worried about the effects of coffee or red meat in your diet, wait a year or so until the next study comes out.

Some things, however, scientists have been able to figure out, and in at least some cases – increasingly many over time, especially with the advent of big data – expert knowledge seems to converge on the truth. The problem relevant to our discussion, then, is not that there is no such thing as expert knowledge, but rather that the knowledge experts have is general, not particular. It is about averages, aggregations, composites, and macro-level predictions, not about specific individuals and their peculiar situations. That means that their general prescriptions can be fruitfully applied to individual situations only once the particularities of those situations are known – and therein lies the rub.

It may be true, for example, that people should save for their retirements. But how much should you or I save – not the "average person," but you or I? It may be true that investing in the stock market tends to give the best overall long-term return on one's investments; does that mean, however, that you should invest in the stock market? Maybe, maybe not. How old are you? How risk-averse are you? Are you married? Do you have children? Do you need money now to pay off student loans or to buy a car or to send your children to college or to care for your ailing parent or grandparent? Similarly, it may be true in general that people should drink alcohol in moderation, eat well, and exercise regularly. It may also be true that people should not have too many (or perhaps too few) children, should not go too far into debt on their student loans, and should spend less now to save more for a rainy day. But none of that tells you whether you should have a second glass of wine at the party tonight (are you driving?), whether you should have fried chicken for dinner (the only time this month?), or whether you should go for a run today (were you unexpectedly called into an important meeting?). Similarly, claiming that people should not have too many (or too few) children does not tell you how many you should have, and claiming that people should save more does not tell you how much or where or what constitutes a "rainy day" that justifies spending now.

Such examples could be multiplied almost indefinitely, but their point is simple: whatever knowledge experts have about saving and investing, health and nutrition, and so on does not suffice to put them in a position to know what you – or *any other individual* – should do, because the experts do not know you, or the other individuals to whom their policies would apply. To know what any given individual should do requires detailed knowledge of her specific situation. The right decision for her would depend, in fact, on a whole range of factors unknown to the experts – factors like what her goals, ambitions, preferences, and values are; what her responsibilities, duties, and obligations are; what her opportunities and limitations are; what she enjoys and what she dislikes; what her personality and temperament are, what risks she is willing to take or not take, which tradeoffs she is willing to make and which she is unwilling to make. In other words, the experts do not know any of the factors that go into making you *you*, as opposed to simply a fungible substitute for anyone else.

One might reply, however, that Google, Amazon, Facebook, and other companies know, or are figuring out, quite a lot about us already – and more than ever before. That is true; yet consider two important points.

First, what they are learning about is our past choices, and they are making predictions about what we will choose in the future based on what we chose in the past. They will never reach the point of making perfect predictions, however, because human beings are unpredictable. We sometimes make choices that are completely different from what we did before; we change our minds as a result of everything from the article we read this morning to the text message we got from our long-absent friend to the off-hand comment our colleague made. Sometimes we make choices in the face of unanimous disagreement from our family members. Sometimes we go along with the crowd, sometimes we buck fashion and trends. Sometimes we plan to do something and fully intend to follow through, and then something unexpectedly comes up that completely changes our plans.

An anecdote from my own life illustrates the predictable unpredictability of human life. When I was in graduate school, I wanted to write my PhD dissertation on the moral theory of my philosophical hero, David Hume. As I was beginning work on it, I discovered that Hume had been friends with Adam Smith. I had heard a bit about Smith when I was an undergraduate student, and I had even read some excerpts from his *Wealth of Nations*, but I remembered next to nothing about him or his work other than the phrase "invisible hand." But because I thought any friend of Hume's was a friend of mine, I decided to spend a few minutes investigating this Adam Smith. I discovered that Smith had written another book, *The Theory of Moral Sentiments*, published some seventeen years before *The Wealth of Nations*. For a reason I cannot now recall, I decided to read *The Theory of Moral Sentiments*. I could not put it down – it was so full of insights, intriguing examples, and fascinating arguments and claims that I raced through it. I then rushed to the library to see what other philosophers (my discipline) had written about it. To my great surprise, I discovered that they had written almost nothing! Some economists had written about Smith, but most philosophers apparently thought that he was either not worth reading or writing about, or possibly that if he had anything interesting to say it was probably already said by his friend Hume (and probably better). Perhaps some philosophers thought of Smith as "only an economist," and hence not worth philosophical examination. Whatever the explanation, I decided to write my dissertation as a systematic reinterpretation of Smith's moral philosophy, along with comparisons to and contrasts with Hume's moral philosophy. That changed the entire direction of my graduate studies, and of my subsequent career – all because of a series of accidents, none of which anyone, including me, could have predicted.

My guess is that you will have similar stories to tell about your own life, about chance encounters or accidental discoveries that had outsized effect on the subsequent course of your life. Everyone else will have similar stories as well. The point of mentioning them is that these are constitutive parts of who each of us is, of our full and unique identities – and they were accidents that could not, even in principle, be predicted. There is no expert knowledge that could enable anyone to predict these kinds of events that have a material effect on our lives. Even more than that, there is no expert knowledge that would enable anyone to know what any of us should do when these unpredictable events occur. Which of these surprise opportunities should we take, and which should we decline? This can be extremely difficult even for us to know for ourselves; what chance does a distant nudger or paternalist have of getting them right for us? And if a government nudger or paternalist undertakes to guide or even compel our choices, how many potentially serendipitous opportunities, how many fortuitous happenstances, how many happy accidents would we either not experience or not be able to pursue?

There is, unfortunately, no Great Mind who can survey the totality of one's life, who knows all the possible courses one's life might take, who can anticipate all the surprises and accidents that emerge in one's life, or who, therefore, can know what you should do. (Maybe God could do this, but He is unfortunately not running for office.)

The second thing that distinguishes the cases of Google, Amazon, Facebook, and so on from paternalistic nudging is that Google, Amazon, and Facebook cannot make anyone do anything. If you are worried about their effects, or simply do not like them or what they do, then you are free not to use them – ever. You can use DuckDuckGo, Walmart, or Instagram if you would rather; or not. People often talk as if companies like Google, Amazon, and Facebook were unavoidable, either because they are just so big or because so many others already use them. It is true that they are big and that many people use them, but no one is required to do so. If you use them because they are easy or convenient or popular, then that is a choice you are making, which you are free to make or not make. By contrast, government nudging happens whether you want it or not. Once paternalistic nudging gets enacted into law or regulation, its requirements must be obeyed, whether they benefit any particular person or not. I can exercise my opt-out option with Google and Instagram (as I in fact do), but I cannot exercise my opt-out option – I am allowed no opt-out option – regarding whether I want to subsidize other people's purchases of electric vehicles.

The impulse to trust experts and to give them authority over us is a venerable one, perhaps indeed having evolutionary roots in our development as a small-group species whose survival in evolutionary times might well have depended on our willingness to submit to and follow a single leader (Rubin 2003 and Rose 2019). The stories of quasi-divine leaders and lawgivers (and pharaohs, emperors, kings, and Dear Leaders who often claimed, and were credited with, divinity) from the past might be instances of a natural inclination not only to submit to powerful, larger-than-life leaders, but to believe them to be endowed with superhuman wisdom. Similarly with various figures who have claimed special abilities to communicate with the gods, divine their will, or interpret their signs – and who enjoyed elevated status in their communities in light of their purported divine favor. A dispassionate look at the actual historical results of obedience to such all-too-human leaders, however, should temper our enthusiasm. History is replete with atrocities committed by people following such leaders, everything from raping and pillaging to conquest, enslaving, and killing. The exceedingly rare exceptions of leaders who were actual moral exemplars, like Jesus or Washington perhaps, nevertheless prove the rule. We should therefore exercise caution when someone claims that he knows better than we do how we should lead our lives, and when he proposes to intervene in our decisions, even against our wishes, to superintend our choices.

There is another consideration, however, connected to the second aspect of the Great Mind Fallacy indicated at the outset of this chapter. When people like Thaler and Sunstein, Ubel, and Conly describe their recommended versions of paternalism – whether the soft version of "libertarian paternalism" or the hard version of straight paternalism – they seem to assume that the people who would administrate their recommended powers of nudging and paternalism would do so only in good faith, with wisdom, justice, and humanity. In fact, their policy recommendations could actually achieve the beneficial effects they describe only if the required agencies were managed and controlled by people who not only had superior cognitive abilities to the rest of us but whose characters were also more virtuous than those of the rest of us. If there is no Great Mind, however, then the first of these criteria fails; the relative rarity – not to say nonexistence – of Supremely Virtuous Beings, especially in sufficient numbers, would seem to warrant skepticism about the second. There are indeed genuine moral exemplars, but how many of them are there? And would they find their ways into, would they even be attracted to, positions of superintendence over the lives, choices, and fortunes of others? Or should we rather expect that the people who will be attracted to these positions and will find their ways into them are likely to be different kinds of people, indeed perhaps exactly the wrong kind of people?

Adam Smith claimed that such power over others would "nowhere be so dangerous as in the hands of a man who had folly and presumption enough to fancy himself fit to exercise it" (1981 [1776], 456). History suggests he may have had a point. But we can draw a more general conclusion. Telling us how beneficial a set of public policies would be if they were administered and staffed by such rare individuals tells us little of practical value. What seems required instead is to tell us how beneficial the public policies would be – that is, how much net benefit they would create, given the opportunity cost – when administered and staffed by the common run of humanity, complete with all the biases, errors in reasoning, prejudices, and self-serving motives that Thaler and Sunstein, Ubel, and Conly themselves identify and document. In fact, it would seem that their argument suffers from a rather awkward embarrassment: if human beings really are as short-sighted and biased (and so on) as they contend, then that would seem all the more reason to be wary of giving any of them such extensive power over others.

Planning

The ancient Greek philosopher Aristotle (384–322 B C) argued that human beings, perhaps alone among creatures on earth, had not only a hierarchy of ends but could also deliberate on them as well. We have near-term, or proximate, goals that we seek to achieve; but our proximate goals in turn serve medium-term, or intermediate, goals; and our intermediate goals themselves in turn serve long-term goals. Given this, Aristotle reasoned, there must be some final or ultimate goal, in the service of which and for the sake of which we do everything else but that itself does not serve any further goal. This final goal would then fix and order, or should then fix and order, all the subordinate intermediate and proximate goals we have. What is this final goal? Aristotle offered *eudaimonia*. That word is hard to translate. It is often rendered in English as "happiness," "flourishing," or "well-being." It encompasses something like a life well and fully lived, an employment of all one's skills and abilities and resources in the service of a life worth living. Here is the idea: imagine yourself at the end of your life, looking back on what you did and how you lived; if you look back on it and believe, honestly believe, that yours was a life worth having been lived – a life of meaning and purpose serving goals that you believe were worth serving – then chances are you will have lived a eudaimonic life. Once you have imagined what kind of life would lead you to such a favorable end-of-life judgment, the next step is to reverse-engineer, to your best approximation, your intermediate and proximate goals so that the things you do today actually lead to the proper intermediate goals, which themselves in turn enable the achievement of eudaimonia.

What we might call a *rationally ordered moral life*, then, is one in which the activities you engage in today serve the goals (or ends, aims, or purposes) that serve the intermediate ends that themselves enable eudaimonia. One's life is irrationally morally ordered, by contrast, if one is engaging in behaviors and actions, and if one is making choices, that either conflict with or do not advance one's progress toward eudaimonia. Hence, one has to figure out what a eudaimonic life would be for one – and, of course, different people will have different appropriate eudaimonic lives, entailing different courses of life – and then plan one's daily, weekly, monthly, yearly (and so on) activities so that they are not only consistent with but integrated into a lifetime plan to achieve one's highest aim of eudaimonia.

That means one must be able to plan. It also means one must be free to make choices about not only the ends themselves but among the various available routes to achieving them. This implicates the second aspect of human nature that Aristotle thought distinguished us from other creatures, namely, our ability to deliberate. We have the ability to consider options; to conceive of and imagine various differing courses of life; and to make choices for which we are therefore morally accountable and responsible. If we had no ability to make free choices, we could not be held responsible for them; in that case, we would not be moral agents – we would be mere machines or robots or automatons, albeit perhaps sophisticated ones. But we can choose, we can be held responsible, and thus we are moral agents. To respect that moral agency, then, we need primarily two things: the freedom to make choices, and the respect of being held responsible for our choices. This means that others must respect our freedom to choose, and it means that others may appropriately hold us accountable for our choices.

This discussion relates to the Great Mind Fallacy in the following way. To achieve a eudaimonic life, a life worth living and having been lived, you need to be able to make choices and plans. You need to be able to chart a course for your own life, to captain your own journey; and you need to be held accountable for, and feel the consequences (good or bad) of, your choices so that you can learn what to do and what not to do in the future. In this way, and in this way only, can we develop what Aristotle called *phronesis*, or good practical judgment. Judgment is a skill, and, like other skills, it must be practiced under correction in order to develop well. If another person takes responsibility for your choices, or undertakes to remove possible courses of action for you or alleviate the negative outcomes of bad decisions you might make, then she is not only disrespecting your moral agency but she is also jeopardizing the development of your judgment and thus imperiling your chance of achieving eudaimonia.

Sometimes the question between, say, socialism and capitalism is framed as a choice between planning and no planning. Socialism is often described as a "planned economy," whereas capitalism is an unplanned, even free-for-all, economy, so the choice between them is often framed as a question about whether there can or should be economic planning or not. But that is a false dilemma. The question is not whether there will be planning or not; rather, it is who will do the planning and for whom. Every human being plans. As mentioned above, one of the perhaps unique features of human beings is that they are capable of deliberating and making choices about their ends, goals, and objectives. Indeed, on the Aristotelian picture, we would not qualify as fully human if we did not use our reason to assess our lives in terms of the ultimate, intermediate, and proximate ends our actions are serving. For any person to stand a chance at achieving a eudaimonic life, she therefore not only may but must plan.

This planning will include economic planning. Among our resources are our wealth, labor, and skills. We will not achieve eudaimonia, or reliably serve any of our other ends, if we do not expend and conserve our resources in accordance with our considered hierarchy of ends, including our distinctively moral ends. The key, however, is that each of us must do this planning for himself. Only in that way can one develop the *phronesis* or practical judgment that enables decisions that can be "rational," that is, actually leading us toward our ends as opposed to away from them. Of course, we may and often will also rely on the advice, counsel, and opinions – including expert opinions – of others, but it is we who must bear ultimate responsibility both of whom to consult and whose advice to take (if anyone's) as well as what choice to make. Planning, then, is a crucial part of a rationally ordered moral life and, indeed, of a fully human life.

If each of us must make plans for his or her own life, then that also means that we must not make plans for others' lives – for in that case they would not be making plans for *their* lives. That is the difference between the planning involved with centralized economies – some making plans for others – and the planning involved with decentralized economies – each making plans for herself. Allowing people to plan their own lives thus has the triple benefits of allowing each individual to develop his or her own judgment, of respecting their dignity as equal moral agents, and of enabling them to chart a proper path to their own eudaimonia.

Motorcycles and Rationality

Would you ride a motorcycle? Would you jump out of an airplane or go free climbing? Each of these involves both potential reward and potential risk. What is the correct level of risk you should take? Do you drive a car, or have you ever consulted your phone while driving? Have you gone into a building without checking its structural soundness? Have you ever bought food from a grocery store or ordered food in a restaurant – and then actually eaten it? Have you taken your doctor's advice and swallowed the pills she told you to swallow? Consider how many things you do every day that involve risk. Doubtless virtually everything you do involves some level of risk, some small and some large, some of which you know, some of which you do not know, and some of which you only think you know. Which risks should you take? One final aspect of the Great Mind Fallacy is to believe that there is some correct level of risk that you should take, and someone else – some Great Mind – knows what it is.

The former might be true, but the latter is not. Experts in estimating risks will, or at least might well, know better than you do what the actual risks of various activities are. Are you more likely to die by gun violence or by driving your car? (The latter.) Are you more likely to die of a heart attack on an airplane or of the airplane crashing? (The former.) And so on. But what experts cannot know is whether you should buy a gun, drive in a car, or fly on an airplane. The most dangerous part of traveling by airplane is the drive to and from the airport; travel by airplane is, mile for mile, the safest overall way to travel. Now that you know that, however, should you drive for your next long-distance trip or fly? The answer to that question depends on a host of facts about you – what your preferences and goals are, what your resources (including time) are, and what your risk tolerances are. That means that the person best positioned to know what you should do is not the expert but you.

Similarly with a wide range of other decisions you will need to make, everything from what to eat to how much to save for your retirement. To take a somewhat extreme example, consider this question: could one be *rationally* morbidly obese? Suppose you know all the health risks you would run if you were morbidly obese, but suppose also that you really dislike working out and you really enjoy eating, and you are willing to bear the costs and risks associated with being morbidly obese. (Add that you would not thereby impose unwanted costs on others – you commit to paying any associated costs yourself.) Might you then make the rational decision to be morbidly obese? The answer is yes. Perhaps you yourself would not actually make that decision. Perhaps you would not be willing to run the health risks or incur the likely health costs, or perhaps you have moral or other objections to doing so. Fair enough. But should you eat dessert after dinner tonight? Should another person? Different people have different preferences, are willing to make different tradeoffs, and have different risk tolerances. The correct risks any individual should take depend on his unique schedule of value. That means that for any given individual, there will be a correct level of risk he should be willing to tolerate given his goals and values, but the correct level of risk for him might apply only to him, and not to anyone else. The risks you should be willing to take would not necessarily apply to him either.

If we were to empower some people to establish acceptable or allowable risks for others – not merely to inform others of the relative risks, but to determine which risks they may take and which they may not – we would in practice be empowering them to select one person's or one group's idiosyncratic judgment about risk and impose it on others. Because those others are not them, however, there is little chance that what is a proper risk to take for the decider will also be a proper risk for the others. The belief that proper levels of risk tolerance could be determined by some person or persons that would be beneficial or even applicable to others is hence to imagine that they know something about us and our lives that they do not, and cannot, know. I cannot know whether you should ride a motorcycle. I might be able to know whether I should ride a motorcycle – whether, considering the risks involved and my values and preferences, it would be worth it for me – but how could I possibly know whether you, a person I have never even met, should? And how could regulators or government officials, however expert in their fields, know, given that they do not know you either?

Yet many seem to believe, or have faith, that there exist people who do, or at least can, know what risks would be proper to take for people they do not know. This is to commit the Great Mind Fallacy, to believe that there exists some Great Mind, or Great Minds, who know more about us than they possibly can. Believing in a Great Mind can be psychologically comforting, relieving us, as it would, of the burden of having to make at least some decisions for ourselves. If we let others make these decisions for us, we bear neither the responsibility for the decisions nor the psychological or any other costs involved in making them. Perhaps we think that the psychological or other cost involved is high enough for us that we are willing to forgo the perhaps onerous responsibility of making such decisions for ourselves in exchange for giving others the authority to make them for us.[3] Even that decision runs a risk, however – namely, the risk of following a course of action that might not lead to benefit for us. So, we cannot escape the necessity of taking risks regardless of what we do. The question, then, remains: Which risks should I take? Unfortunately, there is ultimately only one person who can determine that for me. And only one person who can determine it for you.

Conclusion

Because people are unique, and because their situations – including their ends, desires, and values – are unique, there is no single path to a truly flourishing, or eudaimonic, life that is appropriate to all persons. There is, moreover, no one in possession of the knowledge required to determine the best path to eudaimonia for you – other than you. There is, therefore, no Great Mind who possesses this knowledge and hence can make good decisions for you, or who can construct public policies that would guide each individual on her own unique path toward eudaimonia. The issue is not about whether there

---

[3] That is the tradeoff that, for example, Conly 2013 and 2016 is willing to make – which is her right. The problem arises from the fact that she is proposing to enforce the same tradeoff for the rest of us as well.

will or should be planning or not, but, rather, who will do the planning and for whom. In most cases and regarding most issues, individuals should plan for themselves and their own lives.

There is such a thing as expert knowledge, however, and what Aristotle calls the *phronemos*, or the person of good judgment, will seek it out and employ it liberally. But the person of good judgment will still have to decide whose advice and counsel to seek out, and how to apply it properly to her own life.

Unpredictable changes in our lives, however, down to the level of chance encounters with others, will have, and often should have, an important effect on the paths we take. No distant third party, however expert, can predict these occurrences or know in advance how we should respond to them. Similarly, no third party, however expert, can know what risks we should take to achieve our goals or what our proper risk tolerances should be. There is, alas, no Great Mind, which means that such decisions should properly be left to the individuals themselves, using their judgment as best they can.

4

Progress Is Not Inevitable

*Not only the prejudices of the publick, but what is much
more unconquerable, the private interests of many
individuals, irresistibly oppose it.*

Adam Smith, *The Wealth of Nations*

Introduction

We live in an age of superabundance. Between 1980 and 2017,
the real (inflation-adjusted) price of commodities worldwide
declined by an average of 36.3 percent. During that same
period, real average annual per-capita income rose 63.2 percent, and population-adjusted average annual hours worked
per worker declined by 9.4 percent. That means that real
average hourly income per worker increased by a whopping
80.1 percent. And during that same period, the abundance of
resources worldwide, despite a population growth of 170 percent, increased by an incredible 479.6 percent (Pooley and
Tupy 2018). A person born after 1980 – part of the so-called
Millennial generation – could therefore be forgiven for believing not only that we live in an age of plenty (which we do) but
that the engines of growth will churn forever, more or less
regardless of what we do or what policies we adopt.

But progress is anything but inevitable. For approximately 99.9 percent of human existence on earth, there was

virtually no economic progress.[1] For most of that time there was also no progress in science, literature, or the fine or mechanical arts. Literature has been with us, at least as far as we know, for less than 4,000 years: the *Code of Hammurabi* dates from around 1750 BC; *Enuma Elish* is thought to date from approximately 1700 BC; the Judaic creation story that became the first book of the Bible is thought to date from as early as the twelfth or eleventh century BC; and Homer's *Iliad* dates from perhaps the eighth or seventh centuries BC. Philosophy and science may have begun around the sixth century BC, perhaps with Thales correctly predicting an eclipse in 585, but it did not come into its own until some two millennia later: Copernicus's *On the Revolutions of Celestial Spheres*, which suggested a heliocentric rather than geocentric model of the solar system, was published in AD 1543; Galileo's defense of the Copernican system initiated his Inquisition trial in 1615; Francis Bacon's *Novum Organum*, which suggested an empirical basis for science, was first published in 1620; and Isaac Newton's *Principia Mathematica*, in which he proposed his universal law of gravitation, appeared in 1687. These events may seem as though they happened a long time ago, but if *Homo sapiens* emerged approximately 350,000 years ago, which is a current estimate, then even these earliest texts appeared only within the most recent 1 percent of human existence.

Human prosperity, however, began its unprecedented rise only in the eighteenth century. It had antecedents in the previous century, however, so, estimating generously, we can

---

[1] As Roberts 1997 points out, even the *idea* of progress is relatively recent.

say that the general increase in human prosperity began only in the most recent 0.1 percent of human existence. This suggests that our prosperity has not been the result of any biological or psychological changes in human nature – it is far too short a time span for any significant evolutionary changes to have occurred. Nor is it likely to have been caused by any climatological changes, since during the existence of *Homo sapiens* climate has changed significantly – and yet there was no overall economic development until very recently. These facts suggest that something else, something new and momentous, has been at work in the past 200 years or so. What could it be?

Culture, then Institutions

If you want to have or acquire something, there are three general ways to achieve your goal: (1) you can make it yourself, or *produce* it; (2) you can steal it from someone else, or *extract* it; or (3) you can engage in voluntary trade, exchange, or partnership, or *cooperate* for it. As long as you own or have title or permission to the resources you use to make something, there typically arises no moral issue regarding (1). Regarding (2) and (3), however, a moral issue does arise because in these cases you are dealing not only with yourself but with another person as well. Because others are equal moral agents to you, you must, as I argued in Chapter 1, get their permission. That means that only (3) is morally acceptable. Despite humanity's long love affair with (2), only (3) shows respect to others as moral agents equal in dignity to you and everyone else, and hence only (3) is a morally acceptable way to deal with others.

That may seem obvious, but it has not been obvious to most human beings throughout most of their history – and it is apparently still not obvious to many. Consider how much extraction goes on yet today, everything from restrictions on who may enter markets to who may hold property to what occupations people are allowed to have to what kinds of partnerships or employment arrangements into which people are allowed to enter. And, of course, there is more direct extraction as well, everything from confiscatory taxation to property appropriation to territory occupation. If, however, all adults, regardless of their sex, ethnicity, religion, and so on, are equal moral agents, then all these restrictions are morally improper. For they all amount to privileging the rights and liberties of one group over those of others. I take it as all but self-evident that people should have equal rights and liberties,[2] but to understand why prosperity began to increase when and where it did, as opposed to some other place and time in human history, perhaps it is worth making the case.

There are two general ways one might try to do so: as a matter of *right* and as a matter of *utility*. That is, one might claim that people have a right to equal moral agency and should be accorded respect as such as a matter of principle; or one might claim that treating people this way leads to various beneficial consequences and hence that they should be accorded respect as such because doing so leads to good

---

[2] Qualifications include children, adults who lack capacity, and people duly convicted of crimes, but they are exceptions that prove the rule. The rest of the discussion addresses adults who do not satisfy these disqualifying criteria, which constitutes the vast majority of adults in the world.

ends. In Chapter 3, I suggested an argument for the former, claiming that treating people as equal moral agents respects their status and capacity as moral agents, reflecting their natures as free and responsible beings capable of making choices and being held accountable for them. But perhaps one is not convinced that people are such agents, or at any rate not convinced that they should always be shown respect, and held accountable, for the choices they make. In that case, perhaps one wants to know what the utilitarian argument would have to say. I am pleased to report a happy coincidence: both arguments point in the same direction. A market economy is most consistent with the assumption of equal moral agency, because it is in a market economy that people are free to make choices based on their respective schedules of value, including moral value, given the constraints they face. Moreover, a market economy leads to the best overall – though of course not perfect – results in terms of welfare benefits or prosperity. Thus, as John Locke wrote in his *Second Treatise of Government*, it turns out that "right and conveniency went together" (Locke 1980 [1690], chap. 5, sect. 51, 30).

What has changed over humanity's recent history is not biology, psychology, physiology, ecology, or geography. What has changed, instead, is their attitudes. As economic historian Deirdre McCloskey has demonstrated in her magisterial three-volume investigation under the general title *The Bourgeois Era*, the most salient factor distinguishing the post-1800 era from everything that went before is the attitudes people held toward others. Before that period, the standard background assumption people had was that some people are superior to others – more specifically, one's own people are superior to those other people – and hence people believed they were under no obligation, moral or otherwise, to treat all human beings as their moral equals. What began as an inkling in the sixteenth century, gained some traction in the seventeenth century, and then began to spread in the eighteenth century, was the idea that cooperation was not only allowable, but morally appropriate; and not only with some people, but with ever more people and ever more groups of people.[3] As that idea spread, more and more cooperative behavior was engaged in, leading to mutually beneficial exchanges and partnerships, which launched world prosperity on the precipitate upward slope we have seen since.

If people are to engage in voluntary transactions and partnerships with one another, however, they also need to trust one another. They need to be confident that the other parties to the transactions will uphold their ends of the bargains. Thus, trust is required, not only in each other but also in the public institutions themselves. If people believe that the politicians and regulators setting policies, the police enforcing them, or the courts adjudicating disputes – or all of them – are corrupt or otherwise untrustworthy, then all the destructive

---

[3] One early example: Englishman John Lilburne (1614–1657) wrote in his 1649 *The Free-man's Freedom Vindicated* that "every particular and individual man and woman" is "by nature all equal and alike in power, dignity, authority, and majesty, none of them having by nature any authority, dominion, or magisterial power one over or above another"; he further claimed that equal freedom of all humankind entails that no one may exercise any power or authority over another except "by mutual agreement or consent" (Otteson 2003: vol. 3, 105).

behaviors created by the prevalence of extraction come roaring back to the fore. We have, then, two separate but linked kinds of institutions that are required: we need properly configured public and legal institutions, honestly administered, to protect people in their persons, property, and promises; and we need cultural and moral institutions that incline us to trust both one another and our institutions. Institutions do not enforce themselves, and if citizens do not believe that other citizens can be trusted (regardless of the public institutions in place) or if they do not believe that the institutions themselves can be trusted, or are worthy of trust, then the institutions will be unable to effect the benefits they otherwise could.

Following McCloskey, I argue that, although both are needed and reinforce each other, the attitudes of citizens take pride of place – both historically and practically. Historically: it seems that it was changes in the attitudes of increasing numbers of people that allowed them to engage in what McCloskey calls "mutual betterment," or mutually voluntary and mutually beneficial transactions with more and more people – including people outside their own bands, tribes, races, and religions. Practically: if people do not believe in or support their public institutions, then they will be dead letters. The 1936 written constitution of the Union of Soviet Socialist Republics had a provision in it guaranteeing the security of private property.[4] It made little difference, however, because

---

[4] "ARTICLE 10. The right of citizens to personal ownership of their incomes from work and of their savings, of their dwelling houses and subsidiary household economy, their household furniture and utensils

no one inside or outside the government believed it. In the eighteenth century, David Hume argued that all authority ultimately rests on opinion (Hume 1985 [1741], 32). That may seem counterintuitive, but reflection reveals he might have had a point. No dictator can coerce all his people by himself. Instead he must rely on his ministers, advisors, soldiers, henchmen, and so on. But when he issues them orders and commands, why do they do his bidding? Because they believe he is in charge. And when they in turn issue orders and commands to other citizens, why do the citizens obey? Because they believe their orders have authority, because they believe they might be punished if they disobey, or both. Either way, however, they act the way they do because of their beliefs – or, as Hume put it, their opinions. So, the king's power is based on the beliefs of many levels of people that he has authority that must or should be obeyed.

The point this makes is that what people believe has an enormous effect, perhaps the entire effect, on what they do. And the combined effects of people's beliefs are what ultimately determines the signature and nature of their culture. The public social institutions a country has clearly also have an effect, but ultimately it is people's beliefs about their institutions – and about each other – that affect their behavior and shape their culture.[5] What this suggests is that as people's

and articles of personal use and convenience, as well as the right of inheritance of personal property of citizens, is protected by law." See Union of Soviet Socialist Republics 1936.

[5] As Samuel Smiles wrote in the nineteenth century, "In the order of nature, the collective character of a nation will as surely find its befitting results in its law and government, as water finds its own level. The noble

beliefs began to change about how they should relate to one another, and how they should interact and coordinate with others, the public institutions they supported also changed. More specifically, as they came to believe that others deserved respect and that voluntary transactions were not only acceptable but even morally praiseworthy, and as the scope of people included in their beliefs about who should be accorded this respect expanded, their behavior changed, leading not only to increasing numbers of positive-sum transactions and thus increasing overall prosperity but also to creating institutions that protected and encouraged such interactions. In other words, people's beliefs and thus their culture changed, and then institutions caught up.[6]

Moral Attitudes and Culture

What is the connection between this discussion and the fallacy with which this chapter is concerned, namely, the Progress is Inevitable Fallacy? It is this: culture is critically important for growing prosperity, but culture can change – and quickly. The culture that enabled the growth in worldwide prosperity we have experienced over the last two centuries is not only recent but rare. And it is fragile. One look at the upheavals of the twentieth century, well into the age of enlightenment and the supposed age of democracy, should

---

people will be nobly ruled, and the ignorant and corrupt ignobly" (Smiles 1996 [1859], 2).

[6] As economist David Rose (2019) has recently argued, thus "culture matters most."

suffice to disabuse us of the idea that human beings cannot, or can no longer, be violent, brutal, and inhumane toward one another. Moreover, to follow the recent economic histories of places like North Korea, Cuba, Argentina, Libya, Venezuela, Zimbabwe, Cambodia, Myanmar, and many other countries throughout the world, especially in the so-called developing world, is to see not only the difficulties involved in creating and sustaining economic prosperity but how thoroughly the wrong cultures or institutions can destroy it.

Douglass North (1981, 1990, and 2005), Nathan Rosenberg and L. E. Birdzell Jr. (1986), David Landes (1999), Deirdre McCloskey (2006, 2010, 2016, and 2019), Eric Beinhocker (2007), Joel Mokyr (2009 and 2016), Angus Deaton (2013), Deepak Lal (2013), Edmund Phelps (2013), Joshua Hall and Robert Lawson (2014), Steven Pinker (2018), Hans Rosling et al. (2018), Stephen Davies (2019), and others who have studied the various aspects of human well-being and tracked their courses over time have demonstrated that on almost every measurable margin things are getting better overall. Worldwide, people are living longer, are healthier, are wealthier, are more literate, are more hopeful about the future, and are happier than they have ever been.

As this empirical work shows, these unprecedented improvements have been achieved precisely because people's beliefs have changed.[7] People have gone from a default of

---

[7] It should be noted that the sources cited in the previous paragraph are not all in agreement about the particulars of the story of development, including whether institutions or culture is more important. I believe they may all be fairly represented, however, as holding that both institutions and cultures are crucial. My own account follows McCloskey's most closely.

regarding people different from them with suspicion and as likely enemies to a default of viewing them at least neutrally and even as opportunities. They have gone from viewing trade, commerce, and mutually voluntary and mutually beneficial exchange as unworthy of virtuous human beings, to viewing it neutrally, to, finally, viewing it as at least possibly worthy of dedicating one's life to. They have gone from viewing human beings as fungible atoms in undifferentiated masses to seeing them as unique and precious individuals possessing moral dignity and deserving of both liberty and respect. They have gone from viewing violence and torture as acceptable, even natural, ways to treat and engage with others to believing that violence should be a regrettable last resort – and that torture is inhumane and should be minimized, if not abandoned altogether. And they have gone from automatically distrusting everyone they meet but do not know to increasingly being willing to extend others, even strangers, the benefit of the doubt. Liberal political policies that respect and protect individual rights and give people not only a say over their own lives but a say, or at least a vote, over the shape their governments take, as well as economic policies enabling free trade, commerce, and innovation, as well as the opt-out option to say "no, thank you" to any offer or proposal, are the institutions that have followed, and followed from, these changes in attitudes, beliefs, and culture.

Now, I am generalizing of course. Not all people have made these transitions in beliefs; in some places, these what Pinker (2018) calls "enlightened" ideas have yet to fully take hold; and in some places they might lose ground. Indeed, it may well be that there will never be a time when these ideas have fully taken hold once and for all. Why not?

One reason is because human beings are a small-group species. We evolved in conditions that rewarded – meaning, increased the chances of survival of – groups whose members trusted one another but distrusted the members of other groups, that could expect individual members to sacrifice themselves for the group instead of striking out on their own, that subordinated themselves to a single leader who commanded obedience, and that demanded not only a strict hierarchy of authority but a relative equality of wealth. For most of their history, human beings existed in small nomadic bands, most of whose members were genetically closely related and all of whom knew each other intimately well. They also lived at or close to the margins of subsistence, with high mortality rates, high infancy and child death rates, high childbirth death rates, and short longevity expectations. For most of their history, moreover, one prime way that a group could benefit itself was at the expense of other groups: by raiding and killing the members of other groups and taking their land, possessions, and resources. For that reason it paid to be suspicious of members of other groups – better to kill a stranger than to spend the time trying to discover whether he might be friendly, time during which he or his mates might kill you; and it was risky to accumulate anything worth stealing, because it would serve as an enticement to others to steal it from you, and perhaps kill (or enslave) you for good measure.

Because of how close to subsistence human beings were throughout almost all their history, anything they produced, found, or caught was typically shared equally with all members of the band. The chieftain or the best hunter might get the first choice from or the first bite of the successful hunt, but the differences among shares overall – that is, the inequalities – were quite small in absolute terms, and in any case it was clear to everyone why anyone who did get more was entitled to it, meager though it might have been. All this was required for the survival of the band. But suppose one member of the band, or one family in the band, began to accumulate a bit more than others. There would have been primarily two ways for this to happen: either the prospering individual or family had found a cache of food or resources and was not sharing; or they were cavorting – treasonously! – with another band. Either of these possibilities, however, would have constituted a threat to the unity and hence survival of the band, and so everyone would have been on the lookout for it. If any individual or family was discovered to have more than others, then, it would have been punished swiftly – and often mercilessly. Because unity of purpose was a requirement for survival of the band, an immediate suspicion of inequality would have provided an important advantage to these early small groups of humans. An instinctive suspicion of inequality, along with its attendant suspicion of strangers, would thus have been selected for under such conditions.

We today are the inheritors of these psychological instincts. That may help to explain why we are so immediately suspicious of any person, group, or country that has more than we do, even before we know anything about how they got what they have; and why it is so easy for us to become suspicious of strangers, before knowing anything about who they are and whether they mean us good or ill.

These instincts were indispensable for survival in our evolutionary periods. But they are entirely out of place today. We no longer live or associate only in small groups. We no longer interact, associate, and trade only with people to whom we are related or whom we know personally. Our small-group instincts enabled our forebears' survival, but at the cost of inhibiting general prosperity from appearing and growing. What has enabled prosperity for the last two centuries or so, by contrast, has been a shift in culture that encouraged, and then rewarded, people for suppressing and inhibiting some of their basic instincts of distrust of strangers and of difference. In that way, commercial society, global trade, and generalized trust of others are all highly contrary to deep-seated instincts *Homo sapiens* developed over millennia of hard-fought evolutionary winnowing. The historically recent willingness to trust, trade, associate, partner, exchange, and transact with others – including people unrelated to us, whom we do not know, and who might look different from us, eat and dress differently from us, and worship different gods – is what has enabled the spectacular increase in prosperity the world has seen over the last two centuries, prosperity that has tracked with a high degree of fidelity the spread of exactly these ideas.

Because these ideas are contrary to our native instincts, however, two important conclusions follow. First, it is our changing attitudes, and our changing culture, that has enabled this prosperity from which billions of us have so greatly benefited. Second, it would be all too easy and comfortable – so seemingly, on a visceral level, right – to renounce these "new" ideas of trust, individual dignity, free choice, and so on and to reestablish the tribal mentality that served us so well in evolutionary times but that could so swiftly destroy the benefits from widespread cooperation that has enriched us in the most recent 0.1 percent of our existence.

Culture, therefore, is crucial. For it is culture that transmits the ideas that shape our moral and other sensibilities. If our culture teaches us to distrust others, our children will grow up distrustful of others. If our culture distrusts all material inequality, it may protect us against extraction from external groups, but at the expense of denying us the innovation, entrepreneurship, mutual betterment, and prosperity that cooperation with increasing numbers of people enables. If our culture values only "our" right to liberty, our moral agency, and our dignity, it will sacrifice and disrespect "their" right to liberty, their moral agency, and their dignity. Increasing prosperity is, therefore, by no means a given. It is not a naturally occurring phenomenon, it will not take place no matter what, and it will not survive chauvinistic, racist, xenophobic, or other prejudicial beliefs that denigrate some while elevating others, at least if such malicious beliefs are sufficiently widespread. And given their evolutionary provenance, incitements to distrust, denigrate, and even hate others will often meet with an unfortunate but emotionally satisfying reception. Or at least they can – unless our culture is sufficiently robust to inculcate in people the second-nature habits of rejecting such disrespect and depreciation of others out of hand.

That issues, I believe, in two moral mandates. First, each of us must work hard to internalize in our own characters a robust default of viewing others not with distrust but with trust, of respecting others' choices (even when different from ours, even when wrong) as their business and not ours, and of granting others a wide scope of liberty to order their lives as they see fit while respecting their moral agency enough to also hold them responsible for their choices. Second, each of us must model this liberal and entrepreneurial spirit for others. That includes for our family, our friends, our associates, and even strangers. We must do this on principle, not as an on-the-spot cost–benefit analysis: we must accept it as a default never to engage in extraction, even when we have the opportunity to do so,[8] and that others may trade, interact, exchange, partner, and associate with whomever they wish on whatever terms they mutually agree to. Only in this way can we put ourselves in a position to discover and chart a course for our own lives that has a chance of achieving eudaimonia. And only in this way can we behave in support of, and model reflection of, institutions that give others a chance at the same, thereby enabling generalized prosperity.

The prosperity you and I enjoy is a rare and precious blessing, a gift that previous generations gave us by adopting new and strange attitudes and beliefs from which we have benefited much more than they. We should not only have gratitude toward our forebears who benefited us in this way, but if we care about the welfare not only of ourselves but of our children and others entirely unknown to us, then we must respect those beliefs and institutions that have made it

---

[8] Even when we encounter what economist Robert Frank calls "golden opportunities." See Frank 1988, 72–5. See also Rose 2011.

possible. Adam Smith's great work was called *An Inquiry in the Nature and Causes of the Wealth of Nations*. Note that it was not an investigation into the *poverty* of nations; it was an inquiry into their *wealth*. Poverty was the natural default of humanity: to be poor, all one had to do was literally nothing. It is wealth, by stark contrast, that required explaining and that requires all the work. If we are to continue enjoying all the direct and ancillary benefits of wealth, and to wish those benefits on others, including future others, as well, then we must learn the cultural and then institutional elements of growing and spreading prosperity, and treat them as the rare and precious gifts that they are.

The Undead Great Mind

The Progress Is Inevitable Fallacy also bears an important connection to the Great Mind Fallacy discussed in Chapter 3. If beliefs, attitudes, and culture are among the primary moving forces behind (among other things) how prosperous a country is, then a country's laws, regulations, and other governmental institutions do not create prosperity: they allow it – or, in the better case, encourage it. All the stories about superhuman lawgivers, like Solon of Athens or Lycurgus of Sparta, and all the claims about the "great men" of history, are, in other words, likely inflated. It is not that leaders have no effect on their citizenry, but, rather, that they tend to be products of their communities, societies, or countries, not progenitors of it. There is such a thing as an influencer of culture, even a "superinfluencer," or people who are admired and whose example can have an outsized effect in influencing others' behavior. The field of marketing has for some time been studying this assiduously and expends a great deal of effort trying to identify these people to predict what products, or what kinds of products, these superinfluencers will exhibit and promote. It is the marketer's dream to identify these individuals and get them to promote the marketer's goods.

Yet the goal remains elusive. It is incredibly difficult to predict either who the superinfluencers are or will be, what their influence is or will be, or what they will like, prefer, or do. No one has been able to quite crack this code yet, and part of the reason is that everyone else – all the people who do or might pay attention to what superinfluencers do – are themselves choosy and unpredictable. Culture changes; fashions and trends come and go; and fortunes are made and lost with good and bad bets about where things will go. All this happens with very little predictive certainty. Nobody really knows where people's preferences for everything from clothing to music to movies to reading to food to electronic devices to travel to home buying will go. This uncertainty underpins one of the arguments for a market economy: the best chance we have to discover what will actually satisfy people's constantly changing preferences and needs is by letting thousands, millions, even billions of people run experiments, creating new businesses, offering new products, reorganizing resources, innovating and building entrepreneurially on innovations, and capitalizing on both successes and failures – all with an eye toward creating or enhancing benefit both to themselves and others.

One potential implication of the Progress Is Inevitable Fallacy, however, is the belief that progress can be guided, and its future course charted, by some Great Mind – and our recurring faith in the powers of leaders, lawgivers, statesmen, regulators, administrators, and so forth, despite a long record of at best mixed success, suggests that many continue to be attracted by a vision of wise and benevolent guidance. But centralized experts are not able to guide progress and prosperity. Not because they are unintelligent or vicious – or at least not any less intelligent or any more vicious than people in other walks of life – but rather because they possess neither the knowledge required to make wise decisions nor the incentives to motivate beneficent policy.

As discussed in Chapter 2, a rational economic order requires that our limited resources be put to their most highly valued uses first, their second-most-highly valued uses second, and so on. To know what those values are, however, and in particular their relative ranking, requires detailed, personalized, and localized information about individuals' circumstances of time and place, value, tradeoffs and opportunity costs, and so on. But centralized lawgivers or regulators do not possess this knowledge about their citizens.

Suppose we determined by some objective measure that you are literally the smartest person in the country. On that basis, I decide that you should make the decision about what I should drink every morning. Suppose there are only two options: coffee and tea. What are the chances that you will make the correct choice – that is, the one that best matches up with my preferences, even my authentic preferences, all things considered? Because you do not know me personally, you will have to guess; the chance you will get it right is thus one out of two, or 0.5. Suppose we add one of my colleagues, so that you decide for both of us; what are the chances then? Answer: 0.25, because the probabilities must be multiplied. If we add a third, a fourth, or a fifth person, the chances you will get the entire decision set correct dwindles quickly – to 0.125, 0.0625, and 0.03125, respectively. Suppose we added a third drink choice; suppose we added drink choices also for lunch and dinner; suppose we added meals as well; suppose we increased the number of people to all my colleagues, or my entire city, or my entire state, or to the entire United States: as quickly becomes painfully obvious, the probability that you could get the decisions right rapidly approaches zero. That is not because you are not intelligent, or not intelligent enough (we stipulated that you were literally the smartest person in the country); it is rather because the knowledge you would need to make good decisions for others, including their (changing) preferences and situations and values, you simply do not possess. That stubborn fact reduces your decisions effectively to random guesses, which, in turn, leads to the chances of you getting it right rapidly plummeting to zero. The same would be true for anyone else as well.

That means that presidents, members of congress, regulators, administrators, and other centralized authorities are ill-positioned to know what decisions any of the rest of us should make. Are they also in possession of bad character? Given their record, or a look at the leaders in most of the world's countries today, one could be forgiven for believing so. But one need not assume that. On the contrary, one can assume that they possess no worse character than what people in other walks of life possess. But one should assume they possess no *better* character either. They are, after all – as we all are – just people.

But they face an additional obstacle to making good choices for the rest of us that we do not face when making decisions in our own cases, namely, they are not as incentivized to get it right for us as we are incentivized to get it right for ourselves. Suppose a regulator or expert makes a decision that turns out not to be a good one for you. Suppose, for example, that the United States Department of Agriculture puts out dietary recommendations for all Americans, and that among their recommendations is a one-cup-equivalent of dairy per day (as it is). But suppose you are lactose-intolerant. Or suppose another of their recommendations is a one-to-two-ounce equivalent of grains (as it is), but you are gluten-intolerant. Or suppose they recommend reducing the amount of sodium in your diet (as they do), but I have a congenital heart condition that requires higher levels of sodium (as I do). Any of their general recommendations, in other words, may or may not be appropriate for any given individual. Even if they are accurately based on averages and aggregated data, there is no way to know whether they do or should apply to any given individual.

How does this relate to incentives? Centralized experts will typically not be able to know what decisions any given individual should make in her own case. But suppose they get it wrong – what then? Well, they do not bear the cost or suffer the negative consequences of their decisions: others do. That is because their policies apply not only to themselves but to others as well. And if you or I were to follow them and suffer costs or other negative consequences, it is we who would bear them, not they. The centralized experts most likely would not even know. So even if they had only the best of intentions, they would not get the feedback they need to refine their judgment to make better choices or that would discipline them to get it right. By contrast, when you or I make decisions in our own cases, since it is we who get the feedback and enjoy the rewards or suffer the consequences (as the case may be), we are much more strongly incentivized to revise our judgment and adjust our behavior accordingly.

The double-whammy confronting centralized decision-makers puts them, therefore, in an almost impossible position: they are exceedingly unlikely to know what choices their millions of citizens, almost all of whom are unknown to them, should make; and if their policies lead to negative outcomes for others, they are but weakly incentivized to correct them. Even if they somehow could know or miraculously get it right – given the infinitesimally small probabilities, it would indeed be a miracle – their incentives are not such as to motivate them to actually implement it correctly. If, however, their job is to make policies regardless, they will come up with something. But whatever they come up with is likely to be some combination of, on the one hand, general and aggregated averages applicable only to literally average people, and, on the other, their own personal preferences (or those of their colleagues, friends, and so on – which, unless you are actually in one of those groups, are not likely to be your own preferences).

The Soviet Union began in 1917 with committed leaders, vast territory and land and resources, and a large population with varied skills – many of the elements, in other words, that one might think are required for a successful launch to a prosperous society. For decades, researchers, scholars, and commentators – including Nobel laureates[9] – predicted not only the U.S.S.R.'s success but its eventual triumph over the United States and the rest of the West.[10] And for some time, including throughout much of the Cold War, it appeared that the Soviet Union was indeed a formidable presence, growing in both wealth and power. But then the Berlin Wall fell suddenly and unexpectedly in 1989 – because the Soviets could no longer support its defense. Why couldn't they? Because they were, in a word, broke. As subsequent revelations showed, by the time of the Soviet Union's official demise in 1991, its economy was moribund, its resources were squandered, its environment was despoiled, and its people – those whom it had not, in Lenin's chilling phrase, "liquidated," to the tune of perhaps as many as 62,000,000 souls (Rummel 1997; Courtois et al. 1999; Conquest 2000; White 2012; Niemietz 2019) – were impoverished and immiserated.

Now, if one should object that the Soviet Union was founded and led throughout much of its existence by murderous madmen, not by wise and benevolent statesmen, that is

---

[9] Including, for example, 1970 Nobel laureate Paul Samuelson; see Peart and Levy 2006.

[10] Similarly confident predictions about the future economic and moral success of China, Cuba, North Korea, Cambodia, Albania, East Germany, and, more recently, Venezuela were also made by academics, journalists, politicians, artists, and authors. See Hollander 2016 and 2017; Monnery 2019; and Niemietz 2019.

correct. Lenin and Stalin were merciless mass murderers; Stalin's democide count far exceeded that of Hitler, to a level not seen again until Mao. But the example of the Soviet Union, as well as that of other murderous regimes of the twentieth century – including the German National Socialist regime, China, Vietnam, North Korea, Cambodia, Cuba, and Zimbabwe – shows, among other things, that prosperity, not to mention life, liberty, dignity, and humanity, can be slowed, reversed, and even crushed, even under the banner of "scientific" reforms and in the name of "the people." This gives us strong reason to be wary of granting extensive authority to centralized administrations over the choices, not to mention the lives and liberties, of their citizens.

Conclusion

Progress and improvement are not inevitable. In fact, growing, generalized prosperity did not begin to appear in the world until the most recent 0.1 percent of human history, as a result of changing attitudes about cooperation and extraction. The newly developing idea that cooperation is moral and extraction is immoral then began to spread and change the culture, which in turn led to changes in institutions. Thus, progress, improvement, and prosperity depend on people having the right attitudes, in particular moral attitudes; they depend on having the right institutions, which they can trust and which engender trust in one another; and they depend on allowing people the scope to engage in trial and error to discover the right paths for themselves and to learn from both their successes and their mistakes. Remove, threaten, or weaken any of these, and progress and improvement are themselves jeopardized.

There is no Great Mind to whom we can safely entrust guidance of our prosperity, and neither progress nor prosperity are natural or inevitable. We must make our own choices, in voluntary cooperation with others whom we can and do trust, and we must learn, understand, and then uphold and protect the institutions that recognize and respect the dignity and liberty of individuals and that enable prosperity.

5

Economics and/or Morality

All the different members of [human society] are bound together by the agreeable bands of love and affection, and are, as it were, drawn to the common centre of mutual good offices.

Adam Smith, The Theory of Moral Sentiments

Introduction

Economic calculation and cost–benefit analyses can seem cold and even cruel, possibly valuing "profits over people," as opposed to the other way around. When a company lays off some of its workers while giving its CEO a bonus, it can seem that the company is placing a higher value on an ignominious goal – profit motivated by greed – than it places on what should matter more – the people involved. If economic calculation is about nothing other than searching for ever more efficient ways to allocate resources, and if firms allocate resources based on nothing more than impersonal cost–benefit analyses, then it can seem to discount the value of human beings, and their wishes, desires, goals, and welfare. But no system of economics is worth supporting that places an amoral, or even immoral, search for profit above the welfare and value of human beings. It is ultimately, after all, human beings who matter most; it is their welfare and well-being that should therefore be of paramount concern. Firms and businesspeople who get the proper priorities reversed out of a misguided reliance on cold economic calculation are therefore making a moral mistake. If economics encourages such mistakes, then so much the worse for economics. It would be at best amoral, if not outright immoral.

Perhaps you have heard economics called the "dismal science." The origin of this epithet is worth noting. It was Thomas Carlyle (1795–1881) who dubbed economics a "dismal science," but not because he found it boring. Rather, he found it depressing because the political economists in his day and earlier, including people like Adam Smith and John Stuart Mill, had suggested that their principles would hold for *all* human beings. Why would Carlyle find that depressing? Carlyle believed in a natural superiority of some races (namely his own) over other races. Because he believed himself and the members of his own race superior to members of other races, he believed it was his responsibility, even his moral duty, to superintend the lives of his alleged inferiors. But if, as people like Smith and Mill were suggesting, members of all races could improve their own lives if given the opportunity to do so, then there would be no role for Carlyle and his co-conspirators to play as their masters. As hard as it is to imagine, Carlyle believed in what he called the "beneficent whip" and in what he considered to be the necessity of people like him using it – literally, if need be – to control and train others.[1]

It is to their great credit that political economists, and economics in general, have never accepted this odious

---

[1] The text to read on this is Peart and Levy 2001. See also Peart and Levy 2005.

assumption of natural superiority or inferiority of races, and have instead insisted that all human beings, of whatever race, are capable of improving their own conditions – if just given the opportunity to do so, instead of keeping them under the thumb, or boot, of people imagining themselves to be their betters. So, economics has from its beginnings been based on an assumption of moral equality among human beings, which means that, morally speaking, it got off on quite the right foot.

In this chapter, I argue that economics is in fact neither amoral nor immoral, and that economic reasoning is not a cold and inhumane, or "dismal," process of remorseless calculation but is instead a way, in many circumstances the only way, of enabling us to show proper care and respect for people – all people. The belief that economics is amoral or immoral is a fallacy.

People Over Profit

Consider the complaint people sometimes raise to some of the activities in market economies captured by the slogan "people over profit." What does it mean to advocate "people over profit"? According to its advocates, it requires placing a higher value on the people affected by decisions about how to allocate resources than on the search for profit alone.[2] If a firm decides to downsize, lay workers off, relocate, or

---

[2] As, for example, the nonprofit People Over Profits puts it, "We must put the interests of working people ahead of quarterly profits, shareholder dividends, and stock buybacks" (People Over Profits n.d.). See also Chomsky 1999.

otherwise shift its resources, or if it decides not to pay its workers more or give them more generous benefits, the "people over profit" demand implies that the firm is valuing money more than it does the workers involved, that the firm is valuing its profitability higher than any individual workers that it might fire or dislocate. In this way, "people over profit" seems like an important reminder that what matters – not just in a firm, or even in an economy, but in life – is the welfare of the people who constitute the firm, economy, or society. To sacrifice them in a search for greater profitability thus not only seems to have the priorities wrong but seems to subordinate a worthy end of benefiting people to an ignoble end of satisfying greediness.

That might be how it seems, but that is not how it is – or, at least, not necessarily how it is. On the contrary, to advocate "people over profit" is itself to endorse an objectionable selfishness. Let me explain.

In a properly functioning market economy or commercial society, the paradigmatic way one can make a profit is by creating some good or offering some service that others value enough to part with some portion of their time or treasure to procure. In other words, profit is an indicator that one is creating a net value surplus for others – providing them some value that is greater than whatever they have to give up for it. It is a net benefit to them. Otherwise they would not do it. Similarly, if you judge that it is worthwhile to you to create a good or provide the service in exchange for what someone else offers to give you for it, then that means you are getting a net value surplus for it as well – what you are getting constitutes more value to you than the time or treasure you are giving up. Otherwise you would not do it. On the other hand, if you create something that is costlier in time or treasure than what others are willing to give you in exchange for it, then that means that they do not value your creation sufficiently to give you what you ask or need for it. It does not necessarily mean that they see no value in your creation (though they might not): rather, it means that in their eyes your creation's value is not sufficient to compensate them for the sacrifice they would have to make for it. If you put your resources in this direction nonetheless, the result would be not profit but loss for you. Temporary losses are sometimes justifiable for future gains, but this cannot – and should not – go on forever, or else it is just loss. Thus, the desire for profit is really a desire for value surplus; loss, by contrast, results from actions and decisions that do not lead to a value surplus.

Goods and services arise from human labor, which means that goods and services arise from costs in time or treasure, usually a combination.[3] But these resources are scarce and could have been expended in other directions, which means that we cannot simultaneously serve all our goals at the same time; choices must be made among competing ends, and tradeoffs must be made. The scarcity of resources thus entails that some goals, even worthy goals, must be forsaken in the service of other, more important, goals. If we do not think carefully about the ranking of our

---

[3] There are cases where one stumbles upon a diamond, gold nugget, pool of oil, and so on, and can then trade or sell it without having contributed much labor (or hardly any at all). Such cases are rare, however, and typically still require human labor to turn them into something others want, can use, and so on.

goals, then we might end up putting resources toward a less-important goal at the expense of a more-important goal – which would be inconsistent with our own hierarchy of goals or schedule of value. That a goal or value is important or good is therefore necessary but not by itself sufficient: it must be more important or better than something else. Merely good is not good enough.

It is important to note that this is no one's fault. It is a permanent feature of our world that resources are limited, and a permanent feature of the human condition that no good or service can be created – nothing that we can consume or use can be enabled to be consumed or used – without the expenditure of cost to some person in time or treasure. As more people create ever more value surplus, the resources available to create yet further goods or services to serve yet further goals or ends increases; this is the definition of grow-ing prosperity, or what Phelps (2013) calls "mass flourishing." As long as resources nevertheless remain finite, however, and as long as our desires – our goals, ambitions, values, wishes, and preferences – continue to outstrip the resources we have to satisfy all of them, having to make choices, sometimes painful choices, among our goals will remain part of the existential condition of human nature.

What does this have to do with "people over profits"? People making this claim do so because of situations in which they wish they or others either: (1) were better compensated for their creation or labor; or (2) continue to be paid wages for the labor they wish to do. But recall that the desire for profit is really a desire for net value surplus. If a desire for profit leads some firms, individuals, or other entities to choose not to patronize you, not to hire you, or not to be willing to do so at the price or rate of exchange that you desire, it means that they do not believe such an exchange or partnership would create for them a net value surplus. For them, it would be a net value loss. In that case, if you demand that they give you what you want regardless, you are in effect demanding that they suffer what they consider a loss in value to them to satisfy your ends. Because a loss to them entails a decreased ability to achieve their own ends, however, such a demand entails that you believe that your ends are more important than theirs. A demand of "people over profits" is thus in reality a demand that you be accorded greater consideration than others, regardless of others' desires, needs, values, responsibilities, or obligations. That is not only selfish, but objectionably so.

I base this judgment on the premise with which we started, namely, that people are equal moral agents and therefore should be accorded exactly the same scope of freedom – the maximum scope compatible with granting the same scope to others – that everyone else has. If anyone has a right to make free choices or if anyone has a right to have her choices respected by others, then everyone else does as well. Consider the alternative: at least one person, Sally, has a right to make free choices and have her choices respected by others, but at least some other person, Paul, does not have the same right. It follows that Sally has a scope of agency that, in at least some relevant respects, is greater or wider or more efficacious than that of Paul. It follows that Sally's moral agency is privileged above that of Paul. In the absence of some special qualification, however – if Paul is a minor, a medically or psychologically incapacitated adult, a convicted criminal, and so on – then privileging of Sally's agency over Paul's violates the foundational moral principle of equal moral agency. Thus, if Sally demands respect of her agency over that of Paul, Sally's demand issues from an assumption of moral superiority to Paul and an assumption of greater moral importance than Paul. Such a claim from Sally would be not only selfish but objectionable because it violates the equal moral agency principle.

I will not here argue further for the soundness of that moral principle,[4] though I would point out that denying it would seem to open the door to morally objectionable behaviors like racism, sexism, xenophobia, and so on. That would seem at least strong prima facie reason to accept the principle of equal moral agency and to reject a claimed exception to it and conferral of superiority on any Sally.

Of course, sometimes people make poor or unfortunate choices about which firms to patronize, whom to hire, partner, or exchange with, or in which firms or financial instruments to invest; sometimes they themselves recognize their mistake after the fact. And sometimes firms make poor or unfortunate choices about how to allocate their resources: they pay some people too much (CEOs, perhaps[5]), sometimes they do not pay others enough, and sometimes they decide to produce goods or services that do not repay the requisite investment of resources. All such

---

[4] But see Chaps. 1 and 6; see also Otteson 2006.

[5] The economist Tyler Cowen has recently argued, however, that despite the increasing returns to CEOs over the last several years, they might nevertheless still be undervalued. See Cowen 2019, chap. 3.

poor decisions result in losses of, or at least forgone gains in, value. Often, however, it is difficult to know in advance which decisions will have been the right ones. We live in a world of profound uncertainty, which means that many decisions we make, even with due deliberation and in good faith, will end up having been wrong or bad – will result, that is, in losses.

Much of that uncertainty results from uncertainty about what other people want or will want. We do not know what others' goals, ambitions, and desires are; we do not know what opportunities others have or what constraints they face; we do not know what obligations or responsibilities others have; and we do not know what other factors might affect the choices others make. And all these things are in continuous flux: people's desires and opportunities and obligations are constantly changing, often as a result of yet others' choices, which neither they nor we can predict. It is partly for this reason that nearly 80 percent of all new business ventures fail within two years: what seemed like a good, even great, idea turns out not to seem to others to be surplus value-creating. Sometimes this happens because of luck: people happen to hear, or happen not to hear, about what we are offering; chance encounters with other people change people's minds; unpredictable shifts in culture or fashion change people's preferences; other people's or firms' choices and offerings and innovations suddenly alter people's desires or opportunities.

But the fact that luck figures into the eventuality of our relative success does not mean that it is any less a result of others' choices. And as moral agents equal in dignity to us, they should be accorded respect for their choices based on their desires and goals that is equal to the respect we demand for ours. If they do not want to buy from us, do not want to hire us, do not want to pay us more, and so on, they are entitled to make those decisions – even when we disagree with their choices, when we believe they are mistaken, when we believe they themselves will come eventually to see the error of their ways, and even when we are right that their choices are incorrect. They are entitled to make their own choices, even incorrect choices, exactly as we are.

Profit is a signal that people are making choices about the allocation of their resources of time and treasure that in fact lead to net value surplus, that in fact give others more value than what they must sacrifice to get what we are offering. Profit is the feedback we need in order to know that, amidst our profound uncertainty, we have hit upon something valuable; just as loss is the feedback we need to know that we should consider turning our attention to something else. Because profit and loss are based on feedback from others, which itself issues from the choices others make, seeking profit and avoiding loss are in their essence putting others' choices – and their needs, desires, goals, ambitions, and so on – on par with our own. It is a recognition of the importance of others as being equal to ourselves. We are free to undertake whatever ventures we want and to offer whatever goods or services we want; others are free to decide whether to accept or decline our offerings. A mutually voluntary exchange or partnership is thus a transaction among moral equals, among moral peers, with neither party occupying or presuming to occupy a position privileged over the other.

A demand to privilege "people over profit," then, is thus in reality a demand to privilege some people over others. It is to say that what I want is more important than what you want because I want it and I do not care, or do not care as much, about what you want. A claim that what I want is more important than what you want can be justified, however, only if I am more important than you. It is hence to express an objectionable selfishness.

Why should a CEO make so much, however, when entry-level workers make so comparatively less? Why am I being laid off when an executive is getting a bonus or share-holders are getting a dividend? If a CEO is making ten times, or a hundred times, more than I am, it is easy to think that a small reduction in her pay would, if transferred to me, create a far bigger benefit to me than the loss would constitute to her. Or if we see that a firm that has a multi-billion-dollar market capitalization or billions of dollars in sales or revenues, it is easy – even seemingly self-evident – to conclude that it can afford to pay me more or retain me in its employ. If such a firm decides not to pay me more or to keep me in its employ, this seeming disrespect of my situation or my interests might lead us to conclude that the firm is privileging its profitability over my welfare – that it is privileging "profits over people," instead of the other way around.

But the issue is not what the firm could in principle afford to do, or even whether I am providing or could provide value to the firm. The firm's mission is, or should be, to create as much net value surplus as it can, given its resources. Because it has limited resources, however, it cannot put resources toward all purposes that might be good or create value; it must put those resources toward those purposes that it believes are best or create the most value. That means that it must necessarily forgo not only projects that would lose value but even some that would create value – but not enough value as other projects. Something's being a good idea is therefore not enough: as argued in Chapter 3, it must be a better idea than other good ideas. Like every decision any individual makes, the firm must consider its opportunity cost: what is it (or am I) giving up in order to attempt to achieve this? Because a firm, like a person, wants to survive and even flourish – a firm may even have a legal or fiduciary responsibility to do so – it must dedicate its resources to purposes that it believes in good faith will lead to greater benefit than whatever it is giving up. Such decisions are made at the firm's or individual's risk and are made under uncertainty; they are also typically made at the margin, where the question is not regarding an estimation of total value but of the next increment of value. These facts mean that mistakes will often be made. But a firm that is not constantly making these comparative judgments of marginal value is one that will end up putting at least some of its limited resources to purposes providing less benefit (or even loss); this will mean forgone gain or loss, which no firm – or individual – can continue to do and hope to flourish, or even survive.

Thus, the claim that the firm could afford to keep me in its employ or pay me more may be true, but the question is: What would the firm have to give up in order to do so? If a firm will not employ me or will not pay me more, it means the firm has decided that, at the margin, the potential value I could provide the firm is not worth whatever else the firm might do with those resources. Either it would lose value, or it would not gain as much value as it could otherwise. To repeat, these are very difficult decisions to make – not only because it can lead to disappointment, hardship, or dislocation but also because it is simply extremely difficult to know in advance what the best use of limited resources is. And, also to repeat, mistakes often get made, even in good faith: that is why so many businesses fail.

The other important point to keep in mind, however, is that we are not entitled to others' resources. As equal moral agents, we are all equally entitled to make choices about how we think we can best achieve our ends and purposes, given the constraints we face, and no one of us – and no one group of us – is entitled to demand or mandate that others allocate their resources in ways other than what they choose. If you own a coffee shop, which I have been patronizing every day, but another coffee shop opens up across the street from yours, and I – as well as, perhaps, many of your other customers – decide to patronize your competitor, should you be entitled to compensation for the loss of revenue from me and other customers as a result of our choice no longer to patronize your shop? The answer is no: you have no more right to my resources than, to use our example from Chapter 1, Jack has to Jill's affections. Your disappointment may be real, but it does not trump my (or Jill's) right to make such choices. And if you have to lay off some of your workers due to the decline in revenue as customers go to your competitor coffee shop, if the laid-off workers were to demand to keep their jobs by claiming "people over profit," they would be claiming a right to your resources, and by extension to those of your former patrons who have changed their preferences. But they could make this demand only by claiming an exception for themselves to the principle of equal moral agency. Because we are all equal moral agents, others – Jack, coffee shop owners, everyone – must respect the choices we make, even when our choices result partly from luck, even when they lead to disappointment for at least some parties, and even if we are making mistakes.

To demand otherwise is to privilege ourselves over others, to claim an importance and authority that we deny to others. The demand of "people over profits" is premised upon exactly such an assumption. Profits result from people's choices; hence, the search for profit is the search to create as much value for as many people as possible, while cognizant of the fact that no single firm (or person) can create unlimited value for all others at the same time. The people benefiting from a firm's employment or from the goods or services a firm offers are not demanding "profits over people"; instead, they are people who are profiting together.

It should be noted that this argument would not apply to cases of cronyism, special protections, subsidies, legal monopolies, or other cases of legal intervention into markets or special privileges bestowed selectively upon some market participants. Cases like these are not instances of what I am calling honest profit or honorable business, which operates on the basis of mutually voluntary and mutually beneficial exchange. Rather, they are examples of extraction, which benefit one party to the exchange (or transfer) at the expense of others – exactly as those demanding "people over profits" are desiring. Hence, people demanding "people over profits" are not, in fact, demanding that firms consider the interests of all people, but are demanding instead that the interests of a select group of people be accorded privileged consideration over the interests of others. In a properly functioning market economy, however, profit *means* people: profit results from creating value for all parties to transactions and can arise in no other way.

Selfishness and Cooperation

The second-most-famous passage from Adam Smith's *Wealth of Nations* – after the "invisible hand" passage – is probably this: "It is not from the benevolence of the butcher, the brewer, or the baker, that we expect our dinner, but from their regard to their own interest." Smith continues: "We address ourselves, not to their humanity but to their self-love, and never talk to them of our own necessities but of their advantages" (1981 [1776], 26–7). When you read that, do you hear *selfishness*? Do you hear Smith describing human action in a market as being driven fundamentally, perhaps exclusively, by each participant's self-interest – or perhaps even advocating that we should all be self-interested, never considering the interests of others? Perhaps you think this passage could be the smoking gun, as it were, of capitalism: right there, in just the second chapter of the urtext of capitalism, its founder reveals its prime motivation – self-interest, perhaps even selfishness.

Here is another way to interpret that passage, however, one more in keeping not only with Smith's overall argument but with the logic of market transactions more generally. What Smith is advocating is not *selfishness* but *respect*. Both you and the baker have interests – goals, desires, obligations, and so on – which both of you are trying to serve and promote with your respective limited resources. If you were to appeal to the baker's benevolence to get his bread, or if you were to ask him to take pity on you (that is, if you were to address yourself to the baker's "humanity"), instead of offering the baker something in return that he might value, you are in effect presuming or proposing that your interests are more important than his. Now, in some cases that might be true: if you are starving, for example, or if your children are starving, then perhaps your interests (or your expanded self-interest, which would include the interests of your children) might well be more important than whatever the baker would have done with the money he asks for his bread. But those are exceptional circumstances. In normal circumstances, which cover the vast majority of exchanges or proposed exchanges, we should respect that the baker has his own interests (which also might well include the interests of his children) that we should not presume are less important than our own. Because each of us is a moral agent equal to the other, we should respect one another's choices and wishes. We show that respect by meeting each other as moral peers, which is reflected not in appeals to one another's benevolence but to one another's interests. Our mutual respect is thus encapsulated not only by recognizing that the other has interests and offering to help him achieve them, but by making offers that the other is free to decline if he so chooses.

Buying the baker's bread at his price, a price that is worth it both to you and to the baker, is, therefore, a way of demonstrating mutual respect between you and the baker. Now, your respective interests are not the same: you would like to get the bread for as little as possible, and the baker would like to sell you the bread for as much as possible. Yet both of you would like to exchange, and both of you would probably also like to execute similar exchanges in the future (you will need bread tomorrow as well, and he would like to sell you bread tomorrow too). So, both of you are likely willing to compromise on your interests, until the point where it is worth it to both of you to exchange. If no such intersection of interests is reached – if his price is too high for you or your price is too low for him – then either or both of you will opt out, say "no, thank you," and go elsewhere. If a sufficient intersection of interests is reached or discovered, however, then the exchange is executed and both of you will have benefited from it.

Despite your respectively differing and even conflicting interests, then, you and the baker cooperated. The baker has his interests, which he can serve with the money you might give him; you have your interests, which you can serve with the bread he might give you. After the mutually voluntary exchange, you are both able to serve the interests you each respectively wanted to. In other words, you cooperated with one another to serve one another's interests. We may be self-interested, perhaps in the expanded sense of taking an interest in the family, friends, community, and so on whose "fortune," as Smith wrote in the first sentence of his *Theory of Moral Sentiments*, "render their happiness necessary to" us though we "derive nothing from it but the pleasure of seeing it" (1982 [1759], 9). Nevertheless, market exchanges,

unlike extractive exchanges, are not typically marked by conflict, argument, or violence: they are marked by cooperation.

If you observe the transactions that take place in
markets, you will see this immediately. People typically say
"thank you" to each other after a transaction, even if they do
not know one another and even if they will never see each
other again. A few years ago, I traveled to Hong Kong,
a place I had never been before, where I knew not a soul,
and whose language I did not speak. Yet I walked into
a storefront, handed the stranger working there a small
piece of plastic, and left with a car that I used to drive
around the city. Just contemplate the extraordinary levels
of trust and cooperation involved in that one episode: I flew
in a plane, which I did not inspect (I am no mechanical or
aeronautic engineer, so it would not have done much good
if I had) and whose pilots I did not meet or know; I flew
literally halfway around the world to a foreign country
where I was a complete stranger; and yet someone gave
me a car to use. I trusted the airline and its pilots;
I trusted I would be welcomed and not imprisoned or killed
entering a foreign land; they trusted that my small piece of
plastic would transfer funds to cover the cost of a car, that
I would not steal the car, and that I knew how to use it
without killing others with it; and I trusted that they would
not simply steal funds from me and that the car they gave
me would not explode. At each of these moments, we were
all thankful – and said "thank you" to one another.

On what basis was I, were we all, willing to extend
such extraordinary trust to such complete strangers? It was
not that long ago in human history, after all, that if I had

shown up in distant foreign country I would be viewed with suspicion rather than welcome, that I might as easily have been apprehended or even killed rather than been allowed to use at my disposal someone else's complex and dangerous machine worth tens of thousands of dollars. What changed?

The answer is markets. In markets, people learn to overcome their distrust of others by interacting and exchanging with them for mutual benefit. They learn to curb their selfishness, for otherwise they would not find willing partners with whom to cooperate to achieve their own goals. And they learn to put aside racism, sexism, xenophobia, and other obstacles to human interaction, because indulging prejudices means diminishing their chances of achieving their own goals – both their pecuniary and social goals. The process is not perfect, of course, because people are not and never will be perfect. And, of course, some people might stubbornly decide that their prejudices are worth the cost to them in forgone potential gains that result from continuing to nurse them. But markets in which every person possesses, and exercises, her opt-out option relentlessly uncover and punish such prejudices. In a perhaps surprising way, markets can enable people to capitalize on others' prejudices. If, out of prejudice against me, you will not sell to or buy from me, or will not hire or partner or associate with me, there will be others to whom the cost of prejudice, even if they share it, is too high. And, if they are legally allowed – a big and important "if" – they will be only too happy to have my business, and I will be only too happy to take myself, and my resources, away from you and to them. You may have your prejudices, but in markets they will cost you.

It turns out that empirical study has discovered that the default levels of trust people have for one another vary directly with their exposure to markets: the more people engage in market transactions, the more welcoming and trusting they are toward others. Similarly with concern for others, a sense of and commitment to fair play, tolerance of difference, and a reduced willingness to lie or cheat. By contrast, the less exposure an individual, group, community, or society has to markets, the less trusting they are toward others, the less concern they have for others, the less concerned they are about fairness, and the less tolerant they are of others' differences.[6] Perhaps that surprises you, but it shouldn't, once you consider the extensive cooperation – *voluntary* cooperation – involved and required in markets. Compared with other animals, humans are but weakly equipped by nature with the physical tools necessary to procure what they need to survive. They have no fur, claws, fangs, or wings; they do not run very fast and they are not very strong. What they do have, however, are language and reason, which enable them to coordinate, plan, and cooperate. Add to that their remarkable ingenuity and innovativeness, and their frontiers of possibility are, if not limitless, nevertheless very extensive indeed. Their genes might be, as Dawkins (2016) puts it, "selfish," but what human beings have discovered is that they can best serve

[6] The empirical literature here is large. For a sampling, see Scott 1976; Zak and Knack 2001; Henrich et al. 2004; Bowles and Gintis 2006 and 2011; Zak 2008 and 2012; Gintis 2012; Brennan and Jaworski 2016, esp. chap. 11; Choi and Storr 2016; Ariely et al. 2019; Diamond 2019; and Storr and Choi 2019.

their own goals, even their selfish ones, by cooperating with others. The more others with whom they can cooperate, the more others from whom they can learn, whose ideas and behaviors they can imitate or build upon or avoid if necessary, and the more others with whom they can create ever more complex and dynamic networks of cooperation, the better.

Interdependence, Not Dependence

What markets enable, then, is extensive networks of cooperation. Indeed, the networks can become so vast that it might be literally impossible to know or trace or map them all. Adam Smith claimed – in the eighteenth century – that an attempt to trace out all the links in even a single chain of cooperation "exceeds all computation" (1981 [1776], 22).

Smith's example to illustrate his claim was a plain "woollen coat" that a common laborer in his day wore. It may appear "coarse and rough," Smith says, but it is in fact "the produce of the joint labour of a great multitude of workmen." Just how big is that "great multitude"? Here is how Smith begins the description: "The shepherd, the sorter of the wool, the wool-comber or carder, the dyer, the scribbler, the spinner, the weaver, the fuller, the dresser, with many others, must all join their different arts in order to complete even this homely production." But that is not all – not even close. Who else contributed to the workman's lowly woolen coat? Smith elaborates (I apologize for the length of this quotation, but it is so extraordinary that I could not help myself; I hope you read it all):

How many merchants and carriers, besides, must have
been employed in transporting the materials from some of
those workmen to others who often live in a very distant
part of the country! How much commerce and navigation
in particular, how many ship-builders, sailors, sail-makers,
rope-makers, must have been employed in order to bring
together the different drugs made use of by the dyer, which
often come from the remotest corners of the world! What
a variety of labour too is necessary in order to produce the
tools of the meanest of those workmen! To say nothing of
such complicated machines as the ship of the sailor, the
mill of the fuller, or even the loom of the weaver, let us
consider only what a variety of labour is requisite in order
to form that very simple machine, the shears with which
the shepherd clips the wool. The miner, the builder of the
furnace for smelting the ore, the feller of the timber, the
burner of the charcoal to be made use of in the smelting-
house, the brick-maker, the brick-layer, the workmen who
attend the furnace, the mill-wright, the forger, the smith,
must all of them join their different arts in order to produce
them. Were we to examine, in the same manner, all the
different parts of his dress and household furniture, the
coarse linen shirt which he wears next his skin, the shoes
which cover his feet, the bed which he lies on, and all the
different parts which compose it, the kitchen-grate at
which he prepares his victuals, the coals which he makes
use of for that purpose, dug from the bowels of the earth,
and brought to him perhaps by a long sea and a long land
carriage, all the other utensils of his kitchen, all the
furniture of his table, the knives and forks, the earthen or
pewter plates upon which he serves up and divides his
victuals, the different hands employed in preparing his

bread and his beer, the glass window which lets in the heat and the light, and keeps out the wind and the rain, with all the knowledge and art requisite for preparing that beautiful and happy invention, without which these northern parts of the world could scarce have afforded a very comfortable habitation, together with the tools of all the different workmen employed in producing those different conveniencies; if we examine, I say, all these things, and consider what a variety of labour is employed about each of them, we shall be sensible that without the assistance and cooperation of many thousands, the very meanest person in a civilized country could not be provided, even according to, what we very falsely imagine, the easy and simple manner in which he is commonly accommodated. (1981 [1776], 22–23)

This is clearly a celebration for Smith. (Did you notice all the exclamation points?) And indeed it is an observation whose brilliance is matched only by its accuracy in outlining the phenomenon of human cooperation – cooperation that is so wide, extensive, and pervasive that, like the proverbial fish that doesn't realize it's in water, we virtually never notice. Contemplate that passage from Smith, however, or spend a few minutes trying to trace out the required chains and nodes of cooperation to bring you, say, your iPhone, and you may well appreciate the aptness of Smith's claim that it "exceeds all computation."

We can describe this extensive cooperation that markets enable as *interdependence*. No one of us produces everything she needs or wants; each of us relies on what others produce for us. The more extensive and developed a market economy is, the more goods and services we can use, consume, and enjoy, and the more extensive is our, not *depen*dence, but *inter*dependence. Because each of us requires the cooperation of others, and each of us provides in turn some element or particle that goes into the things others use, consume, or enjoy, we end up being served by others – but only as we serve them. That mutual cooperation and mutual benefit, enabled by our interdependence on one another, Smith felicitously describes as our becoming "mutually the servants of one another" (1981 [1776], 378).

It is important to see why this is not dependence. A dependent relation would be one in which I can get what I want or need only from you, putting me at your behest and perhaps even at your mercy. If I can go nowhere but to you, you have a power over me that exhibits an inequality in agency: what you say goes, because I have no other choice, and thus my agency is beholden and inferior to yours. By contrast, in a market economy I have options other than just you; you, for your part, have options other than just me, which means our agency is leveled and equalized. I may need food, but I do not necessarily need it from you; you may need customers or employees, but you do not necessarily need me in either role. As Smith writes, "Each tradesman or artificer derives his subsistence from the employment, not of one, but of a hundred or a thousand different customers. Though in some measure obliged to them all, therefore, he is not absolutely dependent upon any one of them" (1981 [1776], 420). And, of course, each of us can say "no, thank you" and go elsewhere. As long as there are other options – which, in a market economy, there will almost certainly be – we become interdependent with, but not dependent on, one another, and each of us is therefore incentivized to seek ways to serve the other's needs and wants on pain of not getting what we want.

From Enemies to Opportunities

As we have had occasion to note, most of human history has been marked by mutual suspicion. Because we evolved in small groups whose survival was always close to the margin, one principal way that these groups procured what they wanted or needed to survive was by raiding other bands, often killing or enslaving the other band's members in the process. We therefore learned to be suspicious and wary of members of other bands, and would often kill someone we did not know instead of taking the time to discover whether he might be friendly. The downside risk of taking a chance on a stranger was just too high – it could mean one's death, the death of one's loved ones, or even the death of one's entire band. Hence, there were significant pressures against dealing, trading, or transacting with people outside one's band, and even greater pressures against having any truck with anyone one did not know personally. Although trade has likely been going on as long as there have been humans, the scope of that trade was severely limited, typically to one's own kin, those of whom one had personal knowledge, or, at most, those for whom someone one knew personally could vouch.

In the late seventeenth century and in the eighteenth century, a series of writers, including Montesquieu (1689–1755),

Hume, Smith, and Immanuel Kant (1724–1804), argued that a commercial society with markets and trade could not only increase overall prosperity but – more to the point here – also soften our suspicions of and antagonisms toward others. Montesquieu called it "doux commerce," or tender or kind commerce (Montesquieu 1989 [1748], part 4, bk. 20, 337–53). His argument was that because commerce was motivated at least in part by self-interest, people would, if allowed, be inclined to seek out more and more people with whom they could trade – potentially even people of different nationalities, religions, and races. As long as we were at least tolerably secure in our persons, in our property and possessions, and in our voluntary promises or agreements, our naturally social natures and our drive to improve our own conditions would lead us, even if only tentatively at first, to be willing to make offers of exchange or partnership to others. If we were able to complete beneficial exchanges successfully, this would encourage us to try again in the future and incline us to try with yet others as well. Hume, for his part, argued that commerce would thus make people more "sociable," because regular dealings with others, including very different others, would soften people's prejudices and the vehemence with which they maintained their nationalist, racial, religious, or other biases (Hume 1985 [1754], 271). People engaging in commerce would in this way come to view others with increasingly less suspicion and wariness. Because they wanted to trade with others, they would soon realize that killing, demonizing, or closing oneself off to others would limit their own ability to succeed. You cannot trade with, or profit or benefit from, a person you refuse to speak to or deal with – or whom you kill.

The claim of these early political economists, then, was that a commercial society could give us reason to view others, including strangers, not as enemies but as opportunities. As this process is repeated hundreds or thousands of times, we can come to realize that, whatever differences we may have with others, we nevertheless both want to benefit from each other. When people's persons, property, and promises are protected, our only available choice is to cooperate with others, which requires us to look past our differences and instead focus on our commonalities. In particular, we focus on, and address ourselves to, the fact that each of us wants to improve her condition, and that each of us needs the other to do so. As Smith wrote in the butcher-brewer-baker passage (Smith 1981 [1776], 26–7), we therefore address ourselves not to their humanity but to their self-love, and each of us focuses on what we can respectively do to make the other better off in exchange for bettering our own situation. The more people with whom we might trade or exchange – or, in other words, the bigger the market and the more participants in it – the more opportunities there are to find partners willing to engage in mutually beneficial transactions.

This process has, in fact, two significant benefits. First, the chances that I can find someone willing to transact with me increase with the more potential partners I can approach. If I have unusual tastes in, say, music, pastimes, or religious practices, or if I just have an unusual personality, in a small band or community I might have only a small chance of finding friends or partners who share my interests. If the scope of potential friends or partners were to increase to include members of other bands or communities, the chances

I could find compatible mutually beneficial relations increase. For that reason, the more people who are allowed to participate in markets, and the fewer the trade and migration restrictions, the better for everyone.

Second, the existence of other potential partners means that no one of them has excessive leverage or can demand unreasonable terms. If one person demands too much to transact – either in the price she demands for her goods or services, or the compliance she might demand with her preferences to associate with her – I can exercise my opt-out option and go elsewhere. The other person realizes that, however, so she is incentivized to temper her unreasonableness. This does not guarantee that we will see eye to eye, but it does increase the chances because the presence of options and alternatives introduces competition for both of us for the other's goods, services, or partnership. This competitive process also puts pressure on prices to go down. If prices get too high, people either will not buy or other suppliers will enter the market looking for substitutes or new, and cheaper, ways to produce the goods in question, or both. Either way, markets put pressures on producers and suppliers to constantly search for innovative ways to economize, and consumers are the primary gainers. In a perhaps surprising, even paradoxical, way, then, competitive markets can actually encourage more cooperation – which might help explain why people tend to be more inclined toward fair dealing, word-keeping, and other aspects of cooperative behavior the more exposure they have to commercial societies and markets.

What can derail or corrupt this process, however, is if some enjoy monopoly or monopsony privileges. If there is only one seller or only one buyer in a market, then that person or firm (or even country) can demand, and receive, terms that are better for the monopolist or monopsonist than they could receive in an open, competitive market. In that case, consumers would not be benefited, or not benefited as much as they otherwise would be. Similarly if some favored individuals, firms, or industries get subsidies or are granted protections from competition, those favored will certainly benefit, but at the expense of everyone else – competitors (or prospective competitors) and consumers alike. In such cases, the prices consumers would have to pay, or the costs involved with attempting to compete with already existing, entrenched, or favored firms, are higher than they otherwise would be. Either way, that means that consumers would have to pay more, reducing their ability to satisfy other needs and wants. Such favoritism, or cronyism, has gone on, and continues to go on, in countries around the world, at the ultimate expense of their citizens. They either impoverish their citizens, or they prevent their citizens from becoming as prosperous as they otherwise could.

Note, however, two further aspects of legal privileges like monopolies, barriers to entry, labor restrictions, property ownership restrictions, tariffs on disfavored goods, restrictions on worker mobility, occupational licensing requirements, regulations favored by entrenched firms that make it more costly for new entrants to exist or compete, subsidizing entrenched firms' losses, and so on: first, they are all legal enactments, the results of governmental mandates or prohibitions; and second, they all limit the opt-out options of consumers, laborers, and potential new entrants and competitors. In other words, they are extractive, not cooperative.

Yet if that is so, why, then, do countries and their governments so often engage in it? For several reasons. First, they may subscribe to the Wealth is Zero-Sum Fallacy, falsely believing that if others prosper, it must come at our expense, instead of realizing that mutually voluntary transactions are in fact mutually beneficial. Second, already existing and entrenched firms, who can indeed benefit from cronyist protection and extraction, lobby and get governmental privileges to produce this benefit to them. Competing in open markets is hard, uncertain, and often leads to loss. It is what Joseph Schumpeter called "creative destruction," which allows innovative disruption that often puts others out of business. If a firm has available to it an option to insulate itself from competition and disruption because there exists a governmental mechanism to protect it, and sympathetic politicians willing to do so, then some firms will calculate that it is more cost-efficient to lobby for these legal protections and privileges than to compete in an open market. And so they will do so.

Third and finally, there is the phenomenon Bastiat called the "seen" versus the "unseen." If the government intervenes to save General Motors (GM), for example (as it did in 2008), with bailouts, tariffs on overseas competitors, government-subsidized loans, and so on, what is "seen" is the jobs saved at GM – which are benefits to those workers (and to GM and its shareholders). What is "unseen" is whatever citizens would have done with those resources had the government not taken them and directed them to GM. Because whatever citizens would have otherwise done did not actually take place, it is unseen and hence ignored. When, therefore, a comparison is made between seen benefits and unseen hypothetical benefits (as well as the unseen but real losses), the seen benefits win nearly every time. Politicians get the credit, and the photo ops, for "rescuing" 10,000 jobs at GM, and the papers write articles, with pictures of the politicians, touting the saving of those jobs. It is a win for both the politicians and the GM workers (and, of course, for GM itself). It is a loss for consumers, however, as well as for prospective and existing competitors to GM – as well as their owners, their workers, and their families – but because the latter are unseen, they are unheralded and unheeded.

But those losses are no less real for being unseen. And they result not from cooperation but extraction. The reason GM needed a bailout, after all, is because consumers wanted to put their resources elsewhere – either to GM's competitors or other places altogether. GM was putting too much of its limited resources in directions that did not seem to potential consumers to create net benefit, thus creating loss to GM. If the government steps in to rescue GM, it is hence overriding consumers' choices, taking resources from them by taxation (or debt, which is a future obligation on taxpayers). In other words, government protections, bailouts, subsidies, and so on constitute removal of people's opt-out options, a legally enforced restriction on the scope and efficaciousness of citizens' choices and agency. They constitute, therefore, a departure from the morally and economically superior system of cooperation in favor of extraction to benefit this one firm and its workers at others' expense. It is not a positive-sum transaction, but a zero-sum. Indeed, it is typically a negative-sum transaction because the government takes its cut too. This is cronyism, which is a species of extraction, not cooperation.

One further negative consequence of cronyist extraction that often goes unnoticed and unappreciated is how it endangers Montesquieu's "doux commerce." When firms lobby for government benefits or protections, they are asking for special privileges – privileges accorded to them but not to others, in particular to their competitors. Because these are not cooperative exchanges but extractive, they lead to some benefiting not *along with* others but *at the expense of* others. This pits competing firms, as well as the workers for the respective firms, against one another in a zero-sum scramble. For the winning company will have succeeded not because it provided superior goods or services, was more innovative or entrepreneurial, or benefited consumers better, but because it managed to get the legal playing field tilted in its direction and against its competitors. Thus, entrepreneurs, innovators, new entrants into markets, workers and laborers, and consumers can all conclude that business is about cronyism rather than competition, about extraction rather than cooperation. This breeds distrust, antagonism, and justified resentment. It can undermine support for the market-based commercial society that otherwise provides such enormous benefits, endangering the institutions that enable general prosperity and mass flourishing.

Cronyist extraction therefore leads to several kinds of harm. It is a departure from cooperative exchanges and thus limits the benefits that could otherwise be achieved. It can pit people against each other, inclining them to see others not as opportunities but as enemies. It can change "tender

177

commerce" into "rough extraction." And, if sufficiently wide-spread, it can imperil the attitudes and culture that are required to support the institutions that enable general increases in prosperity. It can incline us to see the world as "us *versus* them," instead of "us *with* them," stoking nationalist antagonisms, religious bigotry, racial prejudice, and a long and sordid list of other ways that people have divided themselves against one another. Of course, one act of cronyism will not by itself plunge us into darkness. As Adam Smith noted, "there is a lot of ruin in a nation" (Smith 1987: 262). But suspicion, distrust, and resentment are easy to inflame and can spread like wildfire, and it is much easier to destroy trust than to build it. That is why our recent and unprecedented increases in prosperity are so amazing – such a stark break from all the rest of our beliefs, culture, and practices. But they are also fragile. Because tribalism calls to us like a siren song, we must therefore remain ever vigilant against it, in all its guises. Cronyism is one species of it, and we should view and treat cronyism with as much disapprobation as we do racism or sexism. We have nothing to lose but our prejudices, and we have peace, prosperity, and human dignity to gain.

The Morality of Economics

We began this chapter by asking what role economics could play in a properly moral life. We raised the concern, voiced by many critics, that economics is cold and calculating, perhaps putting profits over people, and that it therefore is at least amoral if not immoral. Let us close the loop of the argument by explaining why economics is crucial to enabling both a flourishing life of meaning and purpose and proper relations among people – in other words is in its essence moral. There are two parts to the argument. The first connects the tools of economic reasoning to the decision-making necessary to achieve a life of meaning and purpose, both for ourselves and for those with whom we interact. The second connects economics to a market-based commercial society, and thus to the great benefits to humankind that commercial societies have enabled.

The discipline of economics has developed a powerful set of tools to analyze human behavior and the choices human beings make, as well as to measure and assess the effects of, including the costs and benefits of, those choices. It has also made tremendous headway in understanding what the effects are of various public social institutions, allowing us to understand how and why people react to and change their behavior in light of them. Because human beings are, despite their commonalities, nevertheless unique in their goals, desires, needs, preferences, and circumstances, their behavior can never be perfectly predicted – or, at least, the behavior of no single person can be perfectly predicted. But the tools of economics can, and have been able to, develop some fairly stable predictions about how human populations (if not individuals) are likely to change their behavior in response to various changes in their circumstances. The power of these tools is shown in their increasing ability to account for, explain, and retrodict past behavior. Economists are working on attempting to predict more of our future behavior, though humanity's unpredictable nature means that the goal of perfectly predicting our behavior will remain elusive – just as, however well we understand the processes of evolution and the descent of species, we will likely never be able to predict which species, let alone which individual members of species, will survive and flourish and which will not, or what new species will be in the offing in the future.

So, what can the tools of economics do for us? They can help us in at least three important ways, all connected with morality.

First, they can help enable better decisions about how to allocate our resources. Consider these fundamental claims of economics: (1) resources are scarce; (2) this means decisions must be made about how to allocate them; (3) this means that tradeoffs are inevitable; (4) from which it follows that every decision we make involves opportunity cost. Add to those claims a few fundamental axioms about human behavior: (5) human beings tend to be self-interested, not in the narrow sense of selfish, but in the more expanded (Adam Smithian) sense that whatever their goals are, which routinely involve promoting the interests of others they care about, they want to achieve them; (6) human beings tend to be rational, not in the sense of always making wise or prudent or unbiased choices, but in the sense that they possess and regularly employ the ability to figure out what steps would lead to achievement of their goals; (7) their desires are seemingly limitless, in the sense that no matter how much a person has, chances are he wants more – there is almost never a time when they are truly content with their circumstances and situations; and (8) people have a hierarchy of ends and schedule of value, in the sense that some of their ends and some of their values are more important to them than others.

Given these claims, our goal, whether as individuals or as a society, should be to strive to increase our resources so that we can achieve as many of our ends as possible. At any given moment, however, our decisions about how to allocate our resources of time, talent, and treasure should cohere with and follow our considered hierarchy of ends and schedule of value, never sacrificing a more-important end or higher value for a less-important end or lesser value. The first thing economics can do for us, then, is to help us understand the human condition so that we are in a position to make these determinations. Economics might not tell us what our ends or values should be, but, whatever they are, it can help us achieve them. That is a tremendous first step, and, if more widely appreciated and followed, would save us from any number of personal and social mistakes and follies – mistakes and follies not according to others' opinions, but by our own lights.

But consider more carefully point (8) from above. Although many of our ends and values change over our life-times, nevertheless at any given moment we likely will have a relatively stable hierarchy. When we make decisions and choices, and engage in actions and behaviors, our goal is to achieve our ends and values. But what is included among our ends and values? Our *moral* values. We may have amoral ends as well – we like chocolate ice cream better than vanilla, we like coffee better than tea, and so on, and our goals of getting chocolate ice cream and coffee will motivate our actions accordingly (in coordination with all our other goals, of course), without having any particular moral content. And, of course, we also have, if we are to be honest, immoral goals as well – we would like to knock others down a peg or two, we like to punish or embarrass our enemies, and so on. But we also have genuinely moral values – everything from wanting to help others, to improving society, to enriching community, to protecting the environment. Because of the scarcity of resources in the world, and the scarcity of our own resources (including our time), we cannot simultaneously put all our efforts toward all these ends at the same time. We must rank their importance to us and choose accordingly. That is the second step of the value of economics to us: it gives us the tools to reckon and assess the tradeoffs we would have to make and the opportunity costs involved with all the various actions or courses of action we might take.

If our moral values matter to us, then we should want to achieve them. (If we are not interested to achieve them, then they do not actually matter to us.) Assuming we do want to achieve them, the only way we stand a chance of doing so is by allocating our scarce resources appropriately. If, by contrast, we were to disregard scarcity, trade-offs, and opportunity costs, or if we were to choose not to consider them when making choices, then we will end up sacrificing some of our own moral goals for other goals that are either amoral (or immoral) or that are moral but less worthy than higher moral goals. That makes economics essential to achieving not just a rational *economic* order but to achieving a rational *moral* order as well. The tools of economics and the principles of economic reasoning – including cost–benefit analyses – are, then, fundamentally moral when put in the service of our moral ends. Indeed, the more important our moral ends, the more important it is that we figure out how to achieve them given the constraints we face – lest we risk sacrificing our most important moral ends.

The third aspect of the morality of economics is the role it plays in helping us achieve prosperous lives of meaning and purpose. Economics has discovered that market-based commercial societies, for all their various and numerous faults, are nevertheless far better than *all* the yet-discovered and yet-attempted alternatives. The contest between market-based commercial societies, on the one hand, and the rest of the field, on the other, has revealed a clear winner, and it has not been close. As we have seen, by virtually any objective measure, people in commercial societies with freer economies fare far better than their counterparts in countries with less free economies. It is not just that they have more trinkets and widgets. The wealth freer economies produce enables people to address the more immediate and enduring needs of human existence like food, clothing, and shelter, so that they can then turn their attention to other matters that round out, or stand a chance of rounding out, a fuller life of meaning and purpose. In previous eras of human history, the chance of a eudaimonic life was restricted to vanishingly few people; in the last couple centuries, however, and particularly in just the last few decades, this has been democratized to enable ever more people – now approaching seven billion – a chance at eudaimonia. Wealth is not equal to eudaimonia, of course, and does not guarantee it, but it can enable the possibility of it. And there are few difficulties people face that would not be ameliorated by an increase in wealth.

I propose that this means that seeking to increase wealth honorably – that is, through honorable business, honest profit, mutually voluntary and mutually beneficial cooperative partnerships, and mutual respect for equal moral agency – is indispensable to benefiting others. It might even be a moral calling, leading, as it can, not just to the alleviation of misery, pain, and hardship but to the enablement of genuine human flourishing, well-being, meaning, and purpose. What could be more moral?

Conclusion

Economics is often considered to be an amoral or possibly immoral discipline, and the principles of economic reasoning are often accordingly deprecated as cold and heartless. But because our resources are scarce, part of the human condition is therefore that we must make decisions, sometimes hard decisions, about which of our goals or ends to serve first, which to serve second, and so on. Among our goals, however, are moral goals. What the principles of economic reasoning offer, then, are means by which we can assess all our ends, including our moral ends, so that we are better positioned to evaluate them in such a way that we stand a better chance of achieving what actually matters to us.

A demand for "People Over Profit" typically mistakes the issue. Honest profit, which results from honorable – that is, cooperative only, never extractive – business, results from improving others' lives according to the judgment of those others. A person demanding "People Over Profit" betrays, therefore, a selfishness that objectionably presumes that his or her own goals, values, and preferences should be privileged over those of others. We are all equal moral agents, however, which means that no one's ends should be privileged over those of anyone else. Although it will never be the case that all people get everything they want – and thus some will inevitably be disappointed – nevertheless, honorable business is a primary vehicle through which ever more people's needs, wants, and desires can be satisfied.

Cooperative behavior in market economies may be driven by self-interest, but it is not selfish in the sense of disregarding others' interests. Indeed, the only way that exchanges can be successfully executed in a market economy is with the cooperation of willing others. Thus, market economies are as much cooperative as they are self-interested. There is nothing wrong with wishing to improve one's own condition, though seeking to do so at others' expense is indeed morally wrong. Cooperative market behavior, by contrast, allows individuals to seek to improve their own conditions only by simultaneously improving the conditions of others. In markets, we compete with each other to find ways to cooperate with and benefit one another.

Human relations in markets take on the character of interdependence, not dependence, linking indefinitely many people in complex networks of mutually beneficial cooperation. As early political economists like Montesquieu, Hume, Smith, and Kant argued, we can hence come to view others, even others with whom we might otherwise have experienced conflict or toward whom we might have felt prejudice, as not enemies to be opposed but as opportunities for mutual betterment.

The principles of economics and economic reasoning are indispensable for achieving a rational moral order, both personally and publicly. They are therefore necessary for the achievement of our highest moral purposes, and for having a chance of attaining eudaimonia.

6

Equality of What?

Among men . . . the most dissimilar geniuses are of use to one another; the different produces of their respective talents, by the general disposition to truck, barter, and exchange, being brought, as it were, into a common stock, where every man may purchase whatever part of the produce of other men's talents he has occasion for.

Adam Smith, *The Wealth of Nations*

Introduction

Equality is one of our abiding moral concerns. In a 2013 speech, President Barack Obama claimed that inequality was indeed "the defining challenge of our time." There are, however, different conceptions of equality, which raises the question, as Nobel laureate Amartya Sen (1995) has asked, "Equality of what?" Sen argues that various definitions of equality entail satisfying one conception of equality only at the expense of others. You cannot have equality of resources, for example, without sacrificing equality of individual liberty. You cannot have equality of material conditions without sacrificing equality of resources. And so on. Hence, there is no such thing as advocacy for equality full stop: we have to specify which kind of equality we want, and then we have to explain why that specific kind of equality should be advanced above the others.

How does a claim about equality, however defined, count as or relate to an economic fallacy? Equality seems most naturally understood as a moral concern, and claims about it as moral claims, whereas economics is often considered to operate free of moral concerns. I addressed the Economics Is Immoral Fallacy in Chapter 5, arguing that economic reasoning can help us achieve our goals under scarcity, goals that include our moral goals. The fallacy with which this chapter is concerned is, first, the (philosophical) idea that one can simply be an advocate of equality generally. Because competing conceptions of equality conflict, that is impossible. More specifically, however, this chapter argues that one particular, and particularly popular and influential, conception of equality – namely, equality of resources – is in fact undesirable and even potentially harmful. It would require mechanisms that violate fundamental rules of morality, and it would lead to negative economic results. It is also likely impossible to achieve, but even if it were somehow achieved, the costs, both economic and moral, would be so great that we should not endorse them.

Equality of Wealth?

Equalizing wealth might initially sound like a good idea, but examination raises serious questions. To see why, we do not have to rely on a controversial theory of natural rights or a controversial theory of property ownership. The questions instead arise much more straightforwardly, from the claim that inequality of wealth is, or at least can be, a consequence not of something regrettable but of something worth celebrating about human beings: their diversity. Human beings are unique. Each of them has a unique package of gifts, skills, talents, potential, and personality traits; each of them has a unique signature of aspirations, ends, values, and preferences; each of them has a unique set of constraints they face, responsibilities they feel, and duties they owe; and each of them is a node in a unique, complex, and continuously evolving web of interconnectedness with others. Their uniqueness means that they are not fungible: none could be removed without irreplaceable loss, and none could be substituted for any other without change that propagates unpredictably throughout intricate systems of relationships and interdependencies. Despite their manifold connectedness to others, they nevertheless remain independent and unique centers of consciousness, agency, and decision-making. Their uniqueness, their interconnected individuality, and their free moral status are thus not accidental features: they are essential to who each of us is.

Because of their individual uniqueness, and because of the uniqueness of the situations into which they are born, the situations in which they find themselves, and the situations they choose to occupy, their paths through life will be unique as well. The choices they make, both good and bad, will reflect their interests, and hence no two persons' sets of choices or paths in life will be identical. Their diversity and their value pluralism will entail different choices that they make, and different choices that they should make, on their personal roads to eudaimonia. For any given individual, that road may be circuitous, with twists and turns, setbacks, and blind alleys, and it may never reach its final goal. But however it turns out, it will be reflective of their unique identities, and in a deep way will constitute part of their identities. It will represent the special unfolding of their individuality and the expression of their singular souls.

For those reasons we should expect that in most, perhaps nearly all, ways that we can empirically observe or measure, people will be unequal. Their material possessions can become, as Shakespeare's King Lear claimed, not just things they have about them but, rather, external representations of themselves, external manifestations of their unique identities. Differences, and various kinds of inequality, are therefore what we should expect, not what should surprise us. Indeed, if any two people's possessions and situations were equal it would be a stunning surprise, virtually a miracle, one that no doubt would not last another day, as each of them tomorrow would make new choices and decisions that would take them on paths different from wherever they intersected today. The idea that an entire community of people should be equal in their possessions and situations would thus be fantastically unrealistic and inconsistent with the diversity and unique individuality that characterizes human beings – what one might even consider part of the beautiful mosaic of humanity.

But suppose that one did not like these differences or inequalities. Suppose one finds attractive the idea of human beings being the same, or at least more similar than they are now. How could we bring it about? Given the reality of people's individuality and value pluralism, we would have to limit the options people have, take away some of some people's possessions and give it to others, monitor the choices people make, intervene regularly and systematically, and redistribute and re-redistribute continuously. Is there anything wrong with that?

There are, in fact, several things wrong with that. Consider it, first, aesthetically: uniformity and sameness are almost universally boring and ugly. Variety is the spice of life, as the saying has it: it is not sameness but diversity that makes life interesting, even, perhaps, worth living. Now, not necessarily diversity in all things: in some aspects of our lives we like familiarity and stability, even if not perfect sameness. But in life, as in society, as in any living ecosystem, lack of change is death. In a deep way, life *is* change. It is movement, it is progress, it is change. So, difference is both reflective and constitutive of life, whereas sameness is reflective of moribundity.

We might think, however, at least initially, that a society of equality would be attractive. We might be able to imagine a society in which all are the same, or nearly the same, and we might believe, perhaps on some imagined moral grounds, that such a society would be preferable to what we have. But would it be worth the price? For the price would be the diminution of our unique individuality, the constriction of our diversity and variety and pluralism, and the reduction of innovation, of entrepreneurship, of creativity, and of ingenuity. An enforcement of commonality would be the dismantlement of the uncommon. It may prevent people from being worse than others, or being in worse situations than others, but it would thereby also eliminate greatness, excellence, difference, and the opportunity for everyone to seek uncommon achievement. One

191

cannot level the earth by only raising the valleys; one must tear down the mountains as well. An enforced commonality would therefore eliminate uncommon accomplishment and close off the new peaks and frontiers that humanity might climb and traverse. Some trees are taller than others in a forest. If you wanted to equalize them all, you would end up having to cut all of them down to the lowest common denominator – which means eventually all you would have is groundcover, and hence no forest at all. Similarly with human beings.

We do not have to merely speculate or theorize, however, about the human costs entailed by attempts of leveling or equalizing human beings' situations: we have many historical examples and attempts available to us to provide evidence. Consider, as one example, the dozens of country-wide social experiments conducted over the past 100 years under the name of "Communism," which takes material equality as one of its central moral premises and prime directives. The history of Communist experiments has not been pretty. Indeed, as one researcher has put it: "every Communist regime in history killed huge numbers of its own people. If history had seen only one or two nasty people's republics amid a few decent ones, I might accept that a few bad apples gave the whole movement a bad name, but when death and destruction have followed every single Communist regime ever established, there would seem to be a flaw somewhere in the system" (White 2012: 453). This researcher estimates that the twentieth century saw deaths "under Communist regimes from execution, labor camps, famine, ethnic cleansing, and desperate flight in leaky boats" totaling some 70,000,000 people (ibid., 455–6). Is that price, or even risking that price, worth it?

Leveling

If a desire for equality of resources requires us to sacrifice human individuality and uniqueness – and perhaps individual humans as well – then I do not believe the price is worth it. Perhaps you are not convinced, however. Suppose, that is, that you think an equality of resources is a desirable and important moral goal, that current levels of inequality are too great, or that any inequality above some particular threshold is wrong. Perhaps you reject the Communist experiments as being too extreme, and you argue instead for more reasonable and measured steps to be taken to reduce inequality. Hence you conclude that at least some narrowing of inequality is (morally) required.

Fair enough. The next question, then, would be: How would you go about achieving it? The chief vehicle endorsed by most people who are sympathetic to such a position is redistribution via taxation, typically progressive taxation, by which means the government takes wealth from some and redistributes it in cash, goods, or services to others. Most governments in the Western world, and many in other parts of the world, currently engage in precisely such redistribution, and have been doing so for some time. In the United States, this has been going on since Franklin D. Roosevelt's New Deal in the 1930s, which ushered in America's first nationwide welfare and assistance programs; the effort got a significant boost during Lyndon Johnson's War on Poverty in the 1960s;

and it has continued to grow since then. According to Sheffield and Rector (2014), in the first fifty years of the War on Poverty, the United States federal government spent some $22 trillion on its redistributive aid programs. Many other governments similarly collect and then spend large proportions of their citizens' wealth on a variety of such programs. Unfortunately, however, whatever else such programs have done, they have had little effect on either poverty or inequality. According to the U.S. federal government's own poverty statistics, for example, the proportion of people in America officially categorized as at or below the "poverty rate" has remain essentially unchanged during its entire fifty years' War on Poverty. And there is evidence suggesting that such transfers have had at best only little positive effect on the conditions of the poor; indeed, there is evidence suggesting it might have a *negative* long-term effect (Brooks 2008; Dollar and Kraay 2016; Harvey and Conyers 2016).

In one fascinating recent study, historian Walter Scheidel (2017) examined hundreds of societies throughout human history, investigating which of them and at what times in their existence they were able to make substantial and sustained headway toward increasing equality. To his own surprise, his research revealed that the only ways human societies have historically been able to decrease inequality and increase equality to any significant degree have not included progressive taxation, welfare or other kinds of redistribution, or charitable giving. Instead, Scheidel found that there are only four reliable vehicles for decreasing inequality in a society: mass warfare, revolution, state collapse, and pandemic. Accordingly, he called them the "Four

Horsemen" of leveling, because each of them entails wide-spread suffering, displacement, and death. Of all the methods that have been tried through the hundreds of social experiments he reviewed, none of the other methods of taxation and redistribution made much difference. Only the Four Horsemen did. That would seem to put the defender of equality of resources on the horns of an unenviable dilemma: either she must give up her goal of equality, or she must be willing to endorse suffering, misery, and death to accomplish it.

It is not just the economic cost involved, however. It is the moral cost as well. War, revolution, state collapse, and plague are all extremely costly in resources, including human. If you are destroying assets, including people, whether through war, execution, or disease, those are real losses. Even if you can rebuild afterwards, and even if your population will later eventually recover, nevertheless the destruction of assets is a real loss, and your recovery would not bring you to as high levels, or not as quickly, as you could have achieved had you not destroyed them. And the human beings you lose in war, execution, and pandemic are forever lost as contributors to prosperity. Even worse, however, is the moral cost. Those lost humans were irreplaceable souls and uniquely precious moral agents who can never be recovered. And the infliction of misery, suffering, and death on innocents is wrong whatever utilitarian consequences ensue. If progressive taxation and welfare redistributive benefits have little effect in reducing inequality, and if war, revolution, state collapse, and widespread disease are the only effective ways to reduce inequality, then any argument for taking steps to equalize

195

material resources must get over the very high bar of either coming up with some new method of doing so that has never been tried or discovered through hundreds of human social experiments over thousands of years, or of justifying the infliction of misery and death on innocents in the service of one's vision of equality. It is not clear that either of those hurdles can be cleared.

I suggest, then, that equality of wealth is a dubious moral goal and dangerous to set as a goal of policy. Historically, it has been destructive of wealth and prosperity, disrespecting of human individuality and diversity and pluralism, and limiting – even eliminative – of human moral agency.

Be Yourself

There is another, and more promising, way of looking at the issue of equality, however, one that builds on an argument Adam Smith made in just the second chapter of his *Wealth of Nations*. There Smith made two claims that might initially seem to conflict. On the one hand, he wrote: "The difference of natural talents in different men is, in reality, much less than we are aware of"; he continued: "The difference between the most dissimilar characters, between a philosopher and a common street porter, for example, seems to arise not so much from nature, as from habit, custom, and education" (1981 [1776], 28–9). A claim of roughly equal ability across all classes and stations, even across all races and peoples, was a radical one to make in the eighteenth century – even in the nineteenth and well into the twentieth century as well. It is to Smith's credit that two-and-a-half centuries ago he refused to believe that the differences in the comparative wealth of various nations were due to any natural superiority or inferiority of one people compared with another. On the other hand, however, Smith also speaks of the "different genius" that different people have, and he argues that it is these "dissimilar geniuses" that allow us to complement and be "of use to one another" (1981 [1776], 28 and 30). So, which is it – are we (roughly) equal, or do we have differing geniuses?

For Smith, these seemingly differing claims are reconciled by the effects on people of the "habit, custom, and education" that different people seek out and receive. On Smith's account, people are born with similar – if not identical – capabilities, instincts, and psychological equipment. But the natural differences are small relative to our differing experiences in life, and it is our experienced differences that lead us to hone and develop differing talents, skills, and abilities, as well as differing interests, values, and preferences, which in turn accounts for our mature "different geniuses." These developed differences are causes for concern, however, only if we live in societies that are characterized by zero-sum, winner-takes-all, extractive attitudes and institutions. It is such attitudes and institutions that turn our differences into mutual threats, and can sow distrust and suspicion – because if you win, so do your goals and preferences, while I and mine lose. By contrast, if we live in societies that protect our "three Ps" of person, property, and promise, and that allow and reward cooperative interaction and exchange among differing peoples, then our differences are converted from conflicts into complementarities that can enable mutually beneficial interactions and exchanges.

One aspect of Smith's argument concerns what economists today call *comparative advantage*. The opportunity to interact, exchange, and trade with others, including people from other countries, benefits not only wealthier people and countries but those that are developing as well. "The natural advantages which one country has over another in producing commodities are sometimes so great, that it is acknowledged by all the world to be in vain to struggle with them" (1981 [1776], 458). Smith offers this example: "By means of glasses, hotbeds, and hotwalls, very good grapes can be raised in Scotland, and very good wine too can be made of them at about thirty times the expense for which at least equally good can be brought from foreign countries" (ibid.). Because the cost differential is so large, however – a factor of thirty – Smith argues that it would be "a manifest absurdity" in such a case for Scotland "to prohibit the importation of all those foreign wines, merely to encourage the making of claret and burgundy in Scotland" (ibid.). Instead, the Scottish government should allow its citizens to buy from wherever they want, including from foreign countries: "As long as the one country has those advantages, and the other wants them, it will always be more advantageous for the latter, rather to buy of the former than to make"; Smith continues: "It is an acquired [that is, not innate] advantage only, which one artificer has over his neighbour, who exercises another trade; and yet they both find it more advantageous to buy of one another, than to make what does not belong to their particular trades" (ibid., 458–9).

Smith argues, therefore, that we should reject policies premised on the "maxims" by which "nations have been taught that their interest consisted in beggaring all their neighbours"; he continues: "In every country it always is and must be the interest of the great body of the people to buy whatever they want of those who sell it cheapest. The proposition is so very manifest, that it seems ridiculous to take any pains to prove it; nor could it ever have been called in question, had not the interested sophistry of merchants and manufacturers confounded the common sense of mankind" (ibid., 493–4). When Smith concludes, "We trust with perfect security that the freedom of trade, without any attention of government, will always supply us with the wine which we have occasion for" (1981 [1776], 435), he uses "wine" as a synecdoche standing for all the goods and services for which "we have occasion."

Smith's argument is that merchants and manufacturers who would be the principal beneficiaries of special protections – including protections like tariffs and trade restrictions placed on goods produced by their foreign competitors – have managed to persuade people that such protections benefit consumers and domestic citizens. But they do not: they benefit the protected merchants and manufacturers. Such special protections are "carried on for the benefit of the rich and the powerful," while "the benefit of the poor and the indigent, is too often, either neglected, or oppressed" (1981 [1776], 644). If, however, the ultimate purpose of an economy is to increase the prosperity of all consumers and citizens – as it should be – then we should abolish such special protections and allow anyone to trade with, or buy from, anyone he or she pleases.

The primary beneficiary of free trade would be individual citizens, particularly poor citizens, who could now have access to and would progressively be able to afford more of the goods and services they need or desire. The secondary beneficial effect, however, would be to allow people, even whole countries, to specialize in what constitutes their comparative advantage. *Comparative advantage* is when one person, firm, group, or country can produce a good or service at a lower cost than can another person, firm, group, or country. This, in turn, gives the former the ability to produce and sell the good or service at a lower cost. This holds even when one firm or country could potentially be better at producing any number of things than any other specific firm or country. If firm A has highly skilled workers who could do many things well, but firm B has less-skilled workers who would not be as good as those of A at any of those specific things, nevertheless A and B would *both* be better off if A specialized in some particular thing (or range of things), while B specialized in something else that it can do well. That allows A to focus on something it can do particularly well, and to benefit from the fact that B is focusing on something it does particularly well; if A and B are allowed to trade freely, they can then both benefit from each other's respective specializations.

We all have comparative advantages. You might be able to be a plumber, an electrician, a baker, or an app designer; perhaps I could be any of those things too, but suppose you would be better at any one of them than I would be. Still, it would be better for you to focus on whichever one of them whose differential between your ability and my ability is greatest, for me to focus on whichever one of them whose differential between my ability and another person's is greatest, and so on: in that way, all of us get the

greatest production from each person in each line of work –
and we all benefit more than any one of us could if we each
individually tried to do all of them.

What does this have to do with equality? In order for
us, and particularly the poorer of us, to enjoy the increasing
standard of living that results from more goods and services at
lower prices, we need to allow the specialization that results
from division of labor. But that specialization both reflects
and gives rise to our "dissimilar geniuses" – that is, to differ-
entiation and diversity, and hence various kinds of inequality.
It allows people to be different, to pursue different kinds of
experience, training, and education, to go into different lines
of work, and to develop different skills, talents, and areas of
expertise, as well as differing ends, values, preferences, and
even personalities. It might mean that some of us make more
money than others, and that some of us have more wealth
than others, but the preponderance of our differences would
arise from decisions each of us makes about pursuing some
opportunities rather than others, making some tradeoffs
rather than others, and pursuing our individual comparative
advantage to enhance our chances of improving our own
conditions and our own lives the best we can – while, at the
same time, enhancing others' chances to do the same.

In this way, our differences can have not one but two
important benefits. First, they allow us to find new ways to
complement one another and thus to benefit one another,
leading to increasing overall prosperity. Second, they allow
each of us wider scope to find a life path that more closely
reflects his or her own goals and values, and his or her own
characters and abilities. In other words, allowing these

differences to unfold and grow gives ever more people a chance to find and engage in activity that reflects their own identities, who they truly are and want to be. If there are only five different occupations available to me in my small village, the chance that any one of them is a good match for my aspirations and abilities, and would thus provide me fulfillment (let alone eudaimonia), is much smaller than if there are thousands of possibilities in the modern city in which I live. That is partly why so many people today live in cities, and why so much of the global population is currently moving toward urban living: the scope of opportunity is orders of magnitude larger than it is in small or rural towns to live one's life the way one would like,[1] while still being productive both for oneself and for others.

A drive for material equality could choke off that wide opportunity. It is not just about money; it is about fulfillment. The fact that some lines of work are more remunerative than others is true but not equivalent to finding the right line of work, the right vocation and avocation, for any given individual. For a time, I intended to become a medical doctor; if I had done so, I would no doubt have made much more money than I make as a professor. But my comparative advantage lay in becoming a professor, and the fulfillment I get from my chosen line of work is, to me, worth the tradeoff that that choice entailed in getting paid less. My choice would not be right for everyone, of course, in part because other people's comparative advantage lies

---

[1] The economist Eric Beinhocker estimated that in New York City in 2007, the number of stock keeping units, or SKUs, is "on the order of 10^{10}," or some hundred million times as many as those available in a Yanomamö village, whose SKUs number in the "several hundreds, or at the most, in the thousands" (2007, 9).

elsewhere, but the inequality between my pay and what medical doctors get paid is all but irrelevant to the question of whether I made the right decision for me. To proclaim an injustice in my case solely because I am not paid what medical doctors are paid would be to misjudge my situation entirely. And similarly for others who make their own choices of fulfillment and comparative advantage in their own lives. If some people make less money than others or than they otherwise might, that might be simply a result of choices they have made that reflect their own goals, values, and comparative advantage. Unless they were victims of extraction, we are in no position to second-guess, let alone intervene in, their choices. They might well have made, and be making, the best choices in their own cases.

I conclude, therefore, that individuality, variety, difference, and diversity are good things – both for individuals and for the rest of us. And the differences in wealth or resources we might have, when not the result of extraction, can be reflective of our unique identities and the unique person of dignity each of us is.

An Equality Worth Defending

Does that mean, however, that no conception of equality is worth defending? We have been considering one central conception of equality, namely, equality of wealth or resources. Attempting to establish equality of income, of well-being, or of condition would face similar concerns about their potentially harmful tendencies to those outlined above. They might benefit some, but their gains would be temporary, would come at others' expense, and would imperil the attitudes, culture, and institutions that enable the growth of prosperity in the first place. Resources cannot be redistributed unless they are first created – which means someone must create them. There are two ways to get people to create wealth: either we can allow them to do so on their own, as a result of their own motivations, with whichever others they can persuade to cooperate willingly with them; or we can force them. Once again, we see that cooperation and extraction are our only two choices. Extraction is morally wrong, however. That leaves us with cooperation, which – thankfully! – is morally right, but that in turn entails various kinds of inequalities across many margins. That brings us back to our question: is any kind of equality worth defending?

The answer is yes. There is one kind of equality that is consistent with treating all human beings as unique and precious beings of dignity deserving respect and that, by a stroke of amazingly good luck, is also consistent with the institutions required to enable growing general prosperity. That kind of equality is: equality of moral agency. If we treat all people as possessed of a dignity deserving respect, that means that we must respect their ends, their values, and their preferences, as well as the actions they take on the basis and in the service of them. If all of us deserve this respect, none of us should infringe on others' agency and no one should infringe on ours. That means that the scope of each person's agency should be as extensive as possible, consistent with the scope of every other person's similarly expansive agency.[2] If we are

---

[2] As Rawls's first principle of justice frames it: "Each person is to have an equal right to the most extensive total system of equal basic liberties compatible with a similar system of liberty for all" (1971, 302).

all to have the maximum scope of agency, but no one's agency may infringe on anyone else's, then logically that means that we must all have an *equally expansive* scope of agency. In other words, we are all *equal moral agents*.

That is an equality able to be defended not only logically but morally. It is consistent with, indeed follows from, our individual uniqueness, according no one any moral authority over any other. No one may use another person, employ another person, partner or associate with another person, put another person to work, or make use of another's resources – without the latter's consent. All transactions must be based on willing agreement, and each person retains an absolute opt-out option allowing him to say "no, thank you" to any proposal, request, or demand. In this way, respecting others as our equal moral peers demonstrates the dignity of each individual that befits the kind of beings each of us actually is. The prospective result is a community of moral equals, of moral peers – a kind of "kingdom of ends," as Immanuel Kant (1981 [1785]: 39–41) famously and inspirationally put it.

What are the public social institutions required for, and entailed by, this conception of our equal moral agency? They would be institutions that, first, protect our persons, so that no one may assault, kill, or enslave us; that, second, protect our property and possessions, so that no one may confiscate, steal, trespass upon, or destroy our property; and that, third, protect our voluntary associations, contracts, obligations, and promises, so that no one may defraud us out of our time, talent, or treasure. We have called these the "three Ps": person, property, and promise. And we may call the public institutions that protect the three Ps the institutions of "justice." The primary duty of government, then, would be to protect justice, and the proper activities, branches, and functions of government would be whatever is necessary for – but nothing jeopardizing – the protection of justice. If we can manage to have these proper governmental protections of justice, it would, in addition to respecting our status as equal moral agents, also have the great ancillary effect of supporting the proper attitudes and culture necessary to enable growing prosperity. For they would publicly reflect our equal moral agency, they would place primary responsibility for constructing each citizen's path to eudaimonia where it belongs – namely, on each individual as the free and accountable person of dignity each of us is – and they would place the duties to help those in need exactly where it both belongs and where it can be most effective, again on each of us as individuals, singly or in voluntary partnership with others.

I suggest, therefore, that we should resist seeking equality of material conditions. It would be difficult to achieve in any case, but it would also involve us in disrespecting the dignity and humanity of all persons. As numerous historical experiments have shown, it would likely involve using immoral extractive means to achieve, and it would result either in an immiserated populace or in ugly and boring conformity, or both. Instead, the equality we should endorse is equality of moral agency, letting the beautiful variety and diversity of humanity unfold, grow, prosper, and flourish.

Conclusion

There is no coherent way to support equality simply so, because, as Amartya Sen has argued, different conceptions of equality require making tradeoffs against other conceptions of equality. Seeking equality of resources or income for all people, however, ignores human beings' unique individuality, including their respectively unique paths to lives of meaning, purpose, and ultimately eudaimonia. Because people are different, because the values they hold dear differ, and because their situations are different – and are constantly changing, including through luck, both good and bad – we should expect them to take unique, and uniquely different, paths in life. These different paths will entail making different choices, including economic choices, which means that their economic lives will be as unique to each individual as their respective schedules of value are. Enforcing, or attempting to enforce, an economic equality, therefore, not only disregards individuals' uniqueness and the decisions and choices they make as a reflection of their moral agency, but it also would have deleterious effects on their abilities to chart their own proper courses to eudaimonia.

We should therefore not seek equality of resources, income, or wealth. But that does not mean that there is no conception of equality that is worth defending. On the contrary, we should defend equality of moral agency, for all people, out of respect for their dignity as rational and autonomous beings. That means respecting their choices, even when we disagree with them. Although this is a moral, and not strictly speaking an economic, argument, nevertheless respecting people's equal moral agency also enables considerable economic benefit that accrues from the prosperity to which people's individual choices in the search for cooperative mutual betterment can lead.

7

Markers Are Not Perfect

In publick, as well as in private expences, great wealth may,
perhaps, frequently be admitted as an apology for great folly.

Adam Smith, *The Wealth of Nations*

Introduction

Given all the claims we have made about how beneficial
markets and market-based commercial societies are, one
might be surprised at the title of this chapter. Markets lead
to increased prosperity; exchanges in markets are positive-
sum; honest profit is the result of mutual betterment; markets
allow inequality in wealth that we should welcome as
a reflection of human uniqueness and diversity; free trade is
a boon to society and to all parties concerned; and markets
encourage the virtues of tolerance, openness, civility, and
what David Hume called "sociality." And the proof is in the
pudding: on virtually every way we have devised to measure
human well-being – everything from longevity to life satisfaction to peace to prosperity to politeness – the more market-
based a country's economy is, the better its citizens fare. It
sounds as if markets are an unalloyed good, perhaps even
perfect. Is that the claim?

No. Markets are not perfect. They do not meet every
need or desire, they do not have only good effects, they do not

solve all problems, and their features of private property rights, negotiation, exchange, cost–benefit analysis, and voluntary consent are not appropriate in all areas of human life.

Consider families, for example. Imagine trying to run a family on market principles: "How much money would it take for you to let me sit in the recliner to watch the movie?" Or: "Little Mary wants to have only ice cream for dinner every night, so we have to respect her choices." Older brother Alexander offers to trade four one-dollar bills to younger sister Emily for her single twenty-dollar bill, and she agrees because four is more than one. The children want to go to Disney World instead of getting math tutoring or music lessons, want to wear pajamas to the wedding, don't like needles and so don't want vaccinations, and so on. In a family, because some members – like the children – have not yet developed mature judgment, independent autonomy, and thus full moral agency, their desires should not always be respected. Moreover, because the family is small, everyone knows each other intimately well, and they largely share a conception of the good and the good life, centralized decisions (typically made by the parents) about what to do, how to allocate resources, and so on are not only appropriate but necessary. Application of market principles in situations like families would create far more problems than they would solve.

Outside families, however, some of the problems that people identify with markets are not in fact problems with markets per se, but rather problems endemic to the human condition. For example, the fact that resources are scarce and thus cannot be allocated to all good purposes at the same time – that is, the fact that tradeoffs must be made, sometimes regrettable and difficult tradeoffs – is a consequence not of markets specifically but of the nature of the reality we face. It is no more a failure of markets that resources are scarce than it is a failure of engineering that I cannot travel faster than the speed of light. Similarly, the fact that markets do not solve all problems is no more a problem with markets than the fact that modern medicine cannot cure all diseases is a problem with modern medicine. Our knowledge, our abilities, our capabilities, and our resources are limited – there is just no getting around that. We can mitigate the problems by increasing our knowledge, capabilities, and resources, and I have argued that markets – and the wealth creation they enable – can generate more resources with which to address many of the problems we face. But the world is parsimonious, life is risky, the future is uncertain, and our natures are fallen. There will always be problems we cannot solve, including new problems that we have not foreseen or cannot prevent, and, however much wealth might help, it will only be a help, and rarely if ever a once-and-for-all solution.

There are several societal problems we face, however, that seem to be exacerbated, or at least not helped, by markets. In this chapter, we discuss three: collective action problems; inequality; and exploitation. Each of these takes various forms, and there are numerous examples of each that have been raised by critics. Indeed, the literature exploring "market failure" is voluminous.[1] We cannot hope to give exhaustive examinations of these in one short chapter, but perhaps we

---

[1] For presentations of these and other worries about markets, see, for example, Barber 2007; Quiggin 2010; Satz 2010; Sandel 2012; Skidelsky and

can say enough about each to make an at least plausible case that, though they are real, they do not yet defeat the case for markets and market-based commercial societies.

Collective Action Problems

Suppose there is a large lake on which three different parties own land. One is an entrepreneur who wants to let people stay in the lodge she built and go fishing. Another is a naturalist who wants the lake and its environs to remain in their pristine natural state, untouched by human hands. And the third is a nuclear power plant, which wants to use the waters of the lake to cool its reactors. These three potential uses of the lake are mutually incompatible: whoever gets her way means that the others cannot get theirs. Suppose further, however, that each wants the lake to be used in the most beneficial way possible for humankind, and that each genuinely cares about environmental stewardship and sustainability. Who should win? How should we decide?

One way to decide would be to file lawsuits and let a judge or a jury decide. That would be a way to settle the matter – the judge's or the jury's decision would be final – but what reason do we have to think they would get it right? Why would we think their deliberations would stand a better chance of discovering the best use of the lake than if we just picked names out of a hat? The judge does not, after all, have any special powers to foresee the future or determine and

Skidelsky 2012; Stiglitz 2013 and 2019; Anderson 2017; Sunstein 2018; and Deneen 2018.

compare the benefits of each proposed use of the lake – at least
we cannot assume she has any powers that others do not have.
And what ideas, evidence, or factors would the members of
a jury consider that are different from or more objective than
whatever factors the three lake property owners would have?
The three owners have different interests, of course, and their
interests conflict – but the same may well be true of the
members of the jury.

We could put the matter up for a vote, perhaps as
a local referendum. Again, however, why would we think that
would lead to a better result? If history is any guide, most
people will not vote at all; and those who do vote are likely to
have their own special interests they want served. And since
they themselves do not bear the cost, or at least not directly,
and will not enjoy the benefits (again, at least not directly),
they may have little incentive to investigate the matter thoroughly and hence may not be as disciplined to choose well.
They may vote merely aspirationally, as voters often do; but
without themselves facing the possibility of profit or loss, and
without an incentive to consider opportunity cost and tradeoffs, it is unlikely that they will put in the work necessary to
come to a best-all-things-considered decision.

We seem, then, to be at an impasse – as we often are
in winner-takes-all, or zero-sum, situations. There might well
be a single best course of action for all concerned, and perhaps
you have an inkling what that might be, but this is a case
where the scarcity of a desired resource is outstripped by
people's competing and conflicting desires to use it.
A decision must be made: but which, and how should we
decide? It seems we are left with two choices, neither of them

good: either we more or less randomly decide and just hope for the best; or we do nothing, leaving the resource idle and unproductive, and forgo whatever benefit that could have been gained from it.

Consider another kind of case, made famous by a 1968 article by Garrett Hardin called "The Tragedy of the Commons." Suppose ten ranchers jointly use 100 acres to let their cattle graze. Suppose they all want the common grazing area to be used sustainably, so that their cattle can continue to use it indefinitely into the future. Because it is a commons, no one of them may claim exclusive title to it, and no one of them may prevent the others from using it; it is open to all of them to use. But suppose one rancher is considering whether to add a head of cattle to his herd. What effect would that have? The rancher will benefit from the additional head of cattle; in fact, he will get 100 percent of that value, since he can now sell one more head and the profit goes to him. The cost, in the form of slightly more grazing on the land, will redound not only to that rancher, however, but will be distributed among all the ranchers. So, he gets 100 percent of the benefit, but, as only one of ten ranchers using the land, he pays only 10 percent of the cost in extra grazing. That means he is incentivized to add an extra head to his herd. But so are all the other ranchers, who can reason similarly in their own cases. The result might well be that each of them adds another head, and another, and so on, until the grazing land is ultimately exhausted and the resource depleted. If one of the ranchers foresees this inevitable collapse and decides to unilaterally refrain from adding more head to his herd, that merely leaves more grazing capacity for the other ranchers to exploit. The refraining rancher would get the satisfaction of knowing that he had not himself added to the exploitation of the land, but the land would end up being exploited nonetheless, leaving him no better off. Indeed, he would be worse off, because he did not capture that last bit of grazing for himself and the land gets depleted anyway.

What makes the situation even more tragic is that we need not assume that any of the ranchers are evil or have bad intentions. They may have high, even noble, intentions: maybe they want to feed their families, and maybe they genuinely care about the land's sustainability. The logic of the commons, however, leads to depletion regardless – as a result not of mistakes in reasoning but as a result of perfect rationality for each of the ranchers. The result is something none of them wanted, yet to which each contributed given the situation they faced. That is why it is called a "tragedy" of the commons.

What can, or should, we do about such cases? Each of these examples – the lake and the grazing land – are instances of a more general category of problems called *collective action problems*. They result from a limited common pool resource that more than one person wants to use, and whose prospective uses are mutually inconsistent; and they ensue when people engage in rational, self-interested behavior that Adam Smith's "invisible hand" argument suggested should lead to mutual benefit but that in fact leads to either forgone gain or mutual loss. In both cases, then, and in many others besides, self-interested, rational, and mutually voluntary action seems to fail us.

One way to deal with the grazing problem, a solution offered by Hardin himself, is to remove the grazing land from the commons altogether and convert it to privately held land. Let the ranchers buy the land, and whatever they buy they can then use or negotiate with others to let them pay to use. What effect would this have? To use the language of economics, it converts an externality into an internality.

Externalities are effects of my (or our) behavior on unwilling others. They can be either positive or negative. If I mow my lawn regularly, that has the effect of maintaining or even heightening my neighbors' property values; my regular lawn mowing thus generates a positive externality on them. On the other hand, if I let my lawn go wild, that can diminish my neighbors' property values, generating a negative externality on them. Externalities are everywhere and easy to see once you start looking for them. If I open a coffee shop, this will create externalities for others in the area, perhaps positive (more convenient coffee, jobs, and so on), perhaps negative (more traffic); if I perform open-air concerts, it creates an externality, which again might be negative or positive; if I buy a house in your neighborhood, it will create a positive externality if I am a good neighbor or a negative externality if I am a bad neighbor; and so on. Positive externalities are typically welcome and hence create no issue to be resolved. It is negative externalities that are unwelcome, hence need to be addressed, and hence get all the attention.

Return to the case of cattle grazing. If my cattle may graze only on my own land, then I am incentivized not to have too many cattle: otherwise, they deplete my resource, and the resulting loss is borne not by others but by me. The same self-interested rationality that led to a tragedy in the commons leads me to become a good steward of the land if it is land

I myself own. Similarly for all the other ranchers. What was before a downward spiral toward destruction becomes now an upward staircase to benefit for all concerned. The costs I might in a commons have distributed on others, constituting a negative externality for them, is now internalized, that is, reflected back on me; this internalization of the externality by converting the commons into private ownership fundamentally transforms the logic of the situation and the behavior of the people involved. In this way, Smith's "invisible hand" returns to generate the overall benefit he claimed it could.

There are some cases in which a conversion of a commons into private ownership is not so feasible, however. Think of air or water. If my factory generates pollution that goes into the air or the water, that constitutes a negative externality for everyone else who wanted to breathe the air or drink or otherwise use the water. But how could we establish property rights in air or water that could alleviate, or even address, such cases? A solution that may have occurred to you is to create a third-party authority – say, an Environmental Protection Agency (EPA) – that could settle disputes, establish regulations and parameters and restrictions and requirements, and punish those who violate them. Is that the best solution? It may be, but in fact it is difficult to say. How, for example, could we be sure that the EPA will know what is best for all concerned? Like a judge or members of a jury, the EPA has no special power to comprehend all the relevant parties' interests or to foresee all consequences of various courses of action, and its employees may have interests of their own that may or may not comport with the interests of others. Thus, they may end up channeling things in directions according to their own preferences and schedules of value, perhaps encouraging some things and discouraging (or penalizing or prohibiting) other things in ways that conflict with others' considered interests and values. Who is right? And, of course, there is also the matter of opportunity cost: the EPA is expensive (its 2018 budget was about $6 billion), and it employs thousands of people with scientific training; what else would that $6 billion and those scientists have done if the EPA did not deploy them, and how would that forgone benefit compare to what the EPA has them do? Perhaps the EPA is in fact the best use of that financial and human capital, but it is hard to know for sure – at least it cannot merely be assumed that it is; it would have to be demonstrated.

Consider again the case of the lake and the conflicting uses to which its property owners would like to put it. Nobel laureate Ronald Coase (1960) suggested a potential way out of the impasse that would not require third-party intervention: let the property owners negotiate with each other for the rights to use the lake. If each owner has an interest in using the lake according to his or her respective wishes, then each should be willing to pay the others to compensate them for the loss they would incur by giving up their own desired uses. If we let them make offers to one another and bargain, the offered prices will likely rise. Eventually, two of the three will accept the third's offer as sufficient to compensate them for their loss, and the third will then get to use the lake for his or her own use.[2] We cannot know in advance who would win,

---

[2] For Coasean bargaining to work, there need to be both clear property rights and relatively low transaction costs. Even then, however, there can

and we cannot know whether whoever does win will now use the lake in the best way possible. But the Coasean claim is that this negotiation will be a discovery process by which the respective owners will be able to clarify just how much their desired use actually means to them, and the fact that each of them would enjoy the benefit or suffer the cost to their own resources disciplines them to make a fair and accurate assessment of their own values.

Coasean bargaining offers several benefits. First, it does not involve coercion or extraction; it would depend on willing cooperation of all parties. Second, because in most instances the respective parties will have to seek support and backing from other private parties – they will need investors, banks, private donations, and so on, each of whom would similarly be risking their own funds – the negotiation would proceed in a sense on the joint judgment of many people similarly disciplined by internalized externalities. And third, it would enable the resource to be used productively, in the hopes of creating mutual benefit. There is still no guarantee that mutual benefit would be created, since the winning party might be mistaken; all such ventures carry risk. But the risk of losing one's own money can focus the mind, increasing the chances that good decisions will in fact be made.

Collective action problems are often discussed, however, as if there is no way to solve them other than by third-party mandates and impositions. The claim is that private

be holdouts, who might prevent a successful bargain. But offers of increasing value have a way of softening people's initial refusals, so such cases in practice are less frequent than one might expect.

parties, pursuing their private interests with their private property, either cannot solve such problems or will engage in behavior that is suboptimal, even by mutual agreement of the parties themselves. And from this, the conclusion many draw is that markets often fail – and thus are not the panacea that some seem to imagine. What seem indisputable are that collective action problems are real, that they arise in many walks of life, that they are often difficult to resolve, and that they can sometimes lead to "tragic" consequences. Sometimes resource privatization, negotiation, or Coasean bargaining can resolve or mitigate the problems; sometimes third-party intervention, even coercive intervention, is required; some- times it is not clear how to address them.[3]

I suggest, however, that they are often a product of two enduring features of the human condition, the scarcity of resources and value pluralism, that are not themselves pro- ducts of markets or market-based commercial societies. What markets instead do is increase resources (or, more accurately, allow people to increase them), giving people wider scope to act on their various competing values and increasing their capacity to deal with the problems that arise. There is no single set of behaviors or policies or principles that will solve all problems human beings face, and no matter how many pro- blems we solve there will always be more to address. Markets, then, like every other human creation, are not perfect. But we should not let the perfect be the enemy of the good. And

---

[3] For discussions of historical cases of common pool resource problems and the perhaps surprisingly inventive ways local populations have addressed them, see Ostrom 1990 and 2005.

markets have been pretty good, particularly at allowing us to generate increased resources with which to tackle an increasing array of problems – including some collective action problems previously thought to be intractable.

Inequality Redux

We discussed inequality in Chapter 6, where I argued that material inequality arising from cooperative behavior was a positive and beneficial expression of human individuality, uniqueness, and diversity. Material inequality that arises from extraction is a violation of justice and therefore requires prevention, punishment, and redress, but material inequality arising from mutually voluntary cooperative behavior is mutually beneficial and therefore requires freedom, scope, and protection. Perhaps you were convinced by my argument. Even if you were, however, you might have at least two further concerns about inequality that we have not addressed: (1) the psychological anxiety that can be caused by awareness of (sufficiently) large inequality in wealth; and (2) the potential political instability that (sufficiently) large inequality might portend for a community, society, or country. Consider these in turn.

Imagine a society that has a large degree of material inequality but in which each person's level of wealth, whatever it is, resulted only from mutually voluntary and mutually beneficial cooperative transactions. In such a society, there would be no cause for a claim of injustice, because by hypothesis no injustices – understood as the use of force, fraud, theft, or other extractive and involuntary actions that worsened the ex-ante position of others – took place. There has likely been no such actual society, and there likely will be no such society. However widespread a moral commitment to engage only in cooperative and never extractive behavior becomes, people being people there will always be at least some who will, on at least some occasions, engage or attempt to engage in extraction. But let us imagine such a society nonetheless. Even in such a society where all the inequality is by hypothesis innocent, one might nevertheless still worry that great inequality would cause some people psychological discomfort and anxiety – which is a real cost on them. One might conclude that this cost is sufficient to warrant addressing, or at a minimum not simply disregarding.

One response to psychological anxiety arising from the mere presence of innocent inequality is that it is nothing to be proud of. If no injustice occurred, on what grounds, one might ask, could one justifiably still be anxious? Might it result from envy? Envy is a real and persistent feature of human psychology – but not a virtuous one. It is, one might be tempted to say, one of the Seven Deadly Sins for a reason. So, one line of response to the worry about the anxiety, or envy, caused by innocent inequality would be to say that that is a problem with you, not with society. Consider these analogies. Suppose one is a racist and feels psychological anxiety about interracial marriages; or suppose one is a homophobe and feels psychological anxiety about same-sex couples. What should society do in response to a racist or homophobe who voices such concerns? Is the proper response to accord this anxiety, even when real, deference and respect and thus to change the institutions, denying others the freedom to engage in the personal voluntary partnerships they wish to, because some others who are not directly involved might otherwise become upset about it? If your answer is no, that it is not sufficient reason to prevent others from such relationships, then perhaps that applies here as well: just because it makes a person upset that others want to patronize your coffee shop and not other coffee shops, thereby generating more wealth for you than for the owners of other shops, does not give us the right to prevent you from profiting from your coffee shop or to prevent your patrons from voluntarily buying your coffee.

But let us put aside that line of reasoning, which in any case runs the risk of alienating people who feel, or worry about others feeling, this anxiety and generating a needless and perhaps counterproductive divisiveness. There is another response that I believe is as decisive as it is benign. There are still today in the world approximately 600,000,000 people who live at what the United Nations defines as "absolute poverty," or under $3 per person per day. As we have seen, that level is the approximate historical norm for all human beings for some 99.9 percent of their existence, and the great good news is that in recent years nearly 7 billion human beings have ascended out of that level of straitened, precarious existence. What is now, or should by now be, uncontroversial is that what has enabled over 90 percent of humanity to ascend out of absolute poverty is the existence of markets and market-based commercial societies, and the allowance of ever more human beings to participate in them, experience their liberating and enriching benefits, and improve their circumstances. At the same time, however, those same institutions also allow inequality. So, we seem to face the following dilemma: either we can be rich, though unequally so; or we can be equal, but equally poor.

My proposal, given this apparent reality, is the following: until all human beings have risen above the levels of absolute poverty, the issue of material inequality, and the anxiety it can and does cause, are of secondary concern. Whatever psychological cost is involved with discomfort arising from perceptions of the unfairness of inequality, it does not compare to the difficulties, hardships, and miseries attendant on those people living in absolute poverty. That means that poverty, in particular absolute poverty, should be our primary concern. Once we have solved that problem, then we can turn our attention to other, less pressing though still real, concerns, including anxiety over inequality. If you are a person who feels that anxiety, I would thus ask you: does the discomfort it causes you constitute a weightier concern than alleviating absolute poverty? If you had to choose between alleviating your psychological discomfort and anxiety about inequality, or allowing those in absolute poverty to rise out of it, which would you choose? I speculate that you would choose the latter, as I suspect virtually everyone would. If I am right, then I suggest that we not disparage or deny the anxiety some feel about inequality but instead propose merely that we put it on a back burner. As soon as no one is any longer in absolute poverty – and, thankfully, it looks as if this will happen in the not-too-distant future – we can then turn our attention to other matters, including anxiety over inequality.

The other issue regarding inequality is that it could lead to political instability. This arises chiefly from the worry that people in the lower echelons of wealth might believe that they have been treated unfairly, that various injustices have prevented them from having more than they do and have enabled others to have more than they should, or that those with more wealth will unjustly tilt political mechanisms in their favor. Such beliefs can lead to unrest and, if sufficiently widespread or sufficiently deeply believed (or both), it can lead to conflict, uprisings, even revolt. And as numerous scholars have documented and demonstrated, conflict, including, in particular, violent conflict, is a great destroyer of value, both economic and human (North, Wallis, and Weingast 2009; Scheidel 2017). Perhaps, then, if out of nothing other than prudential self-interest, we should seek to minimize inequality and thus reduce the chances of conflict and violence.

This seems like a plausible argument. There are two further thoughts to adduce, however. One is that conflict seems to arise primarily from injustice, not inequality. People who object to inequality typically object that the inequality arose, or is believed to have arisen, from some form or other of extraction; the gravamen of the objection, then, is not to innocent inequality that arises from cooperative exchange but to some having enriched themselves extractively at others' expense. The best way to address such legitimate concerns would be to address the cause and not the symptom: eliminate extraction; protect the "three Ps" of justice; abolish special privileges, special legal favoritisms, and all instances of cronyism. In that way, any inequality would be honestly and honorably earned inequality, to which there can be little if any objection, and which (I conjecture) would diminish both the vehemence and justice of claims about unfairness that could portend instability in society.

The second relevant consideration is that rates of violence have in fact been decreasing dramatically over the same time that market economies have spread and are now at all-time lows worldwide. As Steven Pinker (2011 and 2018), for example, has demonstrated, the rates of violence, and in particular death by violence, of virtually all kinds – individuals killing one another, war or combat, state executions, terrorist acts, and so on – have been on a worldwide centuries-long decline, and today, despite and including the warfare deaths of the twentieth century and the deaths by terrorism in the twenty-first, are nevertheless the lowest they have ever been. This has coincided with the spread of markets, and perhaps the logic of market exchanges we discussed earlier, which Montesquieu, Hume, Smith, and Kant predicted would lead to a softening of antagonisms, have indeed played the beneficial role they predicted. We might not know for sure what the causes are – Pinker himself points to humanist enlightenment, of which market economies are but a part – but the numbers nevertheless are what they are, namely, low and declining. I suggest that this means that the worries about civil unrest, violence, and other forms of social instability are, or should be, decreasing. People will still be unsatisfied with their lots in life, and, as long as extraction still exists and plays any role in worsening some people's life prospects through no fault of their own, there will always be the seeds of unrest, including justified unrest. But its main cause remains extraction in all its various forms. If we can minimize or eliminate extraction, then this will go some way toward mitigating the causes of unrest, especially violent unrest. And those causes seem at their core to be the extraction itself, not the inequality that is a perhaps unwelcome symptom of it. I say treat the disease, not the symptom. Eliminate extraction, and many, if not all, the remaining seeds of discontentment will ebb.

Exploitation

Many criticisms of market economies focus on various ways that they enable exploitation. Exploitation can take many forms. It might mean that people exploit the environment, using up natural resources or using them in inefficient or unsustainable ways. Or it might mean that people exploit asymmetries of knowledge, with some taking advantage of others' lack of expert knowledge. A financial advisor, for example, might take advantage of the fact that customers do not understand, or do not understand fully, how various financial instruments actually work, and can profit from products or services that customers would not pay for if they knew what the advisor knows. Or it might focus on the extent to which employers can take advantage of employees, or potential employees, who have few options. Sweatshops, for example, are often criticized on such grounds: if people are poor and have few options, sweatshop employers might be able to offer them unconscionably low wages or benefits because the workers have few or no other options. Some critics raise similar worries about at-risk populations like poor women, who can be induced into sex work or into selling ova or body parts because they too have few options, which can lead them to make seemingly voluntary choices to engage in transactions they otherwise would not want to or that are destructive for them.[4] Exploitation concerns are also raised about price gouging: if firms raise the prices of essential goods after a natural disaster or other emergency, they can take advantage of consumers who suddenly need these goods and have nowhere else to turn.

If free markets allow such activities – as they do, or at least can – then, the critics maintain, this is a failure of markets and requires third-party, or governmental, intervention to prevent or punish such abuses and to help ensure that markets actually provide the benefits that their advocates claim they can and should, without enabling some to profiteer at others' expense.

In Chapter 2, we discussed Hayek's argument about what constitutes a "rational economic order," and what is necessary to enable one. Hayek claimed that although we all want, or should want, a rational economic order, it is impossible to achieve if we rely on some person or group of persons to organize the economy centrally. Instead, he argued, the only chance we have at approximating a rational economic order is to let individuals make decisions about allocating their resources on their own, that is, decentrally. As we saw, this claim was based on a "local knowledge argument," which held that using resources wisely requires particularized knowledge of time, place, and value, and that the only people who possess this knowledge are individuals themselves about their own situations. Centralized decision-makers, however expert, do not, Hayek argues, possess this knowledge about

---

[4] Satz 2010 calls such markets "noxious."

other individuals, rendering them unable to plan an economy efficiently. But even if individuals have knowledge about their own situations that distant third parties do not possess, it still leaves open the question of how they are to decide to allocate their resources, given their situations. If a rational economic order requires knowledge of, among other things, the particularities of available resources, individuals still need to know what the best use of them is given those constraints. How are they to know that?

To address that question, Hayek offers the price mechanism. Prices arise from a complex set of factors, including what people want and how badly, what is required to produce something in both resources and labor, and what substitutes there are or might be to the good or service in question. But there is a difference between what we might call "aspirational" prices and "real" prices. An aspirational price is what you would like to get for your goods or services, or what you would like to pay for someone else's goods or services. I might like to sell my services as a philosophical consultant, for example, for $500 per hour; or I might like to sell my house for $1 million. Because no one would actually pay that much for my consulting services or for my house, however, those prices are mere aspirations. On the other hand, perhaps you would like my services or my house, but you would prefer to pay $5 per hour for the former or $50,000 for the latter. If I will not sell my services or my house to you at those prices, then your preferred prices are aspirational as well. In contrast, prices become real, not aspirational, when two or more parties say "yes": when you and I agree on a price and make an exchange, whatever the price we agreed to is now a real one, because it was what actually effectuated the exchange. Because they arise from actual decisions we make, real prices reflect our actual needs, wants, and constraints. And they include our respective opportunity costs: we could have sold to or bought from someone else, and we could have produced some other good or service or bought something else entirely. If you bought this from me at this particular price, however, that means that both of us believed this was a good use of or return on our respective resources in the service of ends or preferences we actually have. The price at which we exchanged, then, is real in that it arose from our real, not imagined or hypothetical or aspirational, circumstances.

Our circumstances change, however. When they do, a transaction we might have been willing to engage yesterday we might not be willing to engage today, or tomorrow. New circumstances or opportunities arise, often unpredictably, that affect our preferences, reorder our priorities, or heighten some of our values while diminishing others. As a result, the prices at which, or the terms under which, we are willing to exchange also change. Because the factors we consider when we contemplate any transaction are constantly changing, our aspirational prices are also constantly changing – which means that potential real prices change as well. You get an attractive new job offer, so you are suddenly more willing to consider a lower price for your house; your friend invites you to dinner, so you are suddenly willing to go to a more expensive restaurant; a new software program is developed that would make your job easier, so you suddenly are more willing to buy a more expensive laptop that can handle the new program; and so on. Even the weather affects our schedule of priorities: it looks as though this winter will be colder than you anticipated, so you decide to buy a warmer coat, or you decide to go ahead and plan a trip to the beach to get some sun and warmth.

Or a hurricane strikes. When it does, you find yourself without electricity, which means your refrigerator does not work. So, you suddenly have a desire for ice that you did not have before the hurricane. But others also lost their electricity and now also want ice. The local supply at gas stations and grocery stores is thereupon quickly consumed, but, because the electricity is still out, people still need ice. If there were no restrictions on prices, no legal price ceilings or no anti-price-gouging laws, what would happen to the price of ice in such a case? It would likely rise: a sudden increase in demand, without a contemporaneous and calibrated increase in supply, would predictably lead those selling ice to increase their prices. At some point the increases might enter what is considered "price gouging" territory.

What that threshold is varies by jurisdiction and by personal opinion. In North Carolina, for example, state law holds:

> Upon a triggering event, it is prohibited and shall be a violation of G.S. 75–1.1 for any person to sell or rent or offer to sell or rent any goods or services which are consumed or used as a direct result of an emergency or which are consumed or used to preserve, protect, or sustain life, health, safety, or economic well-being of persons or their property with the knowledge and intent to charge a price that is unreasonably excessive under the circumstances. This prohibition shall apply to all parties in

> the chain of distribution, including, but not limited to,
> a manufacturer, supplier, wholesaler, distributor, or retail
> seller of goods or services. This prohibition shall apply in
> the area where the state of disaster or emergency has been
> declared or the abnormal market disruption has been
> found. (Stein n.d.)

The law does not specify what constitutes an "unreasonably excessive" price increase after an "abnormal market disruption," but the attorney general and the courts have decided it means something more than a 5 percent increase in the price of a relevant good or service from whatever its price was before the "triggering event."

The economist Michael Munger (2007) has written about Hurricane Fran's 1996 strike in North Carolina. Fran took a path that was unanticipated, and Raleigh found itself without electricity and its citizens in need of ice. Apparently, some enterprising North Carolina youth from Greensboro, which was unaffected by Fran, saw a market opportunity: they rented a refrigerated truck and chainsaws, bought about 500 bags of ice at their local stores for $1.70 apiece, and traveled to Raleigh to sell it. They cleared the roads strewn with overturned trees (thus creating a positive externality), made their way to a central intersection, and began selling the ice out of the back of their truck to whoever wanted it. They charged more than $1.70 per bag, however, in part to recoup the costs of not only the ice but the truck, gas, chainsaws, their time and labor, and so on. But the demand was still high, and a long line formed. The prices soon rose to $8 per bag of ice, perhaps higher (accounts vary), but, in any case, far above the 5 percent increase allowed by North Carolina law (a 5 percent increase would have been about $1.79 per bag). Despite people being willing to pay the higher price, the police were called to enforce North Carolina's anti-price-gouging law. The enterprising youth thereupon had their truck impounded, the remaining ice destroyed, and found themselves in the local lock-up.

What they did was clearly illegal – it was in violation of North Carolina law. But was it morally wrong? One might be inclined to say that yes, it was morally wrong, because they were exploiting people's sudden need for ice that resulted from the triggering event of the hurricane. Maybe some of the people in line wanted ice merely to keep their beer cold; but perhaps others were diabetics who needed it to keep their insulin cold, which might be a matter of life and death for them. In such a case, would it not be unconscionable for the enterprising youth – Munger calls them "yahoos" – to charge such high prices for something so useful, even potentially necessary for some people's survival? This seems a clear case, one might think, of exploitation, of taking advantage of people in need, of profiteering in the worse sense. And if a market economy allows – or, even worse, encourages – such profiteering, well, then, so much the worse for market economies.

What makes a case like this different from any other where circumstances affect prices? We said earlier that prices reflect people's actual circumstances, and that those circumstances change, leading naturally to changing prices as well. Why, then, is this case any different? Perhaps because in this case there might be people who genuinely need, as opposed to merely want, a particular good. Or perhaps because it just seems unseemly to profit from a disaster. Or perhaps because rising prices mean that only relatively wealthier people might be able to afford the good in question, while relatively poorer people might not be able to afford it at the now higher prices. The ability to pay is, after all, not the same thing as the willingness to pay or the desire to buy. Maybe some people really need the good, but simply cannot afford the inflated, triggering-event-spiked price. Thus, we might conclude that a third party needs to step in. Perhaps we need a law preventing people from charging exorbitant prices, and the attorney general and police need to ensure that anyone who does so is punished. People who need goods or services, especially in dire circumstances like those following a hurricane strike, should be able to get them without being beholden to exploitive prices or profiteering.

But there might be more to consider. In the local Raleigh area before the hurricane, there was plenty of ice to be had at the $1.70 per bag price. So, we can assume that that price was appropriate, given the normal situations people were in before the hurricane hit. There was no shortage of ice, and no one who needed it had a hard time getting it.[5] It was only once the hurricane struck that demand suddenly increased, leading to the shortage of ice that created the opportunity for suppliers to raise prices. Notice, however, that it was only that shortage, and the resulting potential for suppliers (or prospective suppliers) to realize higher prices,

[5] It might be worth noting that the Raleigh citizens were unable to prepare in advance: although they knew a hurricane was coming, it had been predicted to take a different course. Fran's striking Raleigh was a surprise.

233

that induced the enterprising youth to bring ice to hurricane-ravaged Raleigh. In other words, it was the prospect of higher prices itself that led to increased supply. Without that, Raleigh residents would have remained in the situation they were already facing: no ice. So those who truly needed ice would have been able to get all the ice they wanted, as long as it was zero – because all the ice was gone! If we compare, then, the two actual scenarios people needing ice after the hurricane faced – getting ice, but at a higher price; or getting no ice at a lower price – which is preferable? The fact that at least some people were willing to pay the higher price suggests that the higher price was worth it to them, which in turn suggests that they preferred the option of some ice at a higher price to the option of no ice at a lower price.

For people who genuinely needed the ice, say for their insulin and not just their beer, if the higher price is the only way they can get it, then that seems the better, perhaps more humane and even moral, option. They needed the ice; the enterprising youth brought it them, and they would not have had it otherwise. That seems like a real need that was met, in the only realistic way it could have been.

Consider two other, related aspects of the scenario. First, if the price per bag of ice rose much higher than its pre-hurricane level, to a point that would enable a profit over and above the costs of the ice, the truck, the gas, the chainsaws, and the opportunity costs, in that case yet other enterprising entrepreneurs might be induced to get in on the action, as it were: more people would buy their local ice, get a truck, and bring it to Raleigh. The result would be increasing supply. What would happen as the supply increases? There would be competition among the suppliers; people would have more options from whom to buy, and the price would begin to come down – enabling more people who wanted ice to get it. Second, consider the scenario from the perspective of not the suppliers but the buyers. If the price of ice after the hurricane is still $1.70, then lots of people, including those wanting it just to keep their beer cold, will buy the ice – which is precisely what led to the shortage. If the price begins to rise, however, some people will begin to leave the line: the beer drinker might be willing to pay $2 or $3 per bag to keep his beer cold, but not $8 or more. At some point, then, those who whose needs are less pressing will leave the line. Who will remain in the line? Those whose needs are more pressing – like the diabetics who need it for their insulin. That means that there will likely be ice left for them, ice that is not taken and used by people who need it less. Rising prices have, then, two related beneficial effects: they induce higher supplies that help alleviate shortages, and they discourage frivolous uses of the good, leaving more for more pressing needs.

It may well be that Munger's "yahoos" were interested only in their own private profit and gain and were unconcerned about the welfare of people needing the ice or whatever benefit to them the ice would provide. Even despite themselves, then, their actions would have led to benefit for others. And consider: how *else* might we have achieved that benefit? If we prevented the price increases by law, but nevertheless wanted people who truly needed the ice to get it, how would we accomplish that? Would we offer the current supply of ice on a first-come-first-served basis? That is what already happened with the (inadequate) local supply, which led to the shortage; and in any case, there is no guarantee that whoever happens to arrive there first is who actually needed it most. Would we instead distribute the ice randomly, by, say, a lottery? That might seem fairer, but it too would not quadrate with need – it would be distributed randomly, not by need. Would we then decide to distribute it based on need? But how would we determine who really needed it? (Sometimes people are less than truthful, after all.) Would we ask the government to supply it? That could work, though it might be expected to be slower and more inefficient – as numerous actual instances seem to have demonstrated.[6] Of course, we could ask the government to bring in needed supplies *and* allow entrepreneurs to bring in supplies as well – thereby allowing not one but two routes to addressing the needs.

Allowing the price mechanism to operate freely and to incentivize both suppliers and buyers would not be perfect: there would still be inefficiencies, lags, mismatches between the goods and those who need it most, and so on. We might say, then, that it is not a good solution, except for all the others. In real-world political economy, however, we rarely if ever deal with perfect scenarios or solutions.[7] Instead, we must look for relatively better, often indeed the least bad, scenario or solution, in comparison with the other actually available (not ideally imagined) alternatives.

[6] The spectacular failures and inefficiencies of the federal government's response to Hurricane Katrina in 2005 in New Orleans is but one unfortunate, and unfortunately telling, instance. See Storr et al. 2015.
[7] Compare the economist Harold Demsetz's discussion of what he calls the "nirvana approach" to public policy; see Demsetz 1969.

Relate this back to Hayek's argument about the price mechanism, a rational economic order, and exploitation. Unforeseen changes, both small and large, both natural and manmade, both intentional and unintentional, conspire to change our circumstances, our options, and our desires. No central planner can foresee all such changes, account for them, or hope to address them, especially in real time. Market economies in which people are allowed to offer to sell or buy goods or services according to their own judgments will allow people to exploit these changes in circumstances. But that goes both ways: not only might an entrepreneur or firm be able to exploit some new desire or need by raising prices, but consumers might also be able to exploit a downturn in demand for a good or service by waiting for "Going Out of Business" sales or buying at a discount when an entrepreneur or firm has an oversupply. This is the business model of consignment shops and overstock stores, for example.[8] The economic question is not whether we can prevent such shifts and changes and shocks from affecting

---

[8] A personal anecdote. When I was a graduate student, a local used bookseller went out of business. The owner announced that on a particular final day, all books in his shop would be sold at a 90 percent discount. Many of the books I had wanted, but as a graduate student could not afford at their full price, I could now suddenly afford. Before the appointed day, I went to the store and scouted out all the books I wanted. On the appointed day, I arrived early enough to be first in line, and within fifteen minutes of the bookshop's opening I had a large stack of used books that I bought – costing me $30, or what would have been $300 just the week before. I was far from the only person who took advantage of that 90 percent-off sale. It was a sad day for the bookseller, but what a boon for us graduate students!

supply and demand, but, rather, how best to account for them and encourage the flow of our scarce resources continually to their most important uses. Prices, and all the personalized, localized, and changing knowledge that gives rise to them, can help us do just that.

When people have few options, or few good options, someone coming along and offering them an option that is only slightly better, but not significantly better, can seem greedy or exploitive. And maybe it is! After all, it may well be that the only reason you are offering me a job at such low pay is because you can – either because there are many others who would like the job or because you know that I really want this job. But offering someone an option, adding an option to her already existing set of options (however big or small the set is), doesn't make her worse off. It might be a worse option than others she already has, or at least no better than whatever she already has; or it might be only marginally better than what she already has. In the first case, it makes no difference to her: she will choose another option she has that is better than what you are offering. In the second case, where your offer is no better than other options she already has, she may be indifferent to your offer. In the third case, however, you have improved her option set, even if only marginally. In no case, then, did you make her worse off – even if you could, conceivably, have made her an even better offer than you did. This is an important point to emphasize. Suppose a worthy charity is asking you for a donation, and you decide to give $10. But you could have given $100. Given that you would not have actually considered giving $100, does that mean you should instead give nothing? Or is giving $10 a benefit to the

charity, even if it is not as much benefit as you could conceivably have given? Your $10 donation is a real benefit, and
better than giving nothing. So, between the two actual (not
aspirational) options – giving $10 or giving nothing – giving
$10 is much to be preferred.

Similar reasoning applies to numerous other cases.
We might genuinely wish that others had more or better
options than they in fact have. If we feel strongly about it,
we should ourselves provide them with more or better options
if we can. But we should not prevent others from offering
them different options, even options that are not as good as
we wish they would offer or options that we ourselves would
not accept, just because we wish they had yet better options.
Markets can allow people to take advantage of unforeseen
changes, of unfortunate circumstances, and of genuine need,
just as they can allow people to take advantage of less pressing
shifts in desires or circumstances. In cases where we believe
immoral exploitation is taking place, we may have a moral
duty to put our own money where our convictions are and
make people better offers.[9] Or we might choose not to patronize or work for firms that are offering terms that we believe do
not meet minimal thresholds of decency. But we should be
chary of intervening in others' voluntary choices, even when
they engage in transactions at prices or under terms that we
ourselves would not accept or would not even consider.
Others are not us. Our circumstances are not others'

---

[9] That is, we might believe, as I do, that we are obligated to engage in
"charity beyond justice," as Pope Benedict put it in *Caritas in Veritate*
(Benedict 2009).

circumstances, and others' ends, values, and constraints are not the same as ours. It may be that others are making rational and even wise choices, given the constraints they face and the values they have, which are not the same as ours.

As the local knowledge argument demonstrates, it is very difficult to know from the outside whether others are making good choices for themselves. And sometimes what seems to one person an exploitive exchange can be to another a lifeline and a godsend. Not always, of course, but prices can help calibrate people's choices to their actual circumstances, often better than could an uninvolved and distant third party. If in a particular case we are certain that a person would not be making the choice she is about to make if she knew what we knew, then we might be justified in informing her of what we know, even counseling her against the choice. But we had better be sure, and, given how hard it is to know all the relevant information about others' circumstances, caution and deference would seem to be in order. She might be making a mistake, but it is hard for us to know from afar whether she is. And in any case, she is a person of equal moral agency to us, so we would seem to have good reason to adopt as our default the principle of respecting her, and others', choices, and trusting that she has reasons for what she does even if we do not know what they are.

Conclusion

Markets are not perfect. There are many things that markets do well, or at least as well as or even better than other political-economic institutions. But there are many areas of life, and many difficulties that human beings face, where markets are inappropriate, inapplicable, or imperfect. One such area is the family, where something rather resembling socialism would be preferable and more appropriate than market transactions. Other social issues that markets struggle to address include collective action problems and large-scale externalities, the psychological anxiety and social instability to which inequality can lead, and exploitation, particularly of people in situations of need or emergency.

Some aspects of collective action problems, inequality, and exploitation result not specifically from markets, however, but from difficulties and challenges endemic to the human condition. Yet even in such cases, markets can often help. The increasing prosperity to which market-based commercial societies lead, and the coordination of our available resources to our needs that (real) prices enable, generate more resources with which to face these challenges according to their order of importance to us. That puts us in a better position to address, if not always solve, them.

Conclusion

The World and I

> *Though every man may, according to the proverb, be the whole world to himself, to the rest of mankind he is a most insignificant part of it.*

Adam Smith, *The Wealth of Nations*

Introduction

One thing that the relatively new and illuminating field of behavioral economics seems to have discovered is that we take a high view of ourselves. We tend to think we have good judgment, that we make wise choices, that our preferences are good, and that our intentions are honorable. When we face disagreement or conflict with others, we tend to interpret our own words, actions, and intentions far more favorably than we do our adversary's. When something goes wrong in our lives, we tend to place the blame on others, on the world, on systems or laws or processes or institutions, on the gods or on destiny or on karma – seemingly anywhere but on ourselves.

    One aspect of this inflated view of ourselves is that we often assume, typically without thinking about or reflecting on it, that our preferences are what others should have too.

We do not just like the music or books or movies we like, but we think others should like them too; we do not just prefer the political party we support, but we think others should support it too; we do not just think that our religion is the true one, but we believe others are mistaken; and we do not just think that our moral sensibilities are correct, but that people who have different moral sensibilities must be some combination of naïve, simple, or evil. We all have these prejudices, to varying degrees and with respect to varying objects. To some extent they are harmless reflections of our own unique identities and schedules of value, and our possibly evolutionarily selected-for bias toward ourselves. Sometimes, however, these prejudices can indeed be harmful – as when they lead us to treat people differently, and negatively, for failing to agree with us, to believe what we do, or to prefer what we prefer. We can all too easily assume that our own beliefs, values, and preferences are right not just *for us* but are right *period* – meaning that anyone who has differing beliefs, values, and preferences must be making some kind of mistake.

Some years ago, the philosopher Kurt Baier described moral philosophy as often being an extended exercise in intellectual bullying: "Moral talk is often rather repugnant. Leveling moral accusations, expressing moral indignation, passing moral judgment, allotting the blame, administering moral reproof, justifying oneself, and, above all, moralizing – who can enjoy such talk? And who can like or trust those addicted to it?" (Baier 1965, 3). According to Baier, much moral philosophy thus constitutes what we might call moralism rather than moral philosophy – posturing, status-signaling, and self-flattery, rather than the disinterested pursuit of moral truths. We do indeed often seem to fancy ourselves as others' betters, and the smarter we are, the more cleverly and elaborately can we construct portrayals of our own virtue and of others' vices.

I believe that this propensity to inflate our self-importance and to nurse pretensions of our own moral, social, or epistemic superiority is often at work in our economic beliefs as well. It can lead us to assume that the choices others make and the policies others support, to the extent they differ from what we would have chosen or supported, are the result not of others' reasonable assessments of their situations but instead are the result of ignorance, bias, irrationality, vice, or weakness. Perhaps we think those others choose incorrectly because of their own faults or because they are the victims of other people (or of institutions or of society), but we believe their choices are incorrect regardless. And this conclusion makes us much more susceptible to entertaining ideas of intervening. We do not think to ourselves, "I should mind my own business"; we think instead, "We need to help [nudge, force] them to make better choices."

In most cases, however, we should resist that temptation. Our default assumption should instead be that people who make choices different from what we make or would have made must have their reasons, even if we do not know what they are. Our default principle should be, therefore, to respect their choices and recognize them as reflective of their equal moral agency. That does not mean that others are infallible or that we should regard them as such, or that others should be immune from criticism. But it does mean that we should exhibit humility when we judge others, because we only infrequently know the whole story. Even if it is true that you or I make better choices, moral or otherwise, than they do, that does not mean that we are in a better position to choose for them than they are for themselves – let alone that we have a right to do so. We might be our own world, but we are not theirs, and they are not ours.

I call this fallacy the "I Am the World Fallacy." It has surprisingly far-reaching effects and arises in a surprising number of cases. To make the case that it is indeed a fallacy, however, let us begin with the importance of privacy.

Your Right to Say No

It may seem strange for anyone to argue for privacy, especially today. Who, after all, can any longer expect any privacy? Many will wonder: *Do you have something to hide?* Data on all of us are collected by numerous companies and government agencies, both foreign and domestic; our actions are recorded by cameras in virtually every major city in the world; and millions, even billions, of us put even the most intimate details of our lives and our innermost thoughts on social media and other digital platforms that, whatever their security protocols, almost anyone can find, see, and read – and that never go away.

My argument for privacy is not aimed only at the collection of data about us, however, but also, and more primarily, at the necessity of having a space within which we can live unmolested, free of uninvited intrusion from others. Having an identity, a coherent sense of self, is necessary for constructing a life of meaning and purpose. Being beholden to others is inconsistent with what it means to be fully human, fully a moral agent. Thus, if we have any natural rights at all, one of them – perhaps the first of them – is the right to say "no": no to any offer, suggestion, command, edict, or mandate; no to any question, inquiry, or demand for information; no to any person, however high, noble, authoritative, or rich. The right to say no is so intimately connected with every aspect of human moral agency, so foundational to what makes us human, and so crucial for the construction of a life of meaning and purpose that it should be considered sacrosanct. We relinquish it at the risk of losing what makes us unique and valuable creatures, and when we take it from others we compromise their humanity.

It is not enough, however, merely to possess, in some theoretical sense, a right to say no. Two further things are required. First, one must use it. An unexercised right is, in effect, a nonexistent right. You have the right to say no: exercise this right liberally and regularly, and let no one take it away from you. Second, one must respect *others'* right to say no. They are moral agents just like you; thus, they have the same rights as you, and you must respect those rights exactly as you wish to have your own respected. Perhaps you do not like them; perhaps you find their politics or their morals or their religion odious or repellent; perhaps you believe that they would not make the choices they are making if they only knew what you know; perhaps you believe you have wisdom to bestow upon them (and perhaps you are even right): still, they get to say no. They are full moral agents, equal in that capacity to you and to everyone else, and possessed of knowledge about their own situations that is not only unique to them but unknown in its entirety by anyone else, including you. When they make choices and take actions that are different from what you would have chosen or done, it does not follow that they are therefore mistaken. It might be that they are just different from you. And there is nothing wrong with that.

Many believe that liberty is about being able to say "yes." If I want to do x, and if x does not entail – or, as John Stuart Mill (1806–1873) puts it, does not entail "directly and in the first instance" (Mill 1978 [1859], 11) – harm to others, then I have a right to do x. And this is indeed surely a part of what it means to be a free human being. But a right to say yes is itself derivative from the right to say no. Saying yes just means saying no to an indefinite number of other things, and I can say yes to this only if I have already said, and had the right to say, no to everything else. So, before I can say yes, before I can even begin to think about what kinds of things I will say yes to, I must be able to say no – and have my no recognized and respected. It is a supreme act of individuality, a recognition of my personhood and of my unique existence, a reflection of my singular consciousness, of my essence, of my *haecceity* as, above all else, a free and accountable moral agent to act and choose. That means being able to say no.

Nearly a century ago, Virginia Woolf (1957 [1929]) argued that one must have "a room of one's own" in order to be free. Only when I can close my door – and lock it if necessary – can I put limits on others' intrusions into my life and my identity, limits that I myself set as a reflection and instantiation of my unique personhood. The very act of placing such limits on others' intrusions is itself a supreme act of identity-making. I am a person, and I say who I let into my life, under what conditions, and to what extent. In perhaps the most existential sense possible, I am the author of my life; I am the captain of my ship of life. Not you or anyone else. You might be interested in the choices I make and the life I lead, and my choices and decisions might affect you, if not directly then indirectly. If I have directly harmed you, you may have some claim to make. But your displeasure at or disapproval of my choices gives you no grounds to interpose. If I choose to lock my door to you, figuratively or literally, my no means no. You may go away angry or offended or disappointed, but if I say no to you, you must go away.

The political-economic consequences of my person-hood and the right to set boundaries around it are manifold. As I have already suggested, it means that we should respect others' personhood, and the boundaries they set around it, as well. Their choices are their business, and not mine, and unless I am personally involved in an exchange, transaction, partnership, or other direct relationship with them, I have no warrant to interpose without their invitation or permission into their decisions, whether to prevent them or to push them.

Consider one specific application of this principle that might initially seem unconnected. There is currently a debate in the United States about the legally mandated minimum wage. The U.S. federal government's mandated minimum wage is currently $7.25 per hour, which means that by law no one, with few exceptions (like waitstaff and some internships), may accept work for less than that rate. Yet many people argue that $7.25 per hour is below what they consider to be a "living wage," and thus they argue that the legal minimum wage should be much higher. Now, extensive economic analysis, as well as the logic of prices' effects on supply and demand, indicate that raising mandatory minimum wages above whatever the wages would be in an open market will lead to distortions: the higher costs will lead firms to hire fewer workers, leading to an oversupply of labor. This scenario has played out numerous times in places where minimum wages have been raised above the "market equilibrium" or "market clearing" rates: workers are laid off, not hired in the first place, and businesses that employ workers at the minimum wage may go out of business. There is little debate among economists about whether this happens or would ensue upon raising of minimum wages, but there is significant disagreement about whether that price is worth paying. For a small firm that employs, say, ten workers at the current minimum wage, if it is forced by an increase in the mandatory minimum wage to lay off one worker, the result is one worker now without a job and the remaining nine with higher wages (though perhaps also increased workloads). Is the tradeoff worth it? Does the benefit to the remaining workers outweigh the cost to the now jobless worker?

Most discussion of the minimum wage centers on concerns like these. Should we trade off benefits to some against losses to others? If a business becomes less profitable as a result of an increase in the minimum wage, leading it to shift costs in other directions – higher prices to consumers, less profit to the firm's owner(s), delay of planned capital improvements, less reinvestment in research and development, diminished offsets of healthcare costs, and so on – might that nevertheless be worth the increased wages to those workers lucky enough to get them? I propose to sidestep that question, however, which in any case turns on competing claims about value and moral philosophy – utilitarianism vs. deontological rights claims, for example – that may be irreconcilable. An alternative way to address the issue, one that does not appeal to or depend on a controversial claim about value or morality, is based on the issue of privacy. What I am paid, and what jobs I am willing to do for what pay and under what circumstances, is *none of your business*. What others are paid, and what others are willing to do for what pay and under what circumstances, is their business and no one else's. As equal moral agents they are entitled to choose employment and negotiate terms of employment for themselves with other willing partners. And as proper persons they are entitled to make choices about their own paths in life without uninvited interference from others.

Everyone would like to be paid more than whatever they are getting paid now. (I would; wouldn't you?) If someone comes along and tells me that he can get a law passed that would force my employer to pay me more than she otherwise would, I might be tempted simply to reply "yes, please!" and ignore whatever effects this might have on other workers, on people who would pay for my or my employer's services, or on the long-term prospects of the firm itself. As long as I benefit, why should I care? But consider how selfish that line of thought is. Would I feel the same if the mandated increase meant that I lost my job so that others could benefit? Would I feel the same if I now had to pay more for my healthcare benefits, or if I now had to pay more for my food or other things I wanted?

If we are tempted to answer that yes, we would be willing to pay more so that others can get higher wages, then why don't we just donate to charities for them now? Why wait for the government to force us to do so? Perhaps the reason is that we do not believe the cost of the mandatory wage increase will affect us, or will not affect us much, because the costs will be distributed among many people and we expect to hardly notice the difference. And perhaps we would not notice the difference much. But what we are doing is forcing others to pay for things they do not want to pay for. If the benefit would accrue to us directly, then we are endorsing others to be forced to provide us a benefit at an unwelcome cost to themselves. In other words, we are calling for a benefit not from mutually voluntary cooperative exchange but instead through enforced extractive exchange benefiting one party (ourselves) at the expense of another. The fact that we would enjoy that benefit does not change the unsavory mechanism through which that benefit would find its way to us.

People's resources are scarce, and their desires always outstrip their abilities to serve them. We cannot change that lamentable fact by forcing people to pay for things they otherwise would not or by forcing them to bear costs they do not wish to incur. If we are to respect people as equal moral agents, we must accept the choices they make, even if that means they say "no, thank you" to our request or to what we explain to them our vision of morality requires. What we can do by legislatively intervening in people's otherwise free economic choices is to reallocate their resources in directions they otherwise would not have chosen to put them, providing benefits to some and imposing costs on others. But the benefits must come from somewhere, and the costs must be borne by someone. Closing our eyes to the imposed costs or pretending the benefits came at no cost to anyone may assuage our consciences but they do not change the fact that the new allocations of resources our laws mandate are coerced and are extractive. If, however, mutually voluntary cooperation is morally preferable to involuntary extraction, and if extraction is positively immoral, then we should not disregard that, or conveniently forget our commitment to it, when it is we who stand to benefit. To do so would constitute an objectionable selfishness, and to disrespect others' equal moral agency.

Similar reasoning might apply to what we might consider "noxious markets," to things that we believe "should not be for sale," to employment arrangements we believe are not "minimally decent," to demands we might make for "people over profits" or to be paid "living wages," and to other cases where we believe others should be forced to give us more, others should be provided more at yet others' expense, or others should not be able to make the choices, enter into the arrangements or partnerships, or make the exchanges or transactions they want. Others' decisions are none of our business. My decisions are none of your business, and yours are none of mine. If I ask you for your advice or counsel, please feel free to give it; if I do not ask you but you have good reason to believe I would not make the choice I am contemplating if I knew something you know, then perhaps you should, at least within reason, tell me. But if I want to move ahead nonetheless, or if I do not solicit or want your advice or counsel – in other words, if I say "no, thank you" to you and close my door to you – to respect me as a person of dignity, as a moral agent equal to you, as someone fully possessed of personhood with all its moral implications, you must accede to my wishes. No means no, in this case as in every other.

You're Right to Say No

To take one's proper place in the world as a moral agent, one must set boundaries around oneself through which no one may enter uninvited. That means that one must not only have the right to say "no, thank you" but must regularly exercise that right. When people make requests of you, try to talk you into things, try to intimidate or even bully you into doing their bidding, agreeing with them, or assenting to their wishes, you should have your opt-out option ready to hand and prepared for immediate deployment. There is no better way for you to establish your identity as a moral agent, and to assume all the rights, privileges, immunities, and voluntary obligations such a vaunted and precious position entails. The kinds of things people may want from you, the number of ways they will presume to know better than you, and the number and range of things concerning which they will believe their own ideas, values, and preferences are better than yours will be large and in practice endless. And the number of options, possibilities, and opportunities you will face in your life will similarly be virtually without end. If you are to have a chance of constructing a rational economic order for your life, or a rational moral order, or a life of meaning and purpose on a proper path to eudaimonia, you will have to say no to an almost unlimited number of possibilities. Remind yourself often, then: You are right to say no.

But that also applies to our own dealings with others. The number of occasions on which we will be inclined to believe that others are making mistakes, that they are doing or choosing things they should not, or that our own ideas, values, and preferences are superior – even obviously superior – to theirs, will similarly be large and in practice endless. But they are proper persons, just like us, and they are moral agents, just like us. They, like us, are capable of making rational decisions, and though both they and we will often make mistakes, they, like us, are typically far better positioned nevertheless to make decisions in their own cases than we are for them. They will, and should, bear responsibility for their decisions, good or bad, and they will and should experience the feedback from the consequences of their decisions, whether good or bad. If they choose wisely, then they should enjoy the fruits of their good decisions; if they choose poorly, then they should bear the cost of their poor decisions. That is no more being overly generous to them in the former case than it is being cruel to them in the latter: it is respecting them as moral agents and respecting the boundaries and implications of their proper personhood.

If they want or even need our help, morality might require us to give it; but that is not something that can be determined from afar, and in any case each individual bears the responsibility of discharging his moral obligations to others and cannot be coerced into being moral. If you are forced to help another, you get no moral credit for it. It must be freely chosen, something only you can do in your own case,

254

and it can be effective only when you possess the relevant requisite local knowledge, something no other person can ascertain for you. Only in this way can we respect the equal moral agency of everyone, including respecting their development of good judgment and their execution of their moral duties.

Be Private

As the revelations have continued of the extent to which various government agencies have been monitoring us, the issue of privacy – and the putative tradeoff between privacy and security – has moved down the priority list from the level of shock to a shrug of the shoulders. This is partly because most things that pique our political interest travel over time this same path down the priority list, and in any case our attention spans for such things are short. It may also be due to a general impression people have that the horror stories people tell about our loss of privacy are exaggerated. There are several other considerations that further contribute to people's nonchalance about the lack of privacy, including the beliefs that our government is mostly trustworthy; Google and Amazon already do this anyway; I have nothing to hide (do you?); and my life is already an open book (have a look at my Instagram feed).

Yet I contend that privacy is more important than many of us seem inclined to believe. One way we might try to mount a case is by considering the costs involved. The economist Charles Hooper (2014) has run the numbers regarding our fight against terrorism. As he points out, the

Transportation Security Administration's (TSA) own tests of its employees' reliability indicate that TSA agents were able to find only "40 percent of the [staged-for-testing] bombs present on passengers and in luggage." The statistician Nate Silver (2009) estimates that the chance of being on an airplane that is the target of a terrorist attack is approximately 1 in 11,000,000, or approximately twenty times less likely than your getting struck by lightning. That means that the probability of the TSA discovering an intended terrorist attack on your next flight is about 1 in 30,000,000, or roughly fifteen times less likely than the chances that you will die from falling out of bed. Between the 9/11 attack in 2001 and 2014, 3,066 American citizens died from terrorist attacks (including those who died on 9/11 and using a very broad definition of "death by terrorism"). The total amount of money that the United States federal government spent fighting the "war on terror" during that period is estimated at $5.9 trillion. If we were to credit the entire difference between the previous fifteen years of terrorist killings and those during the fifteen years since 9/11 to the "war on terror," the cost is about $2.1 billion per life saved. (For comparison, the payments made for each death from the 2013 Boston Marathon bombing were about $2.4 million – or about 1/875th as much.[1]) Hooper concludes that the National Security Administration's (NSA) marginal cost per real terrorist is high enough that "Simply accusing

---

[1] See Gee 2014. For further comparison, the U.S. Environmental Protection Agency currently fixes the "value of a statistical life" at $7.4 million, or about 1/284th of value implied by the expenditures on the "war on terror." See U.S. Environmental Protection Agency n.d.

everyone in the country [of being a terrorist] would achieve the same result and allow the federal government to save $5 billion per year on the NSA's budget."

The costs involved, therefore, seem far out of line with the actual expected benefit. But because those costs are paid by other people – in our case, it simply adds to our debt, which will be paid by people not yet alive (or at least not yet voting) – then to each person asked in polls whether they support TSA or NSA searching, the cost seems to be zero. That probably at least partly explains why people report that it is worth it to them: at least some benefit, but at no perceived cost. When James Clapper, the former U.S. Director of National Intelligence, said that in order to "find the needle in the haystack" the NSA must gather a lot of hay, people might well think it sounds reasonable. Why not pursue even the most infinitesimally small risks if it does not cost us (i.e., me) anything?

So, a cost–benefit analysis of monitoring, snooping, and searching does not seem to move many people. That fits with a general pattern of political-economic argument. What often seems to matter to people is not what things cost overall, but, rather, what moral values policies represent. The moral value that government monitoring represents is security – and who is against security, except people with bad intentions or something to hide? In other words, if only bad people are against security, then people opposing snooping probably have something to hide. Or so many people seem to think.

Let us consider, then, a different tack. Consider again the relation between economics and moral value. As discussed in Chapter 5, people are often inclined to dismiss economic considerations as being "merely about money," as appealing only to lower, even sordid, motives. Yet economics concerns itself with human behavior in a world of scarce resources, with imperfect human beings trying to make their way in a world that offers them less than what they would ideally like. Those two factors mean that disagreement is inevitable, and disagreement, which can sometimes become violent conflict, can have real costs in human life. Indeed, throughout human history conflict has been one of the main causes of human misery. If economics, or political economy, can figure out a way to mitigate the conflicts, that would be a great good for humanity – and a moral one.

Robert Skidelsky and Edward Skidelsky take a different view of economics, however. They quote Lionel Robbins's famous definition of economics – "the science that studies human behaviour as a relationship between ends and scarce means which have alternative uses" (Robbins 2000 [1932], 16) – and then claim: "Robbins's definition ... brackets out judgments of value" (Skidelsky and Skidelsky 2012, 12–13). Like many others, the Skidelskys envision economic calculations as cold, lifeless, and inhumane, the amoral search for efficient use of resources without recognition that those resources depend on and affect actual human beings. But when Robbins or other economists speak of investigating ways to allocate scarce resources, and then recommend patterns of efficient allocation, we must remember that the decisions about how to allocate these resources are made by human beings and that the resources themselves are the product of human action. They are created by people based on their respective hierarchies of purpose and schedules of value, given the opportunities and resources available to them. Those decisions, in other words, reflect the values of the decision-makers, and those resources result from human labor.

When you decide to spend an hour at the gym rather than at the office, you have made an allocation of scarce resources (your time, for example) based on your schedule of value; when you decide to become a philosophy professor instead of a medical doctor, you have again made an allocation of scarce resources based on your schedule of value. Not only is it not the case that judgments of value are bracketed out, but those decisions could not be made without your schedule of values. And this aspect of economics – its dependence on values – is already implicated in the last part of Robbins's definition: "scarce means *which have alternative uses.*" Your resources – your time, talent, and treasure – might be put to any number of uses, expended in any number of ways. Many of those various uses and ways are mutually incompatible, however, so decisions must be made: How are you – how are any of us – to make them? Based on our (respective) schedules of value.

I have argued that the conception of human moral agency that this school of political-economic thought assumes is one that conceives of human beings as moral agents with two principal and defining features: autonomy and independent judgment. To be human is, first of all, to possess the power of choosing otherwise. What did you wear today? What did you eat? To whose e-mails did you respond, and to whose did you not respond? What car did you buy? Where did you decide to live? Where did you decide to work? In all these cases, and countless others, you could have chosen otherwise. That does not mean that there would not have been costs or difficulties involved. Perhaps you felt pressured by your parents or your friends or a pushy salesperson. Autonomy does not require that there were no influences on you, or that there were no external circumstances to which you responded or that you took into consideration. What it requires instead is that you could have chosen otherwise – and in all those cases, you could have.

This capacity to choose otherwise, or "autonomy," gives human beings dignity and elevates their status above that of non-human animals and inanimate objects. This is perhaps easier to see when we contrast human agency with the lack of it possessed by others. We do not blame the table leg against which we stubbed our toe, and when a bear attacks a human being we do not pass moral judgment on the bear's violent act. Even for the so-called higher non-human animals, we are loath to place moral praise or blame on what they do. In 2009, Charla Nash was attacked by her friend's pet chimpanzee; she suffered horrific injuries, including having her face completely torn off, and she very nearly died. In the many stories and editorials written about that incident, one can find much laying of blame – on Nash's friend, on the treatment of the chimpanzee, on the very notion of private "ownership" of chimpanzees, even on Nash herself. Yet one does not find blame placed on the chimpanzee for what it did. Why not? If it had been Nash's (human) friend who attacked her instead of the chimpanzee, we certainly would have blamed her. The reason we do not blame the chimpanzee is that we do not consider it a moral agent that could have chosen otherwise.

The chimpanzee is sentient, capable of feeling pain, intelligent, even lovable (well, perhaps not this one, but others might be); but it is not a moral agent. It cannot be held morally responsible for its actions, and hence it does not possess the moral dignity arising from autonomy.

The most compelling picture of human agency, I believe, is one that draws on Immanuel Kant and Aristotle to see human beings as, on the one hand, free and responsible individual centers of moral decision-making (the Kantian part), and, on the other hand, possessors of *phronesis* or practical judgment that must be used to develop properly (the Aristotelian part).[2] These two aspects of agency complement one another. To develop one's judgment properly, one first needs the freedom to make decisions for oneself, because judgment, like other skills, must be practiced to develop. But one must also be held responsible for one's decisions, because it is through feedback – negative or positive, as the case may be – that one learns to correct, hone, and develop one's judgment. This two-fold policy of allowing freedom to decide and holding responsible for decisions is appropriate only to those beings who are properly understood as possessing the capacities to decide, to respond to feedback and develop independent judgment, and to give an account of their reasons for deciding the way they did. That is human beings. Indeed, I claim that that is the essence of humanity.

An especially important aspect of our independent judgment relates, therefore, to the authority to say "no." Saying no is often quite difficult. Others can be persuasive,

---

[2] I defend this position more fully in Otteson 2006.

as anyone who has encountered pushy salespeople, author-
itarian officers of the public, bullies, or any other of many
human types who use intimidation to get others to do what
they want. But saying no is also a skill, and thus it too must be
practiced to be vigorous. Because saying no is so crucial to
establishing the boundaries of our selves, and to maintaining
the integrity of our moral agency, it is especially important to
remind ourselves and others that we do in fact possess this
skill, and that we should exercise it. Sometimes the proper
response to bullies or others attempting to intimidate us is
simply to say, in an unequivocal and decisive way, "no." No,
you may not do that; no, I will not go with you; no, I will not
accept those terms; no, I will not answer your questions; no,
I will not accept your offer. Few acts more clearly demonstrate
the power of human moral agency. A defense of privacy is
really, then, a defense of moral equality, the assertion of
a protective boundary around each agent's moral freedom,
moral integrity, and moral identity.

In *A Room of One's Own*, Woolf wrote, "it is necessary
to have . . . a room with a lock on the door if you are to write
fiction or poetry" (1957 [1929], 109). Consider for a moment
that requirement of "a room with a lock on the door" and
contemplate just how profoundly important that is to a fully
human life. Privacy is a crucial element of moral agency. It is
the power to set limits on others' intrusions into our lives,
a boundary against moral trespass, a fence that enables good
moral neighbors. The brilliant insight Woolf had was to see
that my ability to close my door and lock it is really the
freedom for me to open other doors exploring new frontiers
of moral possibility. The real reason, then, to oppose

snooping, spying, monitoring, and other intrusions into people's private affairs is not because of the monetary costs involved, considerable as those may be: It is because snooping into, spying on, and monitoring of their private decisions – like demanding, requiring, interposing, and bullying others in their economic decisions – disrespect and even defeat human moral agency.

A Fallacy?

If you are wondering how, exactly, human personhood, human moral agency, and the need for privacy have anything to do with, let alone might constitute, an economic fallacy, it is a fair question. The connection is not as obvious as were the (alleged) economic fallacies discussed in the previous chapters, but I believe there is an important connection nonetheless. I called it the "I Am the World Fallacy," by which I meant the false belief that one's own ends, values, and preferences, as well as the tradeoffs one is willing to make and the risk tolerances one has, are those that others should have too – and that if others differ, then they are making a mistake, perhaps one that should be corrected by a third party.

My argument is two-fold. First, we are typically not, in fact, in a position to know what others should do, what their ends, values, and preferences should be, or what the tradeoffs or risk tolerances are that they should make or have. Second, even if we did know, that would not by itself justify us in intervening in their lives to alter their decisions, because as equal moral agents to us their decisions should be respected. I suggest that this counts as an economic fallacy – or perhaps as a political-economic fallacy – when it undergirds or provides a basis for policies that artificially alter the decisions people make or the shape or contour of their life paths. When once we accept, or come to believe, that others are moral agents just like us and, also just like us, act on their own beliefs with their own reasons, then much contemporary economic, or political-economic, policy becomes suspect. For a great deal of it assumes that some of our fellow citizens are not, in fact, capable of making good decisions on their own, that someone else is in a better position to know what they should do, and that someone else therefore has a right, even the duty, to intervene into their decision-making and into their lives.

Value Pluralism

As I have claimed, one enduring fact of humanity is value pluralism: people have differing values, and differing schedules of value – and they always will, as a reflection of their unique individuality. The task facing the political economist or the policy-maker, therefore, is not to eradicate that individuality, pluralism, and diversity, or to level the differences among people, but instead to seek ways to minimize the conflict to which they could give rise over our scarce resources. One good way to do so – and, indeed, if history and empirical evidence are a guide, perhaps the best way we know – is to recognize and protect people's "three Ps" of persons, property, and promises, let them interact and trade and exchange and partner according to their respective and individual schedules of value, and to use coercive mechanisms to intervene only in cases of extractive, not in cases of cooperative, behavior. In other words, the proper political system of organization is liberalism, classically understood, and the proper economic system is a market-based commercial society, which follows naturally from a liberal political order.

When we see something go wrong in society, however, if we see deserving people not get what they deserve and we see undeserving people get what they do not deserve, if we see people unable to get what they want or need, or if we see people suffer through no fault of their own or succeed at least in part by sheer luck, in all these cases our natural resentment can be triggered and inflamed and incline us to cry out against what seems like an injustice – a personal, social, institutional, or even cosmic injustice. People should get what they deserve; people should get what they want or need; and people should not suffer as a result of accidents or other chance occurrences. If we can put a man on the moon, one might say, then we should be able to address and even solve any particular instance of unfairness, ill desert, or bad luck. And, indeed, in a wealthy society like the United States, we might well be able to address many, even most, such cases. But we cannot address or solve them all. The scarcity of our resources, and the transaction costs of getting them where they are needed most, continue to frustrate not only our best intentions but also our sense of propriety, of due proportion, of fairness, even of justice.

What we can hope for, I suggest, is not to solve all these problems, but to solve, or at least make headway in addressing, progressively more of them. If we cannot cure

100 percent of the patients with a disease, we should start by curing one, and then another, and so on. In a profound if unappreciated sense, that is what the world has lately been doing with arguably its greatest challenge, perhaps the single greatest dark afflicter of humanity: poverty. The institutions of a market economy, including the morality and culture appropriate to it, have so far proved not only the most successfully salubrious treatment for this ancient disease, but have today nearly conquered it. We have cured some ninety out of a hundred people on earth afflicted by it, and we are well on our way toward curing the remaining ten. The first cured patients have now gone on to have successful, even spectacularly successful lives, some of them doing far better than others. That should be a source of celebration, however, given how well we have done with nearly everyone else. But the final ten patients still require our poverty cure, and the worst thing we could do is to endanger the process that has led us to cure the previous ninety.

The lives of all one hundred remain imperfect, and their individual success in life, even their own self-reported overall life satisfaction, remains uneven – though improving. Even once we have managed to get the poverty cure to the remaining ten, as much a cause for celebration as that will be – and it will, or should, be a cause of joyous worldwide celebration – there will nevertheless remain other problems to address. Life will still be imperfect, people will still face hardships, and injustices will still occur. But we will be far better positioned to address them with the far greater wealth we will have at our disposal than we would be if we were poorer, let alone at humankind's historical levels of extreme poverty.[3] Being wealthy does not equate to or guarantee leading a flourishing, eudaimonic life, and having wealth at our disposal does not by itself mean it will go toward all the right things in the right order. As Kant said, perfection is too much to expect to fashion from so crooked a timber as is humanity. But what a liberal political order combined with a market economy does portend is steady improvement on many margins important for human flourishing. Not perfection, perhaps, but real and steady gains – perhaps the most that can be hoped for with an imperfect and fallible humanity.

Conclusion

Although we may be the most important person in our own lives, we are not the most important person in everyone else's life, and in any case we are not more important than any other person. That means that our interests do not trump those of others, and that our own ends, values, and preferences are not necessarily relevant or applicable to others.

In order to create and establish a coherent identity and sense of self, each individual must have a private sphere of jurisdiction. That is, each individual must have a sphere of private deliberation, contemplation, and decision-making into which others may not intrude uninvited. That means

---

[3] America's growing wealth has enabled Americans to give substantially to others: in 2018, Americans voluntarily gave an all-time high of $428 billion to charitable causes; per-capita giving was $1,300, and per-household giving was $3,289. See Giving USA 2019.

that privacy, moral privacy, is crucial; each person must have, as Virginia Woolf argued, a proverbial – or literal – door to her private conscience that she can shut and lock to others. Each person must be able to say "no" to others when she chooses, and the rest of us must respect that. No means no.

That also means, among other things, that we must respect others' private business as being their concern and not ours. The professional and private dealings into which others enter are their business, and not ours, and we may not intrude or intervene without invitation and permission. Each of us not only has the right to say no but we are also right to say no to indefinitely many opportunities, offers, and proposals. Because of the central importance of our integrated inner selves to both our happiness and the authorship of our own lives, we should regularly and liberally exercise our opt-out option by saying no. Doing so is one principal way of marking ourselves out as moral agents.

The I Am the World Fallacy can issue, moreover, in the belief that others should be like us or that others must hew to or serve our own schedules of value. The principle of equal moral agency reminds us, however, that others are just as unique, precious, and valuable as we are, and that they are as deserving of respect and tolerance – even if not positive approval – for their life choices as we are of ours. To a large extent, each person's life consists in a series of trial-and-error experiments, and of experiencing and learning from the consequences of decisions and choices, to develop the judgment necessary to achieve eudaimonia. Each person's proper path to eudaimonia will be unique to that person, and hence, if we value other people as much as we value ourselves, we should

give others as wide a scope of individual liberty and responsibility as is consistent with the same scope we and everyone
else enjoy. Only in that way can people find innovative,
productive, and creative ways to improve their own lives in
willing cooperation with others, and only in that way can we
all get better – together.

Postscript

The purpose of this book has been to expose central economic fallacies that meet two main criteria: first, they are fallacies that are based on widely accepted foundational principles of economics; second, they are fallacies that, if more widely understood as fallacies, would have positive effects on human life. I believe that that is what I have done in identifying seven central, and another dozen or so ancillary, fallacies discussed in this book. If I have not convinced you that these fallacies are in fact fallacies, or if you have identified errors, either of commission or omission, in my reasoning, I hope I have at least provided sufficiently strong argument that you can see why the (alleged) fallacies might be fallacies, as well as what would be required to refute the argument or to remain unconvinced by it. I also hope I have made an at least plausible case for why continuing belief in these fallacies slows and can even reverse economic growth and the numerous improvements in human well-being it portends, and thus why one might reasonably believe that exorcizing them from our belief systems would enable yet greater improvements in human life.

There is at least one important respect, however, in which I have departed from reliance on economic principles – namely, my discussion of and reliance on a conception of human equal moral agency. It is not that economists necessarily oppose this principle. It is rather that it is a moral, not an economic, claim, and many economists are, in their professional capacities as economists, loath to commit themselves to any particular, and perhaps controversial, moral premise like that. I suspect that most economists share the premise, implicitly if not explicitly, and personally if not professionally. Many of their arguments presume the value of economic growth and of increasing prosperity, for example, though they typically do not argue for that presumption or connect it, as I have, to a fulfillment or expression of humanity's moral agency. Moreover, in both their personal and professional lives, economists routinely treat others as moral agents of dignity and as equally deserving of respect as everyone else, even if their published scholarship typically does not specifically address questions of morality, agency, and dignity.

Insofar as the discipline of economics is dedicated to the improvement of human life, however, as I contend it is and should be, whether for empirical and utilitarian or for moral and principled reasons, I believe the principles of economic reasoning discussed in this book can serve that noble end. In that way, economics is not an unimportant, cold, or merely calculating discipline – let alone a "dismal science" – but is, rather, an indispensable key to enabling prosperity and, ultimately, eudaimonia. Economics may not be the queen of the sciences – pardon me, but philosophy is – but the principles of economics are like the rook, knight, and bishop in the open-ended multiplayer game of human life. We ignore its findings at our peril, to the detriment not only of our own lives but of the lives of others as well. Insofar as we are concerned, then, with human betterment, not only our own but that of others as well, these basic principles of economics are vital. We should learn them, incorporate them into our worldviews, and teach them to our children. Our futures, and theirs, may depend on it.

Preface

Hanley, Ryan Patrick. 2019. *Our Great Purpose: Adam Smith on Living a Better Life*. Princeton, NJ: Princeton University Press.

Hayek, Friedrich A. 1948. "The Intellectuals and Socialism." *Chicago Law Review* 16: 417–33.

Mankiw, Greg. 2009. "News Flash: Economists Agree." *Greg Mankiw's Blog*. Available at: http://gregmankiw.blogspot.com /2009/02/news-flash-economists-agree.html.

Niemietz, Kristian. 2019. *Socialism: The Failed Idea that Never Dies*. London: Institute for Economic Affairs.

Otteson, James R. 2002. *Adam Smith's Marketplace of Life*. New York: Cambridge University Press.

2014. *The End of Socialism*. New York: Cambridge University Press.

Plato. 2002. *Meno*. In *Five Dialogues: Euthyphro, Apology, Crito, Meno, Phaedo*, 2nd ed. G. M. A. Grube, trans. Revised by John M. Cooper. Indianapolis, IN: Hackett.

Roberts, Russell. 2014. *How Adam Smith Can Change Your Life: An Unexpected Guide to Human Nature and Happiness*. New York: Penguin.

Rodrik, Dani. 2015. *Economics Rules: The Rights and Wrongs of the Dismal Science*. New York: Norton.

Rubin, Paul H. 2003. "Folk Economics." *Southern Economic Journal* 70, 1: 157–71.

Sargent, Thomas. 2007. "University of California at Berkeley Graduation Speech," May 16, 2017. Available at: https://eml .berkeley.edu/econ/UC_graduation_speech_2007.pdf.

White, Lawrence H. 2012. *The Class of Economic Ideas: The Great Policy Debates and Experiments of the Last Hundred Years.* New York: Cambridge University Press.

Chapter 1

Acemoglu, Daron, and James A. Robinson. 2012. *Why Nations Fail: The Origins of Power, Prosperity, and Poverty.* New York: Crown Business.

Anderson, Elizabeth. 2017. *Private Government: How Employers Rule Our Lives (and Why We Don't Talk about It).* Princeton, NJ: Princeton University Press.

Bostaph, Samuel. 2017. *Andrew Carnegie: An Economic Biography,* updated ed. Lanham, MD: Rowman & Littlefield.

Chandy, Laurence, and Corey Smith. 2014. "How Poor Are America's Poorest? U.S. $2 a Day Poverty in a Global Context." Washington, DC: Brookings Institution. Available at: www.brookings.edu/research/how-poor-are-americas-poorest-u-s-2-a-day-poverty-in-a-global-context/

Clark, Gregory. 2007. *A Farewell to Alms: A Brief Economic History of the World.* Princeton, NJ: Princeton University Press.

Coyne, Christopher J. 2013. *Doing Bad by Doing Good: Why Humanitarian Action Fails.* Stanford, CA: Stanford University Press.

Davies, Stephen. 2019. *The Wealth Explosion: The Nature and Origins of Modernity.* London: Edward Everett Root.

Easterly, William. 2007. *The White Man's Burden: Why the West's Efforts to Aid the Rest Have Done So Much Ill and So Little Good*. New York: Oxford University Press.

Gwartney, James, Robert Lawson, Joshua Hall, and Ryan Murphy. 2018. *Economic Freedom of the World: 2018 Annual Report*. Vancouver: Fraser Institute.

Hume, David. 1985 (1748). "Of the Original Contract." In *Essays Moral Political and Literary*. Eugene F. Miller, ed. Indianapolis, IN: Liberty Fund: 465–87.

Kharas, Homi, Kristofer Hamel, and Martin Hofer. 2018. "Rethinking Global Poverty Reduction in 2019." The Brookings Institution. Available at: www.brookings.edu/blog/future-development/201 8/12/13/rethinking-global-poverty-reduction-in-2019/.

Locke, John. 1980 (1690). *Second Treatise of Government*. C. B. Macpherson, ed. Indianapolis, IN: Hackett.

Mack, Joanna. 2016. "Absolute and Overall Poverty." Poverty and Social Exclusion. Available at: www.poverty.ac.uk/definitions-poverty/absolute-and-overall-poverty.

Maddison, Angus. 2007. *Contours of the World Economy, 1–2030 AD: Essays in Macro-Economic History*. New York: Oxford University Press.

McCloskey, Deirdre N. 2016. *Bourgeois Equality: How Ideas, Not Capital or Institutions, Enriched the World*. Chicago, IL: University of Chicago Press.

   2019. *Why Liberalism Works: Why True Liberal Values Produce a Freer, More Equal, Prosperous World for All*. New Haven, CT: Yale University Press.

Meyer, Bruce D., Derek Wu, Victoria R. Mooers, and Carla Medalia. 2019. "The Use and Misuse of Income Data and Extreme Poverty in the United States." NBER Working Paper Series, Working Paper 25907. Available at: www.nber.org/papers/w25907.

Mokyr, Joel. 2016. *A Culture of Growth: The Origins of the Modern Economy*. Princeton, NJ: Princeton University Press.

Monnery, Neil. 2019. *A Tale of Two Economies: Hong Kong, Cuba and the Two Men Who Shaped Them*. London: Gulielmus Occamus and Co.

Nozick, Robert. 1974. *Anarchy, State, and Utopia*. New York: Basic Books.

Otteson, James R. 2014. *The End of Socialism*. New York: Cambridge University Press.

———. 2017. "The Misuse of Egalitarianism in Society." *The Independent Review* 22, 1: 37–47.

———. 2019. *Honorable Business: A Framework for Business in a Just and Humane Society*. New York: Oxford University Press.

Phelps, Edmund. 2013. *Mass Flourishing: How Grassroots Innovation Created Jobs, Challenge, and Change*. Princeton, NJ: Princeton University Press.

Pinker, Steven. 2018. *Enlightenment Now: The Case for Reason, Science, Humanism, and Progress*. New York: Viking.

Quiggin, John. 2010. *Zombie Economics: How Dead Ideas Still Walk Among Us*. Princeton, NJ: Princeton University Press.

Rawls, John. 1971. *A Theory of Justice*. Cambridge, MA: Harvard University Press.

Rose, David C. 2011. *The Moral Foundation of Economic Behavior*. New York: Oxford University Press.

———. 2019. *Why Culture Matters Most*. New York: Oxford University Press.

Roser, Max, and Esteban Ortiz-Ospina. 2017. "Global Extreme Poverty." *Our World in Data*. Available at: https://ourworldin data.org/extreme-poverty.

Rosling, Hans, Ola Rosling, and Anna Rosling Rönnlund. 2018. *Factfulness: Ten Reasons We're Wrong about the World—And*

Why Things Are Better than You Think. New York: Flatiron Books.

Rubin, Paul H. 2019. *The Capitalism Paradox: How Cooperation Enables Free Market Competition.* New York: Bombardier.

Schuck, Peter H. 2014. *Why Government Fails So Often: And How It Can Do Better.* Princeton, NJ: Princeton University Press.

Singer, Peter. 2009. *The Life You Can Save: How to Do Your Part to End World Poverty.* New York: Random House.

Smith, Adam. 1981 (1776). *An Inquiry into the Nature and Causes of the Wealth of Nations.* R. H. Campbell and A. S. Skinner, eds. Indianapolis, IN: Liberty Fund.

    1982 (1759). *The Theory of Moral Sentiments.* D. D. Raphael and A. L. Macfie, eds. Indianapolis, IN: Liberty Fund.

Steinmetz, Greg. 2015. *The Richest Man Who Ever Lived: The Life and Times of Jacob Fugger.* New York: Simon and Schuster.

World Bank. 2018. "Decline of Global Extreme Poverty Continues but Has Slowed: World Bank." Washington, DC: World Bank. Available at: www.worldbank.org/en/news/press-release/2018/09/19/decline-of-global-extreme-poverty-continues-but-has-slowed-world-bank.

Yunus, Muhammad. 2017. *A World of Three Zeros: The New Economics of Zero Poverty, Zero Unemployment, and Zero Net Carbon Emissions.* New York: Public Affairs.

Chapter 2

Bastiat, Frédéric. 2017 (1850). *Economic Sophisms and "What Is Seen and What Is Not Seen,"* trans. Dennis O'Keeffe and eds. Jacques de Guenin and David M. Hart. Indianapolis, IN: Liberty Fund.

Benatar, David, ed. 2016. *Life, Death, and Meaning: Key Philosophical Readings on the Big Questions*, 3rd. ed. New York: Rowman and Littlefield.

Canavero, Sergio. 2014. *Head Transplantation and the Quest for Immortality*. CreateSpace Independent Publishing Platform.

Conly, Sarah. 2013. *Against Autonomy: Justifying Coercive Paternalism*. New York: Cambridge University Press.

2016. *One Child: Do We Have a Right to Have More?* New York: Oxford University Press.

Darwin, Charles. 1981 (1871). *The Descent of Man, and Selection in Relation to Sex*. Princeton, NJ: Princeton University Press.

Davies, Stephen. 2019. *The Wealth Explosion: The Nature and Origins of Modernity*. London: Edward Everett Root.

Deaton, Angus. 2013. *The Great Escape: Health, Wealth, and the Origins of Inequality*. Princeton, NJ: Princeton University Press.

Diamond, Arthur M., Jr. 2019. *Openness to Creative Destruction: Sustaining Innovative Dynamism*. New York: Oxford University Press.

Hayek, Friedrich A. 1945. "The Use of Knowledge in Society." *The American Economic Review* 35, 4: 519–30.

2007 (1944). *The Road to Serfdom*. Chicago, IL: University of Chicago Press.

Hirschfeld, Mary L. 2018. *Aquinas and the Market: Toward a Humane Economy*. Cambridge, MA: Harvard University Press.

Landes, David. 1999. *The Wealth and Poverty of Nations: Why Some Are So Rich and Some So Poor*. New York: Norton.

Maddison, Angus. 2007. *Contours of the World Economy, 1–2030 AD*. New York: Oxford University Press.

Malia, Martin. 1994. *The Soviet Tragedy: A History of Socialism in Russia, 1917–1991*. New York: Free Press.

McCloskey, Deirdre N. 2006. *The Bourgeois Virtues: Ethics for an Age of Commerce*. Chicago, IL: University of Chicago Press.

2010. *Bourgeois Dignity: Why Economics Can't Explain the Modern World*. Chicago, IL: University of Chicago Press.

2016. *Bourgeois Equality: How Ideas, Not Capital or Institutions, Enriched the World*. Chicago, IL: University of Chicago Press.

2019. *Why Liberalism Works: Why True Liberal Values Produce a Freer, More Equal, Prosperous World for All*. New Haven, CT: Yale University Press.

Phelps, Edmund. 2013. *Mass Flourishing: How Grassroots Innovation Created Jobs, Challenge, and Change*. Princeton, NJ: Princeton University Press.

Pinker, Steven. 2018. *Enlightenment Now: The Case for Reason, Science, Humanism, and Progress*. New York: Viking.

Pipes, Richard. 1999. *Property and Freedom*. New York: Vintage Books.

2001. *Communism: A History*. New York: Modern Library.

Rizzo, Mario and Glen Whitman. 2020. *Escaping Paternalism: Rationality, Behavioral Economics, and Public Policy*. New York: Cambridge University Press.

Rosling, Hans, Ola Rosling, and Anna Rosling Rönnlund. 2018. *Factfulness: Ten Reasons We're Wrong about the World—And Why Things Are Better than You Think*. New York: Flatiron Books.

Sargent, Thomas. 2007. "University of California at Berkeley Graduation Speech," May 16, 2017. Available at: https://eml.berkeley.edu/econ/UC_graduation_speech_2007.pdf.

Scheidel, Walter. 2017. *The Great Leveler: Violence and the History of Inequality from the Stone Age to the Twenty-First Century*. Princeton, NJ: Princeton University Press.

Sen, Amartya. 1995. *Inequality Reexamined*. Cambridge, MA: Harvard University Press.

Smith, Adam. 1981 (1776). *An Inquiry into the Nature and Causes of the Wealth of Nations*. R. H. Campbell and A. S. Skinner, eds. Indianapolis, IN: Liberty Fund.

　　1982 (1759). *The Theory of Moral Sentiments*. D. D. Raphael and A. L. Macfie, eds. Indianapolis, IN: Liberty Fund.

Thaler, Richard H. 2015. *Misbehaving: The Making of Behavioral Economics*. New York: Norton.

Thaler, Richard H., and Cass R. Sunstein. 2009. *Nudge: Improving Decisions about Health, Wealth, and Happiness*. New York: Penguin.

Ubel, Peter. 2009. *Free Market Madness: Why Human Nature Is at Odds with Economics—And Why It Matters*. Cambridge, MA: Harvard Business Review Press.

White, Mark D. 2013. *The Manipulation of Choice: Ethics and Libertarian Paternalism*. New York: Palgrave Macmillan.

Chapter 3

Ariely, Dan. 2010. *Predictably Irrational: The Hidden Forces that Shape Our Decisions*, rev. and exp. ed. New York: Harper Perennial.

Aristotle. 2000. *Nicomachean Ethics*, 2nd ed. Terrence Irwin, trans. Indianapolis, IN: Hackett.

Conly, Sarah. 2013. *Against Autonomy: Justifying Coercive Paternalism*. New York: Cambridge University Press.

　　2016. *One Child: Do We Have a Right to Have More?* New York: Oxford University Press.

Kahneman, Daniel. 2013. *Thinking, Fast and Slow*. New York: Farrar, Straus and Giroux.

Lomasky, Loren. 1987. *Persons, Rights, and the Moral Community*. New York: Oxford University Press.

Otteson, James R. 2010. "Adam Smith and the Great Mind Fallacy." *Social Philosophy and Policy* 27, 1: 276–304.

   2006. *Actual Ethics.* New York: Cambridge University Press.

   2014. *The End of Socialism.* New York: Cambridge University Press.

Perry, Mark. 2018. "18 Spectacularly Wrong Predictions Made around the Time of the First Earth Day in 1970, Expect More." *Carpe Diem AEI.* Available at: www.aei.org/publication/18-spectacularly-wrong-predictions-made-around-the-time-of-first-earth-day-in-1970-expect-more-this-year-2/?fbclid=IwAR2fBEwxRtyKsx9wLkhKRtoeWZfS8c8bendWx9E3m60Os6SFqPb2uxDF43E.

Rizzo, Mario and Glen Whitman. 2020. *Escaping Paternalism: Rationality, Behavioral Economics, and Public Policy.* New York: Cambridge University Press.

Rose, David C. 2019. *Why Culture Matters Most.* New York: Oxford University Press.

Rubin, Paul H. 2003. "Folk Economics." *Southern Economic Journal* 70, 1: 157–71.

Smith, Adam. 1981 (1776). *An Inquiry into the Nature and Causes of the Wealth of Nations.* R. H. Campbell and A. S. Skinner, eds. Indianapolis, IN: Liberty Fund.

   1982 (1759). *The Theory of Moral Sentiments.* D. D. Raphael and A. L. Macfie, eds. Indianapolis, IN: Liberty Fund.

Stigler, George J. 1961. "The Economics of Information." *The Journal of Political Economy* 69, 3: 213–25.

Tetlock, Philip E. 2006. *Expert Political Judgment: How Good Is It? How Can We Know?* Princeton, NJ: Princeton University Press.

Thaler, Richard H. 2015. *Misbehaving: The Making of Behavioral Economics.* New York: Norton.

Thaler, Richard H., and Cass R. Sunstein. 2009. *Nudge: Improving Decisions about Health, Wealth, and Happiness.* New York: Penguin.

Tomasi, John. 2012. *Free Market Fairness*. Princeton, NJ: Princeton University Press.

Ubel, Peter. 2009. *Free Market Madness: Why Human Nature Is at Odds with Economics—And Why It Matters*. Cambridge, MA: Harvard Business Review Press.

White, Mark D. 2013. *The Manipulation of Choice: Ethics and Libertarian Paternalism*. New York: Palgrave Macmillan.

Chapter 4

Beinhocker, Eric D. 2007. *The Origin of Wealth: The Radical Remaking of Economics and What It Means for Business and Society*. Cambridge, MA: Harvard Business Press.

Conquest, Robert. 2000. *Reflections on a Ravaged Century*. New York: Norton.

Courtois, Stéphane, Nicholas Werth, Jean-Louis Panné, Andrzej Paczkowski, Karel Bartošek, and Jean-Louis Margolin. 1999. *The Black Book of Communism: Crimes, Terror, Repression*. Cambridge, MA: Harvard University Press.

Davies, Stephen. 2019. *The Wealth Explosion: The Nature and Origins of Modernity*. London: Edward Everett Root.

Deaton, Angus. 2013. *The Great Escape: Health, Wealth, and the Origins of Inequality*. Princeton, NJ: Princeton University Press.

Foster, Peter. 2014. *Why We Bite the Invisible Hand: The Psychology of Anti-Capitalism*. Toronto: Pleasaunce Press.

Frank, Robert H. 1988. *Passions within Reason: The Strategic Role of the Emotions*. New York: Norton.

Hall, Joshua C., and Robert A. Lawson. 2014. "Economic Freedom of the World: An Accounting of the Literature." *Contemporary Economic Policy* 32, 1: 1–19.

Henderson, M. Todd. 2019. *The Trust Revolution: How the Digitization of Trust Will Revolutionize Business and Government.* New York: Cambridge University Press.

Hollander, Paul. 2016. *From Benito Mussolini to Hugo Chavez: Intellectuals and a Century of Political Hero Worship.* New York: Cambridge University Press.

2017. *Political Pilgrims: Western Intellectuals in Search of the Good Society*, 4th ed. New York: Routledge.

Hume, David. 1985 (1741). "Of the First Principles of Government." In *Essays Moral Political and Literary.* Eugene F. Miller, ed. Indianapolis, IN: Liberty Fund: 32–41.

Lal, Deepak. 2013. *Poverty and Progress: Realities and Myths about Global Poverty.* Washington, DC: Cato.

Landes, David. 1999. *The Wealth and Poverty of Nations: Why Some Are So Rich and Some So Poor.* New York: Norton.

Locke, John. 1980 (1690). *Second Treatise of Government.* C. B. Macpherson, ed. Indianapolis, IN: Hackett.

McCloskey, Deirdre N. 2006. *The Bourgeois Virtues: Ethics for an Age of Commerce.* Chicago, IL: University of Chicago Press.

2010. *Bourgeois Dignity: Why Economics Can't Explain the Modern World.* Chicago, IL: University of Chicago Press.

2016. *Bourgeois Equality: How Ideas, Not Capital or Institutions, Enriched the World.* Chicago, IL: University of Chicago Press.

2019. *Why Liberalism Works: Why True Liberal Values Produce a Freer, More Equal, Prosperous World for All.* New Haven, CT: Yale University Press.

Mokyr, Joel. 2009. *The Enlightened Economy: An Economic History of Britain 1700–1850.* New Haven, CT: Yale University Press.

2016. *A Culture of Growth: The Origins of the Modern Economy.* Princeton, NJ: Princeton University Press.

Monnery, Neil. 2019. *A Tale of Two Economies: Hong Kong, Cuba and the Two Men Who Shaped Them*. London: Gulielmus Occamus and Co.

Niemietz, Kristian. 2019. *Socialism: The Failed Idea that Never Dies*. London: Institute for Economic Affairs.

North, Douglass C. 1981. *Structure and Change in Economic History*. New York: Norton.

1990. *Institutions, Institutional Change, and Economic Performance*. New York: Cambridge University Press.

2005. *Understanding the Process of Economic Change*. Princeton, NJ: Princeton University Press.

Otteson, James R., ed. 2003. *The Levellers: Overton, Walwyn, and Lilburne*, 5 vols. London: Thoemmes Continuum.

2012. "The Inhuman Alienation of Capitalism." *Society* 49, 2: 139–43.

Peart, Sandra J., and David M. Levy. 2006. "The Fragility of a Discipline When a Model Has Monopoly Status." *Review of Austrian Economics* 19: 125–36.

Phelps, Edmund. 2013. *Mass Flourishing: How Grassroots Innovation Created Jobs, Challenge, and Change*. Princeton, NJ: Princeton University Press.

Pinker, Steven. 2018. *Enlightenment Now: The Case for Reason, Science, Humanism, and Progress*. New York: Viking.

Pooley, Gale L., and Marian L. Tupy. 2018. "The Simon Abundance Index: A New Way to Measure Availability of Resources." Cato Institute Policy Analysis No. 857. Available at: www.cato.org/publications/policy-analysis/simon-abundance-index-new-way-measure-availability-resources.

Roberts, J. M. 1997. *A Short History of the World*. New York: Oxford University Press.

Rose, David C. 2011. *The Moral Foundation of Economic Behavior*. New York: Oxford University Press.

2019. *Why Culture Matters Most*. New York: Oxford University Press.

Rosenberg, Nathan L., and L. E. Birdzell, Jr. 1986. *How the West Grew Rich: The Economic Transformation of the Industrial World*. New York: Basic Books.

Rosling, Hans, Ola Rosling, and Anna Rosling Rönnlund. 2018. *Factfulness: Ten Reasons We're Wrong about the World—And Why Things Are Better than You Think*. New York: Flatiron Books.

Rummel, R. J. 1997. *Death by Government*. New York: Routledge.

Schwab, David, and Elinor Ostrom. 2008. "The Vital Role of Norms and Rules in Maintaining Open Public and Private Economies." In *Moral Markets: The Critical Role of Values in the Economy*, Paul J. Zak, ed. Princeton, NJ: Princeton University Press.

Smiles, Samuel. 1996 (1859). *Self-Help: With Illustrations of Conduct and Perseverance*. London: Institute for Economic Affairs.

Smith, Adam. 1981 (1776). *An Inquiry into the Nature and Causes of the Wealth of Nations*. R. H. Campbell and A. S. Skinner, eds. Indianapolis, IN: Liberty Fund.

Union of Soviet Socialist Republics. 1936. *Constitution of the Union of Soviet Socialist Republics*. Available at: www .departments.bucknell.edu/russian/const/1936toc.html.

White, Matthew. 2012. *The Great Big Book of Horrible Things: The Definitive Chronicle of History's 100 Worst Atrocities*. New York: Norton.

Chapter 5

Ariely, Dan, Ximena Garcia-Rada, Katrin Gödker, Lars Hornuf, and Heather Mann. 2019. "The Impact of Two Different Economic Systems on Dishonesty." *European Journal of*

Political Economy. Available at: https://doi.org/10.1016/j
.ejpoleco.2019.02.010.

Bowles, Samuel, and Herbert Gintis. 2006. "The Evolutionary Basis
of Collective Action." In *The Oxford Companion to Political
Economy,* eds. Barry R. Weingast and Donald A. Wittman.
New York: Oxford University Press.

2011. *A Cooperative Species: Human Reciprocity and Its Evolution.*
Princeton, NJ: Princeton University Press.

Brennan, Jason, and Peter M. Jaworski. 2016. *Markets without
Limits: Moral Virtues and Commercial Interests.* New York:
Routledge.

Choi, Seung (Ginny), and Virgil Henry Storr. 2016. "Can
Trust, Reciprocity, and Friendships Survive Contact with
the Market?" In *Economics and the Virtues: Building
a New Moral Foundation.* Jennifer A. Baker and Mark
D. White, eds. New York: Oxford University Press:
217–35.

Chomsky, Noam. 1999. *Profits Over People: Neoliberalism and
Global Order.* New York: Seven Stories Press.

Cowen, Tyler. 2019. *Big Business: A Love Letter to an American Anti-
Hero.* New York: St. Martin's.

Dawkins, Richard. 2016. *The Selfish Gene: 40th Anniversary Edition.*
New York: Oxford University Press.

Diamond, Arthur M., Jr. 2019. *Openness to Creative Destruction:
Sustaining Innovative Dynamism.* New York: Oxford University
Press.

Gintis, Herbert. 2012. "Giving Economists Their Due." *Boston
Review.* Available at: https://bostonreview.net/gintis-giving-
economists-their-due.

Henrich, Joseph, Robert Boyd, Samuel Bowles, Colin Camerer,
Ernst Fehr, and Herbert Gintis. 2004. *Foundations of Human
Sociality: Economic Experiments and Ethnographic Evidence*

from Fifteen Small-Scale Societies. New York: Oxford University Press.

Hume, David. 1985 (1754). "Of Refinement in the Arts." In *Essays Moral Political and Literary.* Eugene F. Miller, ed. Indianapolis, IN: Liberty Fund: 268–80.

Kant, Immanuel. 1983 (1795). *To Perpetual Peace: A Philosophical Sketch.* In *Perpetual Peace and Other Essays.* Ted Humphrey, trans. Indianapolis, IN: Hackett.

Krugman, Paul. 1998. *The Accidental Theorist: And Other Dispatches from the Dismal Science.* New York: Norton.

Marglin, Stephen A. 2010. *The Dismal Science: How Thinking Like an Economist Undermines Community.* Cambridge, MA: Harvard University Press.

Mayer, Colin. 2018. *Prosperity: Better Business Makes the Greater Good.* New York: Oxford University Press.

Mazzucato, Mariana. 2018. *The Value of Everything: Making and Taking in the Global Economy.* New York: Public Affairs.

Montesquieu, Charles de Secondat, baron de. 1989 (1748). *The Spirit of the Laws.* Anne M. Cohler, Basia C. Miller, and Harold S. Stone, trans. New York: Cambridge University Press.

Ostrom, Elinor, and James Walker, eds. 2003. *Trust and Reciprocity: Interdisciplinary Lessons from Experimental Research.* New York: Russell Sage Foundation.

Otteson, James R. 2006. *Actual Ethics.* New York: Cambridge University Press.

2019. *Honorable Business: A Framework for Business in a Just and Humane Society.* New York: Oxford University Press.

Peart, Sandra J., and David M. Levy. 2001. "The Secret History of the Dismal Science." The Library of Economics and Liberty. Available at: www.econlib.org/library/Columns/LevyPeartdismal.html.

2005. *The "Vanity of the Philosopher": From Equality to Hierarchy in Post-Classical Economics*. Ann Arbor, MI: University of Michigan Press.

People Over Profits. N.d. "Our Values: Worker's Rights." Available at: https://thepeopleoverprofits.org/.

Phelps, Edmund. 2013. *Mass Flourishing: How Grassroots Innovation Created Jobs, Challenge, and Change*. Princeton, NJ: Princeton University Press.

Piketty, Thomas. 2014. *Capital in the Twenty-First Century*. Cambridge, MA: Harvard Belknap.

Ridley, Matt. 2010. *The Rational Optimist: How Prosperity Evolves*. New York: Harper.

Rodrick, Dani. 2015. *Economics Rules: The Rights and Wrongs of the Dismal Science*. New York: Norton.

Schumpeter, Joseph A. 1942. *Capitalism, Socialism, and Democracy*. New York: Harper Perennial.

Scott, James C. 1976. *The Moral Economy of the Peasant: Rebellion and Subsistence in Southeast Asia*. Princeton, NJ: Princeton University Press.

Seabright, Paul. 2010. *The Company of Strangers: A Natural History of Economic Life*, rev. ed. Princeton, NJ: Princeton University Press.

Smith, Adam. 1981 (1776). *An Inquiry into the Nature and Causes of the Wealth of Nations*. R. H. Campbell and A. S. Skinner, eds. Indianapolis, IN: Liberty Fund.

1982 (1759). *The Theory of Moral Sentiments*. D. D. Raphael and A. L. Macfie, eds. Indianapolis, IN: Liberty Fund.

1987. *Correspondence of Adam Smith*. E. C. Mossner and I. S. Ross, eds. Indianapolis: Liberty Fund.

Storr, Virgil Henry and Ginny Seung Choi. 2019. *Do Markets Corrupt Our Morals?* New York: Palgrave Macmillan.

Zak, Paul J., ed. 2008. *Moral Markets: The Critical Role of Values in the Economy*. Princeton, NJ: Princeton University Press.

2012. *The Moral Molecule: The Source of Love and Prosperity.* New York: Dutton.

Zak, Paul J., and Stephen Knack. 2001. "Trust and Growth." *Economic Journal* 111: 295–321.

Chapter 6

Beinhocker, Eric D. 2007. *The Origin of Wealth: The Radical Remaking of Economics and What It Means for Business and Society.* Cambridge, MA: Harvard Business Press.

Brooks, Arthur C. 2008. *Gross National Happiness: Why Happiness Matters for America—and How We Can Get More of It.* New York: Basic Books.

Dollar, David, and Aart Kraay. 2016. "Trade, Growth, and Poverty." World Bank Policy Research Working Paper No. 2615. Available at: https://papers.ssrn.com/sol3/papers.cfm?abstract_id=632684.

Frankfurt, Harry G. 1988. "Equality as a Moral Ideal." In *The Importance of What We Care About.* New York: Cambridge University Press: 134–58.

Harvey, Phil, and Lisa Conyers. 2016. *The Human Cost of Welfare: How the System Hurts the People It's Supposed to Help.* Santa Barbara, CA: Praeger.

Kant, Immanuel. 1981 (1785). *Grounding for the Metaphysics of Morals.* James W. Ellington, trans. Indianapolis, IN: Hackett.

Letwin, William, ed. 1983. *Against Equality: Readings on Economic and Social Policy.* London: Macmillan.

Otteson, James R. 2017. "The Misuse of Egalitarianism in Society." *The Independent Review* 22, 1: 37–47.

Piketty, Thomas. 2014. *Capital in the Twenty-First Century.* Cambridge, MA: Harvard Belknap.

Rawls, John. 1971. *A Theory of Justice*. Cambridge, MA: Harvard University Press.

Sen, Amartya. 1995. *Inequality Reexamined*. Cambridge, MA: Harvard University Press.

Scheidel, Walter. 2017. *The Great Leveler: Violence and the History of Inequality from the Stone Age to the Twenty-First Century*. Princeton, NJ: Princeton University Press.

Shakespeare, William. 2000 (1608). *King Lear*. Stephen Orgel, ed. New York: Penguin.

Sheffield, Rachel, and Robert Rector. 2014. "The War on Poverty after 50 Years." Washington, DC: The Heritage Foundation. Available at: www.heritage.org/poverty-and-inequality/report/the-war-poverty-after-50-years.

Smith, Adam. 1981 (1776). *An Inquiry into the Nature and Causes of the Wealth of Nations*. R. H. Campbell and A. S. Skinner, eds. Indianapolis, IN: Liberty Fund.

Tomasi, John. 2012. *Free Market Fairness*. Princeton, NJ: Princeton University Press.

White, Matthew. 2012. *The Great Big Book of Horrible Things: The Definitive Chronicle of History's 100 Worst Atrocities*. New York: Norton.

Chapter 7

Anderson, Elizabeth. 2017. *Private Government: How Employers Rule Our Lives (and Why We Don't Talk about It)*. Princeton, NJ: Princeton University Press.

Barber, Benjamin R. 2007. *Consumed: How Markets Corrupt Children, Infantilize Adults, and Swallow Citizens Whole*. New York: Norton.

Benedict (Pope). 2009. *Caritas in Veritate*. Rome: Vatican.

Brennan, Jason. 2016. *Against Democracy*. Princeton, NJ: Princeton University Press.

Caplan, Bryan. 2007. *The Myth of the Rational Voter: Why Democracies Choose Bad Policies*. Princeton, NJ: Princeton University Press.

Coase, Ronald H. 1960. "The Problem of Social Cost." *The Journal of Law and Economics* 3: 1–44.

Demsetz, Harold. 1969. "Information and Efficiency: Another Viewpoint." *The Journal of Law and Economics* 12, 1: 1–22.

Deneen, Patrick J. 2018. *Why Liberalism Failed*. New Haven, CT: Yale University Press.

Frankfurt, Harry G. 1988. "Equality as a Moral Ideal." In *The Importance of What We Care About*. New York: Cambridge University Press: 134–58.

Hardin, Garrett. 1968. "The Tragedy of the Commons." *Science* 162, 3859: 1243–48. Available at: http://science.sciencemag.org/content/162/3859/1243.full.

Munger, Michael. 2007. "They Clapped: Can Price-Gouging Laws Prohibit Scarcity?" The Library of Economics and Liberty. Available at: www.econlib.org/library/Columns/y2007/Mungergouging.html.

North, Douglass C., John Joseph Wallis, and Barry R. Weingast. 2009. *Violence and Social Orders: A Conceptual Framework for Interpreting Recorded Human History*. New York: Cambridge University Press.

Ostrom, Elinor. 1990. *Governing the Commons: The Evolution of Institutions for Collective Action*. New York: Cambridge University Press.

2005. *Understanding Institutional Diversity*. Princeton, NJ: Princeton University Press.

Otteson, James R. 2019. *Honorable Business: A Framework for Business in a Just and Humane Society*. New York: Oxford University Press.

Pinker, Steven. 2011. *The Better Angels of Our Nature: Why Violence Has Declined*. New York: Viking.

    2018. *Enlightenment Now: The Case for Reason, Science, Humanism, and Progress*. New York: Viking.

Powell, Benjamin. 2014. *Out of Poverty: Sweatshops in the Global Economy*. New York: Cambridge University Press.

Quiggin, John. 2010. *Zombie Economics: How Dead Ideas Still Walk Among Us*. Princeton, NJ: Princeton University Press.

Sandel, Michael J. 2012. *What Money Can't Buy: The Moral Limits of Markets*. New York: Farrar, Straus and Giroux.

Satz, Debra. 2010. *Why Some Things Should Not Be for Sale: The Moral Limits of Markets*. New York: Oxford University Press.

Scheidel, Walter. 2017. *The Great Leveler: Violence and the History of Inequality from the Stone Age to the Twenty-First Century*. Princeton, NJ: Princeton University Press.

Schelling, Thomas C. 2006. *Micromotives and Macrobehavior*. New York: Norton.

Schwartz, Barry. 2016. *The Paradox of Choice: Why More Is Less*, rev. ed. New York: Harper Collins.

Skidelsky, Robert, and Edward Skidelsky. 2012. *How Much Is Enough? Money and the Good Life*. New York: Other Press.

Smith, Adam. 1981 (1776). *An Inquiry into the Nature and Causes of the Wealth of Nations*. R. H. Campbell and A. S. Skinner, eds. Indianapolis, IN: Liberty Fund.

Somin, Ilya. 2016. *Democracy and Political Ignorance: Why Smaller Government Is Smarter*, 2nd. ed. Palo Alto, CA: Stanford University Press.

Stein, Josh (North Carolina attorney general). N.d. "Price Gouging." Available at: https://ncleg.net/EnactedLegislation/Statutes/HTML/BySection/Chapter_75/GS_75-38.html.

Stiglitz, Joseph E. 2013. *The Price of Inequality: How Today's Divided Society Endangers Our Future*. New York: Norton.

2019. *People, Power, and Profits: Progressive Capitalism for an Age of Discontent*. New York: Norton.

Storr, Nona Martin, Emily Chamlee-Wright, and Virgil Storr. 2015. *How We Came Back: Voices from Post-Katrina New Orleans*. Arlington, VA: Mercatus Center.

Sunstein, Cass. 2018. *Human Agency and Behavioral Economics: Nudging Fast and Slow*. New York: Palgrave.

Conclusion

Baier, Kurt. 1965. *The Moral Point of View: A Rational Basis of Ethics*, abr. ed. New York: Random House.

Coyne, Christopher J., and Abigail R. Hall. 2018. *Tyranny Comes Home: The Domestic Fate of U.S. Militarism*. Palo Alto, CA: Stanford University Press.

Crawford, Neta C. 2018. "United States Budgetary Costs of the Post-9/11 Wars Through FY2019: $5.9 Trillion Spent and Obligated." The Costs of War Project. Brown University Watson Institute of International and Public Affairs. Available at: https://watson .brown.edu/costsofwar/files/cow/imce/papers/2018/Crawford_Co sts%20of%20War%20Estimates%20Through%20FY2019%20.pdf.

Gee, Brandon. 2014. "On Civil Side of Boston Marathon Bombing Fallout, Lawsuits Absent." *Detroit Legal News*. Available at: www.legalnews.com/detroit/1388483.

Giving USA. 2019. *Giving USA 2018: The Annual Report on Philanthropy for the Year 2018*. Chicago, IL: Giving USA Foundation.

Hooper, Charles L. 2014. "NSA Surveillance: A Cost/Benefit Analysis." The Library of Economics and Liberty. Available

at: www.econlib.org/library/Columns/y2014/Hoopersurveillan
ce.html.

Mill, John Stuart. 1978 (1859). *On Liberty*. Elizabeth Rapaport, ed. Indianapolis, IN: Hackett.

Otteson, James R. 2006. *Actual Ethics*. New York: Cambridge University Press.

Powell, Benjamin, and Matt Zwolinski. 2012. "The Ethical and Economic Case against Sweatshop Labor: A Critical Reassessment." *Journal of Business Ethics* 107, 4: 449–72.

Robbins, Lionel. 2000 (1932). *A History of Economic Thought*. Princeton, NJ: Princeton University Press.

Silver, Nate. 2009. "The Odds of Airborne Terror." *Fivethirtyeight. com*. Available at: https://fivethirtyeight.com/features/odds-of-airborne-terror/.

Skidelsky, Robert, and Edward Skidelsky. 2012. *How Much Is Enough? Money and the Good Life*. New York: Other Press.

Smith, Adam. 1981 (1776). *An Inquiry into the Nature and Causes of the Wealth of Nations*. R. H. Campbell and A. S. Skinner, eds. Indianapolis, IN: Liberty Fund.

Snyder, Jeremy. 2009. "What's the Matter with Price Gouging?" *Business Ethics Quarterly* 19, 2: 275–93.

United States Environmental Protection Agency. N.d. "Mortality Risk Valuation." Available at: www.epa.gov/environmental-economics/mortality-risk-valuation#whatvalue.

Woolf, Virginia. 1957 (1929). *A Room of One's Own*. New York: Harcourt Brace Jovanovich.

ACKNOWLEDGMENTS

In writing this book, I have benefited enormously from reading the works of, and having discussions with, numerous people.

These include historical figures like John Lilburne, David Hume, Adam Smith, Frédéric Bastiat, and Karl Marx, as well as near contemporaries I never met, including Friedrich Hayek, Milton Friedman, James Buchanan, G. A. Cohen, and Hans Rosling.

I have also learned a great deal from, and would like to thank, Bradley Birzer, Emily Chamlee-Wright, Thomas Cushman, Douglas J. Den Uyl, Richard Epstein, Daniel Hammond, Mary Hirschfeld, Max Hocutt, Adam Hyde, Rashid Janjua, Paul Krugman, Deirdre McCloskey, Maria Pia Paganelli, Steven Pinker, Richard Richards, Matt Ridley, Gregory Robson, David Rose, William Ruger, Daniel Russell, David Schmidtz, Robert Whaples, Amy Willis, and Matthew Wols. Of course, none of them are responsible for errors in the book; only I am.

This book was composed in the welcoming and intellectually stimulating environment of the Eudaimonia Institute at Wake Forest University. I thank the Institute's staff, research associates, and visitors for the opportunity and for innumerable valuable conversations. I also thank my students at Wake Forest University, Yeshiva University, and New York University, as well as those I have been privileged to teach through the Tikvah Fund's excellent programs, for their patience and their challenges as I tried out many of the ideas that found their way into this book.

I also thank Robert Dreesen of Cambridge University Press and for his encouragement, help, and professionalism. Thanks also go to two anonymous reviewers of an earlier draft of the manuscript for their incisive comments and many helpful suggestions. Again, only I am responsible for any remaining errors.

Finally, I thank my family for their continuing and unflagging love, support, and inspiration. My beloved Katharine, Victoria, James, Joseph, and George are in this, as in everything else, my *sine qua non.*

INDEX

absolute poverty, 29, 30, 54, 61, 64, 222, 223
allocation of resources, 9, 69, 77, 96, 155, 180, 258, 259
Amazon (business), 105, 108, 255
Aristotle, 111, 113, 114, 120, 261
attitudes, 43, 57, 125, 131, 178, 197, 206
    cooperation and extraction, 41, 144, 203
    moving force, 137
    mutual betterment, 127
    prosperity, 134, 136
authentic preferences, 35, 139
autonomy, 102, 207, 209, 259, 260

Baier, Kurt, 243
Bastiat, Frédéric, 72, 73, 74, 175
beneficent whip, 147
Bezos, Jeff, 38, 39, 54, 60
boundaries, 248, 253, 254, 262
Broken Window Fallacy, 72, 75

Cambodia, 130, 143, 144
capitalism, xiv, 114, 156, 160
Carlyle, Thomas, 147
Carnegie, Andrew, 39, 40
China, 37, 143, 144
Clapper, James, 257
Coase, Ronald, 217, 218, 219

collective action problems, 11, 210, 211, 214, 219, 220, 241
commerce, 11, 131, 167, 171
commercial society, 9, 134, 149, 171, 172, 173
commercial society, market–based, 177, 183, 208, 222, 265
    case for, 211
    economics and, 179
    products of, 219
    wealth in, 9, 61, 241
Communism, 192, 193
comparative advantage, 6, 7, 198, 200, 201, 202
consent, 16, 22, 26, 31, 126, 205, 209
cooperation, 41, 162, 164, 168, 176, 177
    attitudes about, 144
    behavior, 126, 173, 185, 220
    benefits of, 135
    chain of, 166
    Coasean bargaining, 218
    competitive markets, 173
    exchanges, 18, 20, 28
    extensive, 165, 168
    extraction vs., 19, 40, 61, 176, 204
    gaining wealth through, 9
    individual liberty, 269
    market exchanges, 163
    markets enable, 166

Printed in the United States
by Baker & Taylor Publisher Services